D0903785

Bodyshop

The Photoshop Retouching Guide
for the
Face and Body

Birgit Nitzsche, Karsten Rose

WILEY
Wiley Publishing, Inc.

Bodyshop: The Photoshop Retouching Guide for the Face and Body

Published by
Wiley Publishing, Inc.
10475 Crosspoint Boulevard
Indianapolis, IN 46256
www.wiley.com

Published simultaneously in Canada

ISBN: 978-0-470-62438-8

Manufactured in the United States of America

10 9 8 7 6 5 4 3 2 1

For general information on our other products and services or to obtain technical support, please contact our Customer Care Department within the U.S. at (877) 762-2974, outside the U.S. at (317) 572-3993 or fax (317) 572-4002.

Wiley also publishes its books in a variety of electronic formats. Some content that appears in print may not be available in electronic books.

Library of Congress Control Number: 2010924565

Trademarks: Wiley and the Wiley Publishing logo are trademarks or registered trademarks of John Wiley and Sons, Inc. and/or its affiliates. All other trademarks are the property of their respective owners. Wiley Publishing, Inc. is not associated with any product or vendor mentioned in this book.

Credits

Senior Acquisitions Editor
Stephanie McComb

Translator
Almut Dworak

Editorial Director
Robyn Siesky

Business Manager
Amy Knies

Senior Marketing Manager
Sandy Smith

Vice President and Executive Group Publisher
Richard Swadley

Vice President and Executive Publisher
Barry Pruett

Media Development Project Manager
Laura Moss

Media Development Assistant Project Manager
Jenny Swisher

Media Development Associate Producer
Marilyn Hummel

About the Authors

The authors are experts of photography and image retouching.
Their emphasis is primarily on practical application, in refreshing contrast to the vast majority of theoretical approaches in today's image editing industry.

Birgit Nitzsche has been working in photography for 20 years. The main focus areas of her work are business and lifestyle. Her experience stems from international photo projects as well as her own studio in Munich (Germany). For the last 15 years, she has been working with the composer and Photoshop lecturer
Karsten Rose (Macromedia Academy of Media, Photoshop-Convention), who is known from his many seminars and workshop. Together they have managed to perfect the interplay between photo-shooting and digital image editing.

Preface

Image editing programs – above all Photoshop – have now become so powerful that almost any conceivable picture optimization and motif manipulation is possible. But we need to ask ourselves if something that is "possible" is also the right choice for the picture we want to edit. Or does the art lie rather in sifting through the multitude of possible choices to select exactly those methods that are most appropriate and best suited to the purpose of the final product?

The more perfect the picture, the better the conditions for digital optimization. However, not every portrait photo is taken after a four-week wellness holiday, and not every production budget allows booking a makeup artist. This book therefore aims to indicate where it is rewarding to invest time into taking a picture, and where it is quicker and more cost-effective to perfect a picture using the computer.

This book is not a theoretical reference work about Photoshop, but a practical handbook allowing the advanced Photoshop-user immediate access to portrait retouching in form of detailed practical exercises. The unusual approach of structuring the exercises "from head to toe" is intended to facilitate orientation and purposeful application for the user. Each chapter can be used independently, as both the basic overviews and the practical exercises are stand-alone and do not follow on from one another.

Bodyshop: The Photoshop Retouching Guide for the Face and Body contains a wealth of different retouching tutorials related to different body parts. All technical specifications in the workshops relate to a file size of about 15 MB. The pictures are present in the Adobe RGB color space. All technical specifications relate to high-quality output, as not everything that appears perfect and brilliant on the computer screen can be printed without losing quality. All images are copyright protected and may not be distributed or reproduced in any way.

We would like to thank our editors Kristine Kamm, Cornelia Karl and Heico Neumeyer for their continued assistance and support during the entire project, and Almut Dworak for providing the English translation. Our special gratitude to Mr Domke of Wacom Europe. Testing the newest devices was a great joy and made our work much easier. Many thanks to Julie Zaffarano, Kevin La Rue and Tyler Graham at Nik-Multimedia for supplying the most recent versions of the creative and workflow filters which are included as trial versions on the enclosed DVD.

Retouching **Tutorials** 10

rotund lithe attractive perfect aesthetic shapeless corpulent fat obese slim trim taut athletic wrinkly unflattering sporty padded flawless sexy overweight styled youthful bulky bare light plump tall short muscular delicate massive heavy strong petite firm ideal vigorous flabby curved straight upright slumped

noble lively attractive vital average common round pinched plain symmetrical asymmetrical rigid unattractive mask-like flabby relaxed strained interesting stressed long wide oval square average

shiny expressive glowing attractive pretty brown bright make-up natural dark lively mysterious big small tired dull brilliant reddened over-worked blue radiant awake effective mystical damp clear open

mystical voluminous pronounced **shiny** matte red attractive beautiful curved colored plain **vivid** glamorous sensuous sexy dark mysterious dull natural smiling thin full big small rough sore wide

fresh tanned pale wrinkly **smooth** shiny matte chapped relaxed beautiful rosy **silky** pastel-shaded young old soft dimply wrinkled impure rough stretched **tender** taught uneven fine yellow pure saggy healthy sun-

shapeless **shiny** strong matte dull healthy scruffy smooth silky full flat gray **colored** tinted brittle worn-out brushed glossy tidy unkempt **styled** red flaky greasy brunette blonde black short long

aesthetic blotchy **tender** chapped **soft** sore gnarled long short youthful large pampered neglected **manicured** wrinkly straight strained ugly dry silky strong fine small rough veiny plump broad beautiful

Retouching
Tutorials

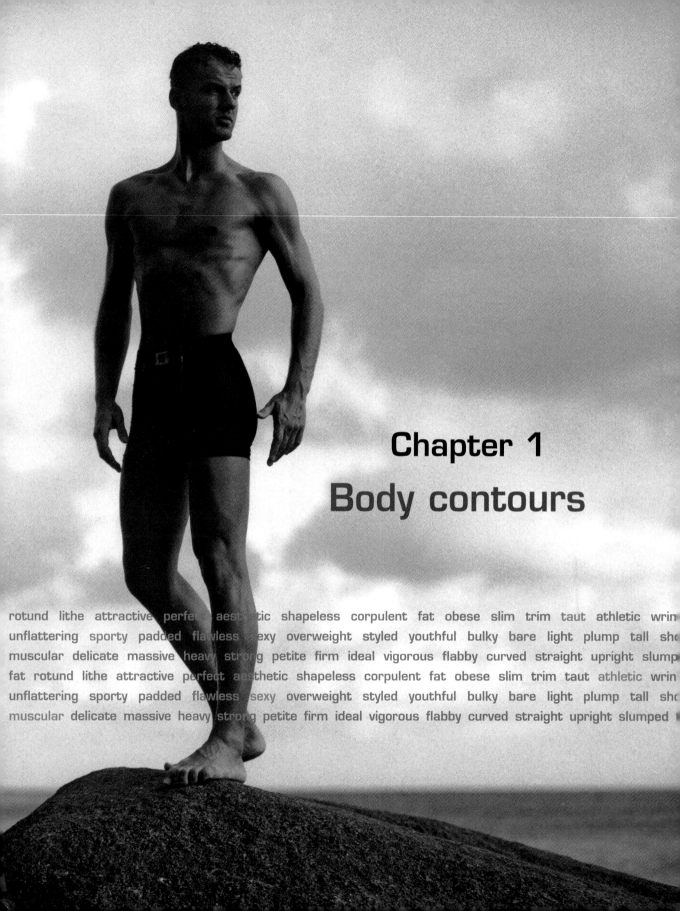

Chapter 1

Body contours

rotund lithe attractive perfect aesthetic shapeless corpulent fat obese slim trim taut athletic wrin
unflattering sporty padded flawless sexy overweight styled youthful bulky bare light plump tall sho
muscular delicate massive heavy strong petite firm ideal vigorous flabby curved straight upright slump
fat rotund lithe attractive perfect aesthetic shapeless corpulent fat obese slim trim taut athletic wrin
unflattering sporty padded flawless sexy overweight styled youthful bulky bare light plump tall sho
muscular delicate massive heavy strong petite firm ideal vigorous flabby curved straight upright slumped

How to slimb limbs

How to improve posture

How to narrow waist and buttocks and create symmetry

How to modulate body shapes quickly and easily

How to change body size

How to lengthen legs shortened by perspective

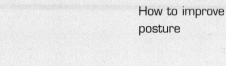

Basic Overview Workflow

How to reduce a big belly

How to change body shapes with light and shadow

How to create harmonious body contours

How to conjure up more muscles in the upper body

How to change body shape without destroying pattern and structures

How to achieve perfect upper body contours

How to replace missing body parts

How to draw with light in order to emphasize body shape

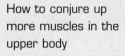

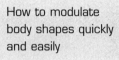

Slim legs against plain background

Picture analysis

❶ Slim legs, maintaining original size of coat

❷ Reduce raised veins and knee wrinkles

❸ Smooth ankles

❹ Adapt skin tone

These legs appear ungraceful not only because of their shape, but also due to other features such as raised veins, strong and hard shade transition between foot and shoe, wrinkles on the knee and the unhealthy skin tone.

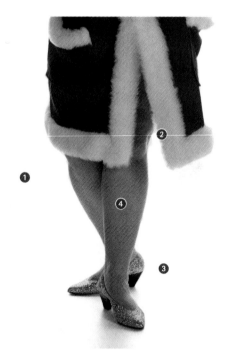

before

after

ch1/santalegs.jpg

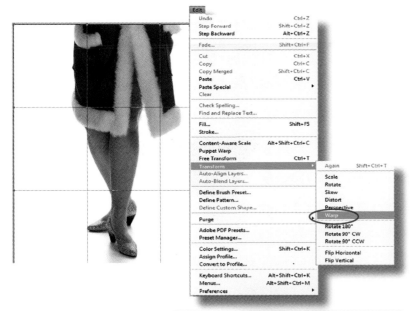

Slim legs

To make the legs and feet slimmer, apply the Warp tool to the entire picture.

Duplicate the background layer to make sure the original pixels remain unchanged. Select EDIT/TRANSFORM/WARP.

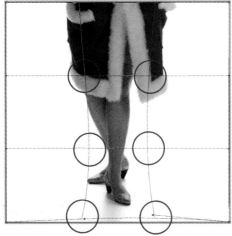

The Warp tool places a grid onto the picture. You can drag any of the intersection and corner points of the rectangles in order to compress or stretch the picture or achieve curves.

Drag the four intersection points of the center square slightly inwards, but keep the points on about the same horizontal. This compresses and thereby slims the legs. Now drag the lower intersection points of the bottom middle square slightly upwards. This slims the feet.

Apply a layer mask by clicking on the mask symbol at the bottom of the Layer palette and paint the coat back in its original size with black (D). Use the Brush tool (B, Size 120 pixels, Hardness 0%, Opacity 50%).

Correct mistakes

Copy the layer "Background" by clicking on it and pressing ⌘/Ctrl+J. Activate the layer "Background copy 2". Merge both layers (⌘/Ctrl+E). Now you can use the retouching tools to correct small flaws on the coat, such as duplicated folds or hard transitions in the fabric. Select these areas with the Patch tool (J) and drag the selection onto a wrinkle-free and smooth area. Quickly check the preview and then let go of the tool.

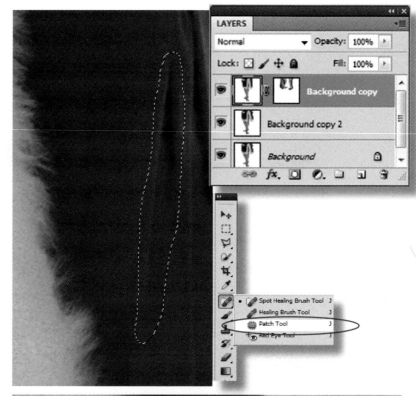

Reduce knee wrinkles

Use the Patch tool (J) again to correct the knee cap and any prominent veins.

First retouch the darkest wrinkles on the knee and then the lighter areas. As the knee has to stand out from the leg by its natural curve, you should not remove all raised areas and wrinkles, but only reduce them as appropriate.

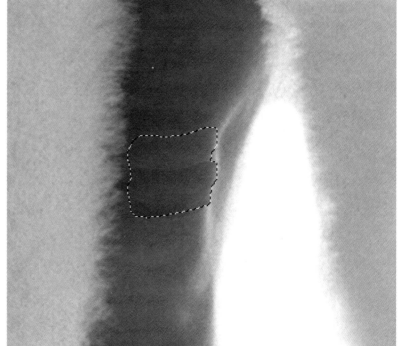

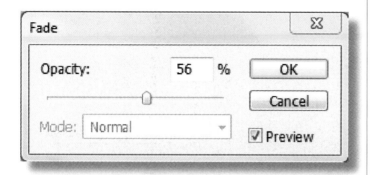

After each correction you can select EDIT/FADE and adapt the opacity of your correction. The more you reduce the opacity, the more the wrinkles and bulges will shine through the editing. Make sure the picture still appears natural. Completely without veins, the leg would appear very artificial.

For the moment you can disregard the transitions between areas of light and shadow around the knee cap. We will later correct these using a different method.

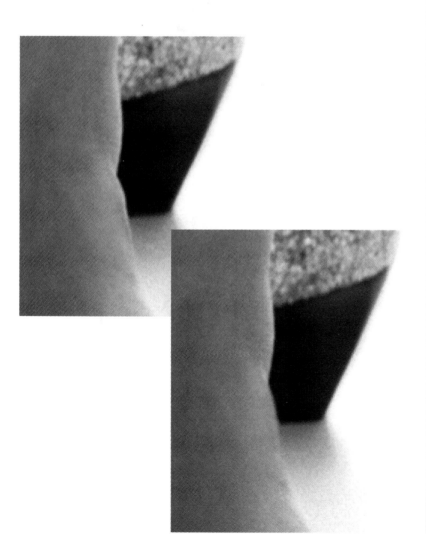

Smooth ankle

The right ankle on the foot in front is very pronounced. You can retouch it using the Clone Stamp tool ([S], Size 12 pixels, Hardness 25%, Opacity 100%) in order to achieve pleasant transitions within the skin. The editing now hides the light border on the foot. Create a new empty layer and change to the Brush tool ([B], Size 6 pixels, Hardness 0%, Opacity 17%). Use white to paint the lost shine back into the edge you just retouched.

The neutral layer

In order to reduce the light edge and several shadow areas on the knee and the foot you could work with the Dodge tool or the Burn tool. These tools are however very inflexible as they are applied directly to the pixels. A better option is working in a neutral layer.

Create a new empty layer and fill it with 50% GRAY by selecting EDIT/FILL. Set the layer's blend mode to SOFT LIGHT. The gray layer does not change the picture's appearance at first. Now you can paint onto this layer with the Brush tool (B). In this case you use white to lighten the shadows and use black to darken the light areas. To work even more effectively and flexibly, you can create two of these neutral layers, one for lightening, the other for darkening. Now you can adjust the opacity of each layer independently and are therefore able to match lights and shadows even more exactly.

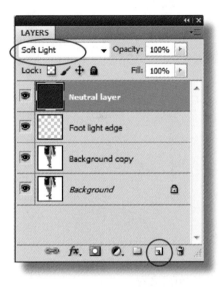

Proceed in the same manner with the dark border between foot and shoe. Use the Brush tool (B, Size 4 pixels, Hardness 0%, Opacity 15%, Foreground Color white).

You should vary the Size, as the original edge also has varying thickness in different places.

For large areas, as for example the knee, select 70 pixels as Size for the brush, set the opacity to 4% and the foreground color to black. Darken the various light flares on the leg, which helps to alleviate bumps and slight dents. You do however need to make sure that the knee still remains visible as slightly raised area.

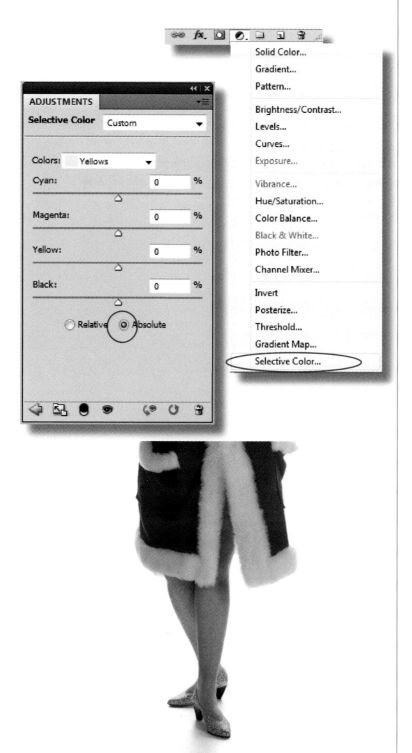

Adapt skin color

The leg shape is now much improved, but the complexion still seems too yellow. The legs should be more reddish in color.

Choose SELECTIVE COLOR from the Layers palette..

Under COLORS, choose YELLOWS and change the color settings to:

CYAN   –9
MAGENTA   +5
YELLOW   –23
BLACK   0

Make sure that the method of this picture is set to ABSOLUTE.

Reduce buttocks and create symmetry

Picture analysis

❶ Reduce buttocks

❷ Adjust left leg

❸ Replace and adjust right leg

❹ Change arm position

This picture is intended to express inner balance and harmony. The message is supposed to be emphasized by symmetry in the arrangement of the picture and the body posture. Unfortunately, the sitting position and the perspective of the shot make the buttocks appear very wide and unflattering. Furthermore, the hard shadow on the right leg and the slightly different leg angle have a negative effect. The leg appears shortened and disturbs the motif's symmetry, as does the arm position which dips slightly to the right.

ch1/buttocks.jpg

before

after

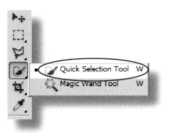

Mask out body parts

Due to the multitude of necessary changes and adaptations it would be most efficient to place the individual body parts onto separate layers. Convert each of these layers to a smart object, for example by using FILTER/CONVERT FOR SMART FILTERS, in order to be able to change the position as many times as you like without affecting the quality. Now you can experiment at your leisure to reach the best result.

The following body parts are required:

– arms and shoulders
– swimsuit minus the hair
– left leg

We do not need the right leg because we are going to use the left leg and flip it over to the right.

Select the first body part with the Quick Selection tool ([W]) by dragging it over the area you wish to select.

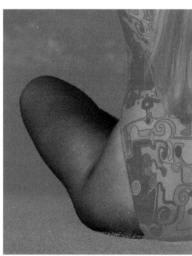

In order to refine the selection, change to Mask mode ([Q]) and correct the mask with the Brush tool ([B], Size 25 pixels, Hardness 60%, Opacity 100%). Change back to Normal mode and copy the body part onto a layer with [⌘]/[Ctrl]+[J].

Proceed in the same manner for the other body parts.

The Layers panel should now look as on the screenshot shown here. Name each layer accordingly.

Prepare background

Hide all layers except for the background. Cover up all body parts which you want to replace with new ones, by copying the background (⌘/Ctrl+J) and using the Clone Stamp tool (S, Size 80 pixels, Hardness 75%). After your corrections, the picture should look something like this.

In order to be able to use the original as reference when transforming the individual body parts, you can copy the background layer (⌘/Ctrl+J) again and position it at the top of the Layers panel. Reduce the opacity until you are just able to see the original contours. Name this layer, for example "Reference Layer". After editing, you should delete it again.

Warp swimsuit

Change to the layer "swimsuit" and select EDIT/TRANSFORM/WARP. Now drag the lower handles slightly inwards horizontally.

In the reference layer you can see exactly by how much you are shrinking the swimsuit. Then hide the reference layer again.

With X you can hide the grid to be able to see the changes more clearly.

Warp left leg

Change to the layer "Left leg" and move the thigh to the right until it touches the swimsuit. Make sure that the layer "Left leg" is beneath the layer "Swimsuit" in the Layers panel. That means you do not have to retouch the edges of the leg elaborately, because they are now under the swimsuit. Now, reselect EDIT/TRANSFORM/WARP and reshape the leg. It takes a little bit of practice until the proportions are just right.

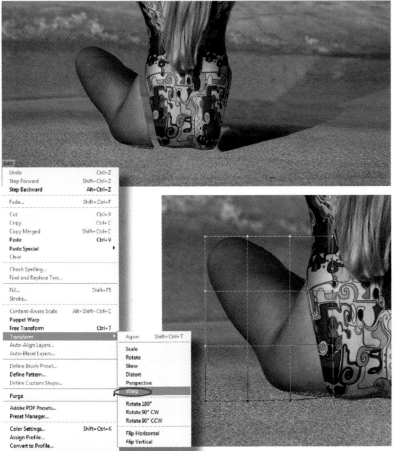

Attach right leg

Copy the layer "Left leg" by selecting LAYER/SMART OBJECTS/NEW SMART OBJECT VIA COPY.

Flip the layer by selecting EDIT/TRANSFORM/FLIP HORIZONTAL and call the layer "Right leg". Adapt this leg accordingly with the Warp tool.

Body shadow

In order to create the impression of a diffuse body shadow on the leg you should darken the leg somewhat.

While holding the Alt-key, click on CREATE NEW FILL OR ADJUSTMENT LAYER in the Layers panel, then click on CURVES. In the following dialog, activate the button USE PREVIOUS LAYER TO CREATE CLIPPING MASK and select LUMINOSITY as mode to make sure that the curve does not result in any unpleasant color changes. The layer thumbnail of the curve is displayed indented. The curve therefore only affects the layer "Right leg".

Drag the center of the curve slightly downwards until you achieve a brightness that looks like it would correspond to the prevailing lighting conditions.

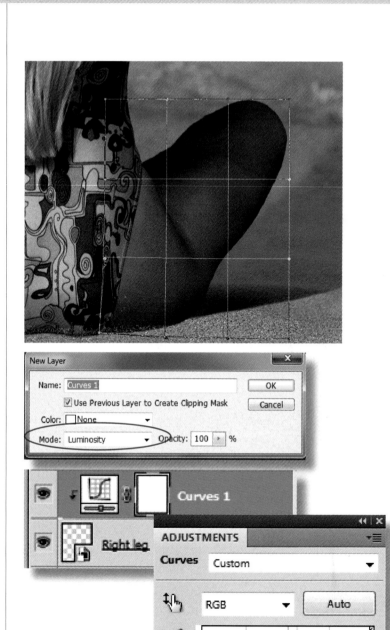

Change arm position and adapt upper body

Change to the layer "Arms". In order to give the position of the arms more symmetry, select the rulers by pressing ⌘/Ctrl+R and pull up a guide. Now you can see clearly that the left arm is too high and the right arm too low. By selecting EDIT/FREE TRANSFORM (⌘/Ctrl+T) you can turn the layer "Arms" slightly to the left, until both elbows are at the same level as the guide line.

Click on the Warp-button at the top and move the various anchor points. Make sure that especially the left arm does not get too wide. Keep correcting by dragging the next point along in the opposite direction. If you drag the left point marked on the picture inwards, you will need to drag the right point marked on the picture outwards.

During this same step, adapt the transitions between skin and swimsuit.

Complete shadows

Because of the changes made to the body, the shadows on the sand are no longer in the right place. Switch to the layer "Background copy". Using the Clone Stamp tool (S, Size 60 pixels, Hardness 45%, Opacity 100%), stamp the light sand over the shadow. Pay close attention to the shape of the original.

Look closely at the original shadows. Check the shadows via the reference layer. Here, the shadows have a sharp edge. The tool tip of the stamp should therefore not be set to 0% Hardness. Experiment with different hardness settings.

Create a new empty layer by clicking on the New Layer icon in the Layers panel. Drag it above the layer "Background copy" and call this new layer "Shadow". Use the Brush tool (B, Size 50 pixels, Hardness 80%, Opacity 100%) to draw a faint shadow at the bottom of the swimsuit. Set the blending mode to LUMINOSITY to avoid color changes. If the shadow is too strong, reduce the layer opacity. When you are finished, check all details of your adjustments once more.

Change body size

Picture analysis

❶ Make man taller

❷ Adapt arm position

At the moment when this picture was taken, the man was bending his knees so much that the woman appears considerably taller. In reality, he is actually 10 cm taller than her. In order to visually recreate this relationship of size, we will need to stretch the man a little bit.

ch1/bodysize.jpg

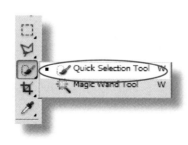

Mask out the man

In order to enlarge the man we first need to isolate him from the background. The question that always arises is how precise we have to be with our selection. In this case, we can afford to be less precise as the man will only be enlarged within the original picture. The surroundings and therefore the difficult transitions in the edges remain the same and do not require complicated adjustments.

Use the Quick Selection tool ([W]) to select the man. Vary the tool settings. Different settings are necessary due to the different brightness values. Then use the [Q] key to switch to Mask mode and improve the mask with the Brush tool ([B], Size 9 pixels, Hardness 60%, Opacity 100%) with black and white. As you can see on the picture on the left, this does not have to be very exact. Switch back to Normal mode with [Q].

The Quick Selection Tool does not have a feathered edge. The selection edges may therefore appear too hard. Click on REFINE EDGE in the Options panel.

Set View to ON LAYERS (L). Enter a Feather of 1 pixel and set Shift Edge to -5% to move the edge inwards. You do not need to eliminate the color fringe completely as the background color does not change during the next enlarging step. Click on OK.

Go back to the Layers palette. Copy the man to a new layer with ⌘/ Strg +J and name this layer "Man".

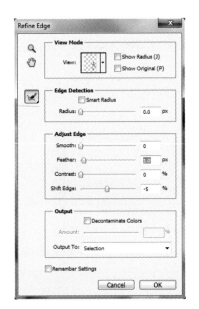

Prepare background

Hide the layer "Man" and activate the background layer. Select the man by drawing around him with the Lasso tool (L) and choose EDIT/FILL.

Set Use to CONTENT-AWARE and click on OK. The selected areas is automatically filled with a suitable content. Deselect the selection with ⌘/ Strg +D and retouch any imprecise edges and transitions with the usual retouching tools.

Transform man

In the Layers palette, go to the layer "Man" and show this layer again. First of all, change the layer "Man" to a Smart Object: right-click next to the layer thumbnail and select CONVERT TO SMART OBJECT. To make sure the man has the correct size, activate the rulers with ⌘/Ctrl+R and pull out a guide from the horizontal ruler. Position the guide on top of the upper edge of the man's head and transform the man's height just slightly with ⌘/Ctrl+T until he is a little bit taller than the woman. Confirm by pressing the ⏎-key. Then when you no longer need the guide, clear it via the VIEW menu.

Adapt hands

When checking the edges, you will notice that there is nothing to correct except for the left hand. Hide the layer "Man" and remove the man's hand completely with the Clone Stamp tool (S, Size 20 Pixels, Hardness 60%, Opacity 100%), if you have not already done so in the step "Prepare background".

Activate the layer "Man" and position it with the Move tool until the two hands look something like on the picture.

Now use the Lasso tool (L, Feather 5 pixels) to select the arm and part of the upper body and copy it onto a new layer with ⌘/Ctrl+J. Name this layer "Arm". After you have copied the layer, it is no longer a Smart Object. Convert the layer to a Smart Object. Hide the layer "Arm" and create a layer mask on the layer "Man" by clicking on the mask symbol at the bottom of the Layers panel. Cover up large parts of the arm in the mask by painting over with black (D).

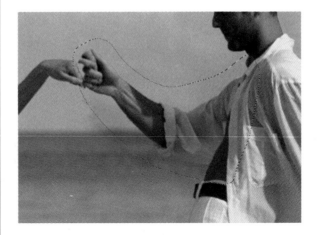

Show the layer "Arm" again and use ⌘/Ctrl+T to rotate the arm. Move the pivot point of the rotation away from the center, towards the shoulder. The arm now rotates around the shoulder joint.

Now rotate the arm until the touching fingers line up.

Create again a layer mask on the layer "Arm" and remove the unwanted areas on the arm and upper body using the Brush tool ([B], Size 20 pixels, Hardness 60%, Opacity 100%).

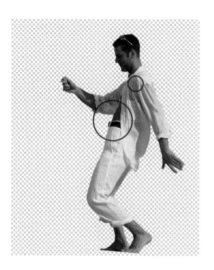

Hide the background to make it easier to spot small inconsistencies, for example in the transition between arm and body.

If you hide the layer "Man" as well, you can see what is left of the arm.

Improve background

After to the initial rough background retouching, we now have to smooth out some details. Check all transitions between the man's outline and the background. We discovered the original toe and several mistakes in the horizon and the clothing. You will of course find different small inconsistencies during your own editing work. The best solution is to retouch the mistakes with the Clone Stamp tool (S, Size 45 pixels, Hardness 30%, Opacity 100%). Feel free to experiment with other tool settings as well.

Optimize skin tone

Finally, we want to correct the color slightly. The skin tones appear too red. But even if you have a well calibrated monitor, appearances can be deceptive. We therefore have to measure the colors exactly. Select the Info panel by pressing F8. Use the Color Sampler tool to set a sampling point (sampler) on the woman's thigh. The Info panel shows you this point as fixed value. Now we know for sure that there is too much red.

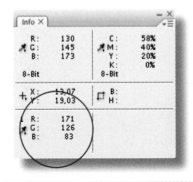

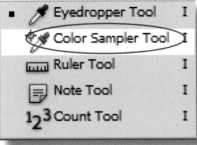

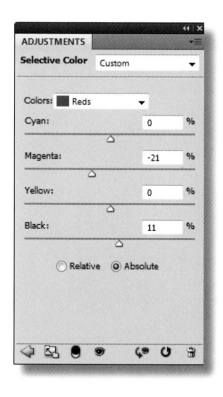

Use the button at the bottom of the Layers panel to create a SELECTIVE COLOR adjustment layer. Correct the REDS as follows.

MAGENTA   −21%
BLACK   +11%

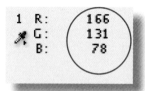

In the Info panel you can see that the values have changed. Red and blue are reduced and green is increased. Red and green, the highest values, make yellow. The skin tone appears more yellow and therefore seems fresher and healthier.

Reduce belly

Picture analysis

1. Remove belly above swimming trunks
2. Narrow contours of waistline
3. Smooth wrinkles and light reflections on skin
4. Tighten swimming trunks
5. Shrink and reposition belly button

To reduce a big belly in side view is fairly easy, you simply stamp it away. With a perspective from the front, you have to deal with several problems at the same time: the side contours have to be straightened, the belly has to be reshaped and the belly button needs repositioning. Finally, the swimming trunks require a different cut.

ch1/belly.jpg

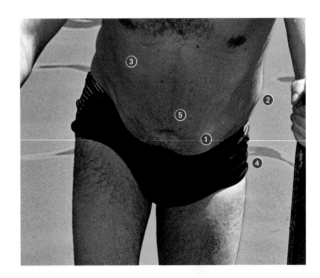

before

after

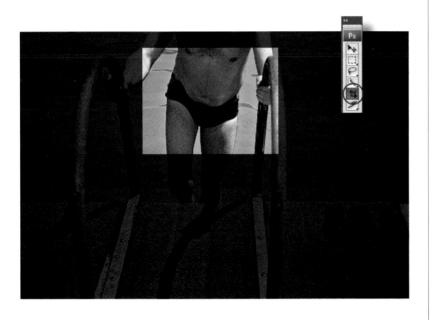

Effective working

If you do not happen to own one of the most modern computers, some editing steps can be rather slow and nerve racking. If you are only working on one small part of the picture, it is worth saving the section that you are editing as separate file. Select the area with the Crop tool (C) and confirm by pressing the ⏎ key. Save this image under a new name. Now the file is much smaller and the finished retouching can be copied into the original picture when you are done.

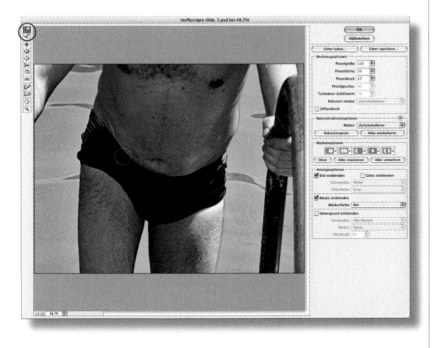

Push waistband "over" belly

First duplicate the background (J) to avoid altering the original. Name the layer "Belly 1". Now use FILTER/LIQUIFY and select the Forward Warp tool (W) which you will find at the top left of the Tools panel to edit the upper edge of the swimming trunks. For the first step, use the tool settings indicated on the picture on the left. Place the tool tip not exactly onto the waistband, but slightly below it in order to push primarily the waistband upwards and not the skin. Now push the waistband up a little. You need to repeat this step several times as the waist is only being incrementally changed.

Improve contours

With the same procedure you can now edit the left and right waist contours.

Edit the edges on both sides of the body with the Clone Stamp tool ($\boxed{S}$, Size 40 pixels, Hardness 60%). If you do not have a very steady hand, you can also create a path for the shape, as described in Chapter 7, Basic Overview – Paths.

With skin retouching in particular you need to make sure that the new skin texture corresponds to the texture being replaced.

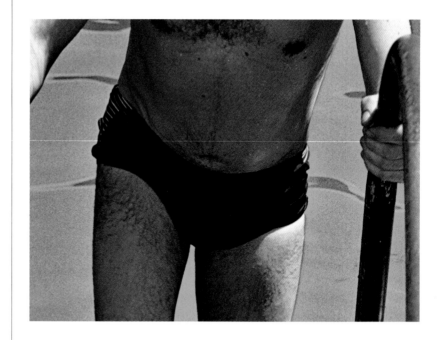

Remove wrinkles and love handles

Remove the wrinkles with the Patch tool ($\boxed{J}$). Move the Patch tool around the dark areas of the wrinkles and drag these onto a smooth area, best of all straight up, where you find the same skin texture with less hair. Use the same method to reduce the light reflections. Now your picture should look something like this.

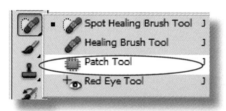

A sporty cut for swimming trunks

The now well-proportioned body also needs suitable swimming trunks. In our example, the cut is less than perfect.

In order to remedy this, straighten the waistband and the side contour on the left. Stamp out the offending wrinkles and bulges. Use the following settings: Clone Stamp tool (S), Size 30 pixels, Hardness 50%. The swimming trunks now look much tauter. Do the same on the right-hand side.

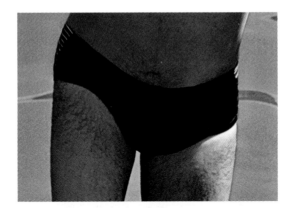

To improve and modernize the cut of the swimming trunks, stamp the leg texture upwards. With a graphics tablet and a little practice you can achieve a nice rounded shape even freehand. Alternatively, you can first create a selection for the shape, just as with all shape modifications.

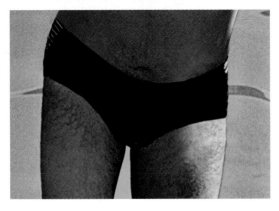

The belly button

The belly button is a small but important detail. Because of the original
shape and size of the belly, the belly
button still sits much too low. In order
to position it in the right place, we
need to know where it should go. In
a slim belly, as on the example on the
far right, the belly button is situated at
the same level as the narrowest point
of the waistline.

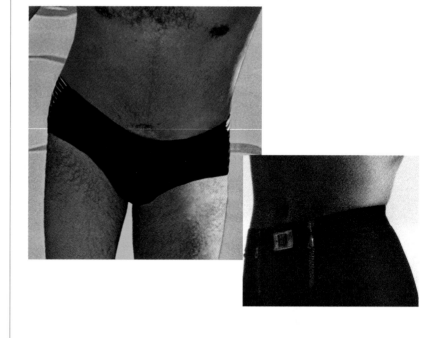

We therefore want to move the belly
button. Select it with the Lasso tool
([L]) with a feathered edge of 5 pixels
and place the belly button onto a new
layer with [⌘]/[Ctrl]+[J]. Right-click
on the layer, then convert it to a smart
object via the Layers panel. Now we
can change the shape of the belly
button at any time in order to match
it better to the new belly. We named
this layer "Belly Button". Drag the
belly button to the same level as the
waistline. Remove the original belly
button from the layer "Belly 1" with
the Patch tool ([J]).

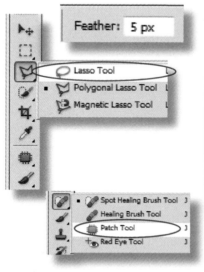

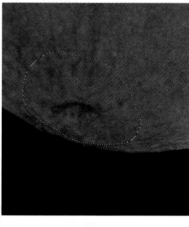

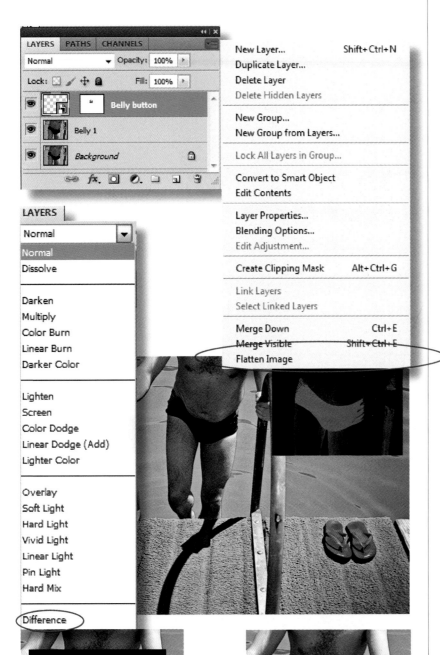

In order to adjust the belly button, create a mask by clicking on the mask icon in the Layers panel and remove the edges of the belly button with black (⎡D⎤) and the Brush tool (⎡B⎤, Size 45 pixel, Hardness 40%, Opacity 100%). Save the picture and then flatten all layers via the pop-up menu in the Layers panel. Select all with ⎡⌘⎤/⎡Ctrl⎤+⎡A⎤ and copy it with ⎡⌘⎤/⎡Ctrl⎤+⎡C⎤ to paste it into your original picture.

Insert retouching

Open the original picture and paste your retouching into it with ⎡⌘⎤/⎡Ctrl⎤+⎡V⎤. Set the blend mode to DIFFERENCE. Now you can insert the retouching accurately.

The retouched area becomes black when it is congruent, and only the altered edges become visible. Then you set the blend mode to NORMAL. Adjust the edges with a layer mask.

Achieve perfect leg contours

Picture analysis

Left lady:

❶ Narrow hips

❷ Narrow thighs, inside and outside

❸ Slightly narrow right calf

Right lady:

❹ Narrow hips

❺ Slim inside of thighs

❻ Narrow inside of knee

❼ Slim calves, inside

If you want to change the leg shape over its entire length, as in this example, you should bear in mind that legs have many differently pronounced curves. It is therefore better to correct the contours with the Stamp tool and not with the Liquify or Image Warp tool. However, to avoid getting dents in the leg shape, you need to have a precise selection. This precision can only be achieved with the Pen tool (P). The resulting path can then be transformed into a selection and edited further.

 ch1/scarves.jpg

before

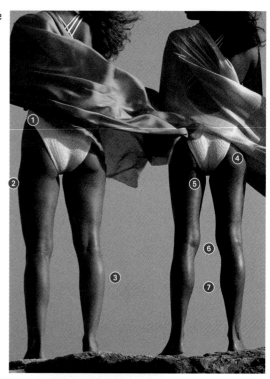

after

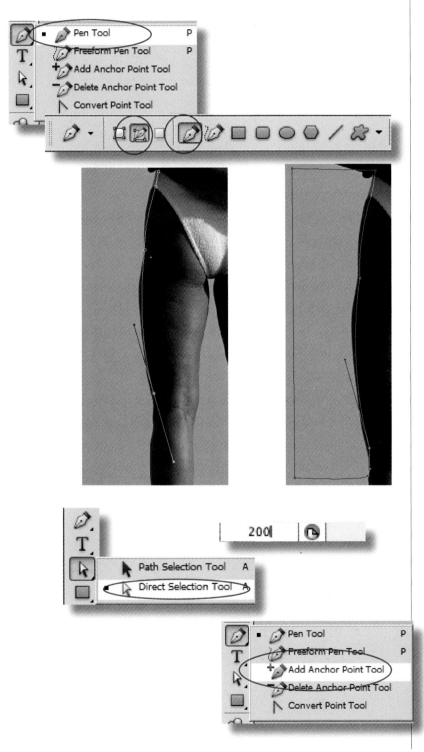

Create the first path

For the first path, select the Pen tool from the Brushes panel ($\boxed{P}$). Make sure that the pen is set to PATHS and the Pen tool in the Options panel, as shown.

Create an approximate path with the Pen tool. The path does not need to be accurate yet. Place the first anchor point at the intersection between scarf and swimsuit. Draw the path, as shown, a little bit inside the leg, so that you already sketch the intended shape. Close the path by returning to the starting anchor point.

Zoom into the picture to 200% by entering 200 at the bottom edge of the picture and press the $\boxed{\hookleftarrow}$ key. Correct the path with the Direct Selection tool ($\boxed{A}$). Now you can use the tool to adapt position and curve of each set anchor point in detail. You can also add additional anchor points with the Add Anchor Point tool, or remove them with the Delete Anchor Point tool.

Save path

Once you are happy with the path, save it in the Paths panel.

Give your path an expressive name, as you will create other paths later.

We named our path:

"Left woman/left leg/left thigh". Abbreviated, it looks like this:

LW/LL/LT.

Create further paths

Now create further paths for the other areas you want to change.

To make sure that the new shape joins up seamlessly to the original shape, you should always set the start of your path at a point where you are not making changes. Start from there and determine the new shape. If the motif permits it, always try to fix the path with two anchor points and then add the new edge.

Do the same at the end of the path, but this time you should finish the path at a point which will not be changed. Close the path by clicking on the first anchor point, then save the path.

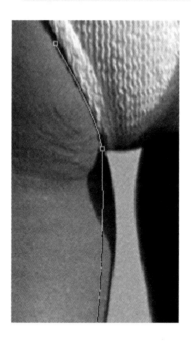

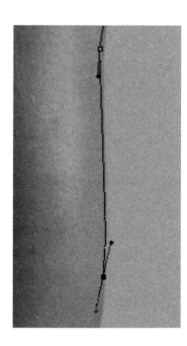

Once you have set all the paths, your Paths panel will look something like this.

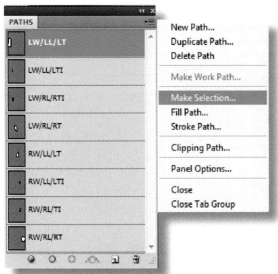

Convert paths to selections

Click on the first path in the Paths panel and create the selection via the pop-up menu MAKE SELECTION.

Set the Feather Radius in the MAKE SELECTION dialog box to 2 pixels. This setting will result in more flowing, less frazzled contours than a radius of 1 pixel.

Slim leg

Duplicate the background to make sure you will be able to use the original picture over and over again in future. Drag the background to the New Layer icon at the bottom of the Layers panel. Now stamp away the areas within your selection with the Clone Stamp tool (⑤, Size 30 pixels, Hardness 0%, Opacity 100%).

During retouching you will notice that the selection edge is too soft. We set the radius too high when converting the path to a selection.

The size of the feather depends on the file resolution and unfortunately, the radius of 2 pixels is too high in this case. To correct this, deselect the selection with ⌘/Ctrl+D and delete the background copy. Create a new background copy, reactivate the path and create a new selection from it, this time with a Radius of 1 pixel.

Once you are happy with the hardness of the edge, activate one path after the other, create a selection with a radius of 1 and simply stamp away the surplus areas. Because of the softness of the selection, the Stamp tool also takes effect slightly beyond the selection, removing a bit more than the selected area. Therefore try to only stamp over the edge once. You can use the effect the other way around as well, if your selection is slightly too small and you want to remove more of the leg.

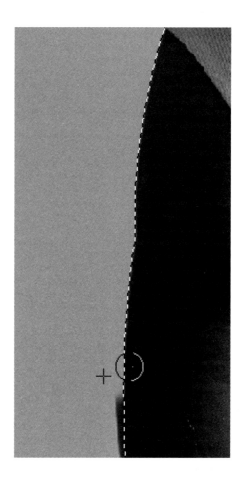

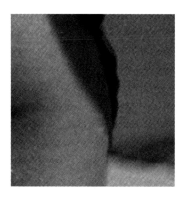

Path versus Liquify Filter

In some places it is not appropriate to use the Stamp tool. For example, if you were to remove the shaded area from this section of the leg as well, the interplay of light and shadow would not look right any more.

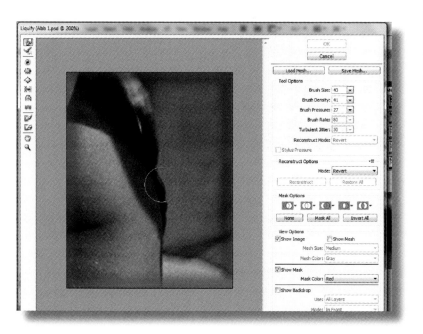

In such cases, the Liquify filter serves the purpose well. Select the area you want to edit with the Rectangular Marquee tool (M, Feather 5 pixels). Without a selection, the entire picture would be loaded into the path and processing progresses only slowly.

Adapt the leg, the fabric and the shadows to the new shape.

In the left leg of the woman on the right, the transition between the leg and the blue fabric cannot be easily adapted with the Stamp tool either. Narrow the left leg as much as possible using paths and Stamp tool, then deselect the selection. As you can see, the fabric has to be moved to the right in order to fit.

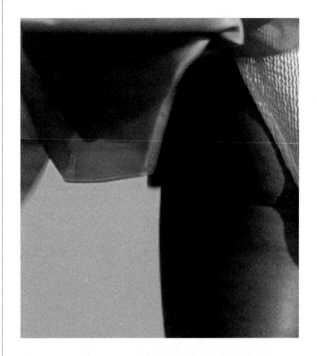

Now select the thigh-scarf-area generously with the Rectangular Marquee, then copy the area with ⌘/Ctrl +J to a new layer "Layer 1".

Move this layer slightly to the right with the Move tool (V), until the fabric touches the leg again. Create a layer mask by clicking on the ADD LAYER MASK icon at the bottom of the Layers panel. Remove all unwanted areas with the Brush tool (B) and black.

Hide the two bottom layers and look at what is left of the leg and the silk scarf.

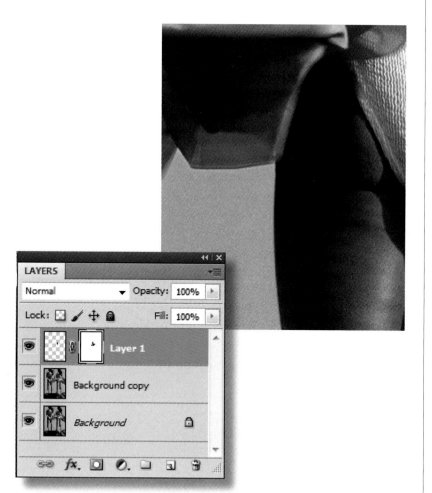

Merge the "Layer 1" with the layer "Background Copy". Do this by activating "Layer 1" and pressing ⌘ / Ctrl +E. If some transitions and edges are still not exact, refine the retouching with the retouching tools.

Always check your editing at 100% zoom by double clicking on the magnifying glass icon in the Tools panel. This allows you to see all details clearly.

Once you are happy with the shape of the legs, you can start editing the skin wrinkles and skin texture (see chapter "Skin").

Slimmer legs against detailed background

Picture analysis

1 Slim legs, preserve structures on tights and wall.

Here we need to pay close attention to patterns and structures, unlike the workshop "Achieve perfect leg contours" (see page 40).

before

after

ch1/legs_against_wall.jpg

Slimmer legs

To reduce the amount of work we need to do to the minimum possible, select the first leg with the Rectangular Marquee tool (M, Feather 5 pixels) as shown on the left. We also selected some of the area surrounding the leg. We will need this area around the leg to make sure the original leg is completely covered up after the streamlining. Place the selection onto a separate layer with ⌘/Ctrl+J and convert it (by right-clicking on the area next to the layer thumbnail, then CONVERT TO SMART OBJECT). This ensures you can later change the shape without loss of quality.

Select EDIT/TRANSFORM/WARP. Now push the left and right borders of the middle blocks in the bounding box inwards, as shown on the picture. Check the background carefully and only move the handles along the horizontal lines of the wall. The bricks need to line up and should not be warped upwards or downwards. Streamline the legs while making sure to maintain the proportions. Do not make them too thin.

Proceed in the same way with the right leg as you just did with the left: SELECTION, NEW LAYER, WARP.

When we now check our picture, we are going to find some areas which were affected by the streamlining (marked in red on the picture). The feather boa has double contours, the brick wall has extra grooves and slightly distorted transitions, the skirt also has an imperfect edge and the double contour on the shoe is immediately obvious. Make sure to check your picture carefully. You are likely to find completely different flaws in your image as you probably did not select exactly the same area or the same degree of warp.

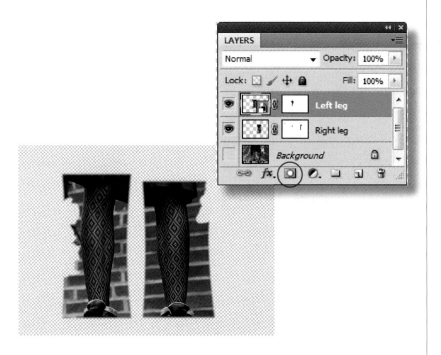

Fine retouching

We can correct the feather boa and the shoe with a layer mask. Create a mask on each layer by clicking on the ADD LAYER MASK icon at the bottom of the Layers panel. Remove the duplicated feathers and the shifted shoe by using the Brush tool and black. When you hide the background, the feather boa should be almost completely gone from the layer "Left leg" and there should be no more shoe visible in the layer "Right leg". Now make the background visible again.

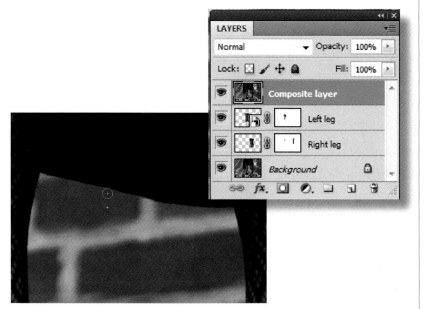

We will remove the edges in the wall and the skirt with the normal Clone Stamp tool. We therefore need all layers merged into one layer. Activate the top layer and press the keys ⌘/Ctrl+⇧+Alt+E. All layers are now merged into one composite layer. Now you can correct the remaining mistakes with the Clone Stamp tool. For the skirt we use a Size of 15 pixels, Hardness 40% and Opacity of 100%. Vary these settings according to your own needs for the different image areas.

Replace missing body parts

Picture analysis

1 Insert foot

Taking picture when someone is in motion can be tricky. Quite often, just when mimics, image composition and sharpness are at their best, another important detail in the picture does not fit. In our case, the woman's right leg is obscured due to the perspective. As there is no suitable woman's foot to be found in the entire photo series, we need to make do with the man's foot.

ch1/foot.jpg

before

after

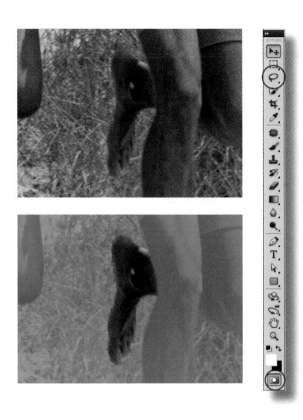

Select foot

Select the foot with the Lasso tool
($\boxed{L}$, Feather 0 pixels). For now,
the selection does not yet need to
be completely accurate.

Now switch to Mask mode with
the $\boxed{Q}$ key. The surroundings of
the selection are shown colored
in red as red is the masking color.
Refine the mask with the Brush
tool ($\boxed{B}$, Size 20 Pixel, Hardness
20%, Opacity 100%). Paint with
black to apply the red masking
color. With white you can remove
it again. When you are finished,
switch back to Normal mode by
pressing the $\boxed{Q}$-key once more.

Use $\boxed{\mathcal{H}}$/$\boxed{\text{Ctrl}}$+$\boxed{J}$ to copy the
selected foot to a new layer, name
the layer and position the foot on
the woman's right leg. Before you
adjust the foot's size and shape,
convert the layer with FILTER/
CONVERT FOR SMART FILTERS.

Adjust shape and size

We now need to turn the man's foot into a dainty lady's foot. Transform the foot with ⌘/Ctrl+T. Reduce it slightly more in the vertical than in the horizontal and rotate the foot clockwise. Now warp the heel and the toe with EDIT/TRANSFORM/WARP as shown.

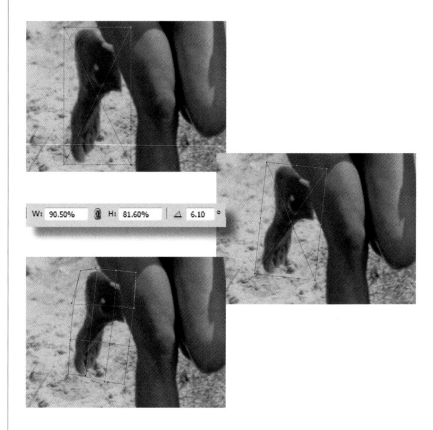

Motion blur

Despite our adjustments, the foot still seems too chunky. We will therefore use a little trick.

Use FILTER/BLUR/MOTION BLUR to place a blur on the foot. With a smart object, this is only possible with Photoshop CS3 onwards. If you are using an older version, you first need to rasterize the Smart Object by right-clicking on the layer. The Angle has to be adapted to the direction of movement. The Amount has to be selected accordingly to make sure the foot is still recognizable as such.

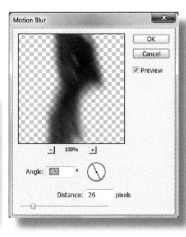

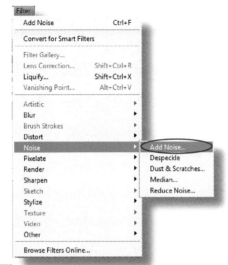

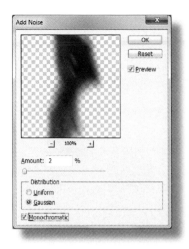

The filter has made the foot's texture disappear. Apply a slight noise to the foot with FILTER/NOISE/ADD NOISE. Refer to the original image for comparison.

The new foot still sticks out over the left leg. Create a layer mask by clicking on the mask icon at the bottom of the Layers panel. Use the Brush tool ($\boxed{B}$, Size 20 pixels, Hardness 20%, Opacity 100%) and black ($\boxed{D}$) to remove any parts of the foot that stick out over the leg.

Due to the Motion Blur filter, the foot might now be too big again. Select the Warp tool once more to correct shape and size of the foot. Now you are done.

Improve posture

Picture analysis

❶ Replace the man's head

❷ Straighten upper body

❸ Remove hip kink

❹ Intensify and darken colors

The posture of our couple at the beach is less than perfect. Fortunately we can choose from a whole series of photos with this motif and therefore have the option to exchange individual body parts. Analyze carefully what causes the bad posture to be able to correct the problem with the appropriate methods.

ch1/posture.jpg

ch1/posture2.jpg

before

after

Select the head

We managed to find a better head for the man in our photo series and are now going to insert it into our picture. To do this, open both pictures and select the head you want to paste (ch1/posture2.jpg) with the Quick Selection tool (W, Diameter 10 pixels, Hardness 100%). Refine the selection in Mask mode (Q). Also include the shadow on the left between shirt and neck in the selection. You will see the reason for this in the next step. Once everything is masked, switch back to Normal mode (Q), copy the selected head with ⌘/Ctrl+C and insert it into the original image (ch1/posture.jpg) with ⌘/Ctrl+V.

Duplicate the background with ⌘/Ctrl+J. The layer is now called "Background copy". First remove the original head with the Stamp tool.

Insert the head

Now you can position the new head with the Move tool ($\boxed{V}$). Again you can use the small shadow as a reference point. It can really be that quick, but you are not completely finished yet. In order to be able to change the head at a later time without loss of quality, select CONVERT TO SMART OBJECT from the menu in the Layers panel.

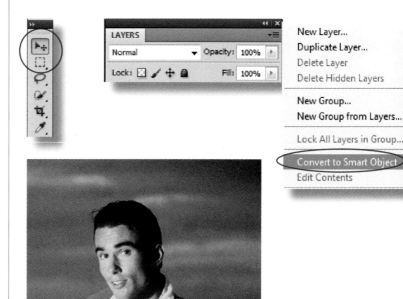

The head needs to sit a bit more upright on the shoulders. Rotate the head slightly clockwise with FREE TRANSFORM ($\boxed{⌘}$/$\boxed{Ctrl}$+$\boxed{T}$) - we used 9.7 degrees, as you can see in the Options panel – until it sits straight, then push it up a little.

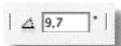

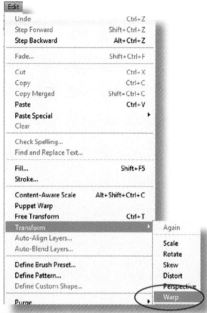

Lift shoulders

The Smart Object allows us to make additional corrections without repeated loss of quality, so that we can approach the result step by step. First we take care of the man's drooping shoulders. Activate the background layer and select the upper body with the Rectangular Marquee tool. Copy it onto a separate layer with ⌘/Ctrl+J and convert it to a Smart Object with the pop-up menu in the Layers panel. Use the Warp tool to lift the shoulders. Pull the two upper corner handles horizontally upwards until you are happy with the shape of the shoulders. Create a layer mask with the ADD LAYER MASK icon in the Layers panel and remove the distorted background with the Brush tool (B). Also watch out for distortions on the model, for example the pocket on his jacket. If you hide the background you can see the retouching more clearly.

Reposition the head and refine the transitions on the neck with a layer mask. Hide the background to be able to see the edges more clearly.

Please note that in older versions of Photoshop, a layer mask on a smart object layer is not linked with the image. If you change the transformation, the mask will not be changed and you have to adapt it separately. This changes with Photoshop CS4 onwards, where the link between mask and Smart Object remains intact.

Narrow waistline

The strong frontal flash has nearly eliminated all shape-enhancing shadows. This creates the impression that the woman has bad posture. As a result, her upper body seems to lack contours.

In order to narrow her waistline, select the waist and surrounding areas with the Lasso tool ([L], Feather 3 pixels) and copy it onto a separate layer with [⌘]/[Ctrl]+[J] then turn it into a Smart Object. We name this layer "Waistline". Use the Warp tool to give the waistline a new shape. Push the right side slightly inwards, as on our picture.

You do not necessarily have to click on a cross point, you can also move the image within each rectangle. Confirm the transformation.

Now the hands and arms no longer fit. Hide the layer "Waistline" and switch to the layer "Background copy". There you can remove the woman's arm with the Clone Stamp tool ([S], Size 50 pixels, Hardness 60%, Opacity 100%).

Now show the layer "Waistline" again and use a layer mask to hide all unwanted and distorted elements.

Hide all other layers in order to check the retouching.

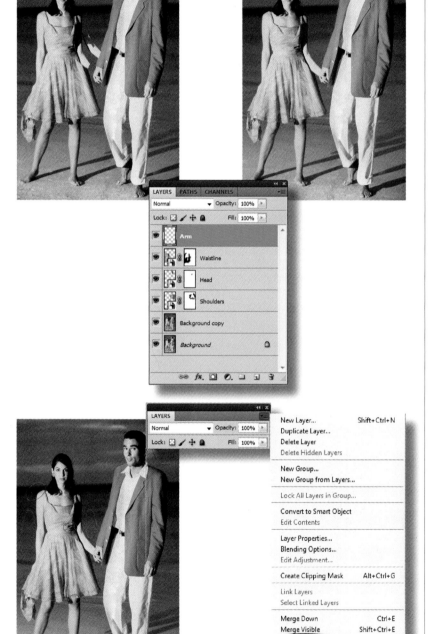

Attach arm

In order to reposition the woman's arm, hide all layers except for the background. There you select the original arm with the Lasso tool (⌊L⌋, Feather 3 pixels) and copy it onto a separate layer with ⌘/⌈Ctrl⌉+⌊J⌋. Now move that layer to the top of the Layers panel.

Position the arm and adapt it with a layer mask.

All major changes are now done. For the other touch-ups you need to have all corrections on a composite layer. First, save the image with all its layers. Then flatten all layers with the panel command FLATTEN IMAGE and save this image under a new name.

Go to 100% view by double-clicking on the magnifying glass in order to check the image for errors, distortions and other unwanted elements, such as the large wrinkle on the abdomen, and retouch these.

Change contrast and color

Often you can achieve pretty, color-intensive effects by switching to LAB mode.

For these changes, switch the image to LAB with IMAGE/MODE. Click on IMAGE/APPLY IMAGE. Try out all three channels in the dialog: BRIGHTNESS CHANNEL, A CHANNEL and B CHANNEL. Also experiment with the various blend modes.

In this example we get the most beautiful evening atmosphere by selecting B CHANNEL with the blend mode SOFT LIGHT.

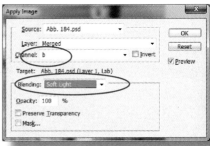

Curve with luminosity mask

To finish, we darken the image slightly with a Curves adjustment layer. In order to enhance the evening atmosphere even more, we want to emphasize the shadows more than the highlights. To make sure the changes affect mainly the dark tones in your image, create a luminosity mask. Switch to the Channels panel and click on the RGB icon while pressing ⌘/Ctrl+X. The luminosity is loaded as a selection. The lighter tones are selected more strongly. Invert the selection with ⌘/Ctrl+⇧+I.

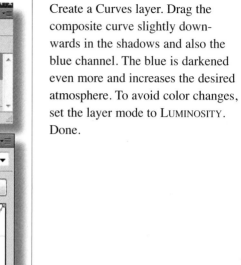

Create a Curves layer. Drag the composite curve slightly downwards in the shadows and also the blue channel. The blue is darkened even more and increases the desired atmosphere. To avoid color changes, set the layer mode to LUMINOSITY. Done.

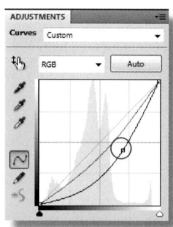

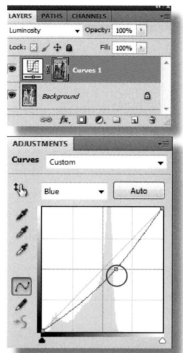

Body modulation

Picture analysis

❶ Lighten shadows on body

❷ Improve modulation

This picture was taken with very diffuse light conditions without any illumination from the front. The very soft light transitions cause the modulation of the muscles to disappear almost completely. You can bring out facial features and enhance muscle structures with a simple method.

ch1/athlete.jpg

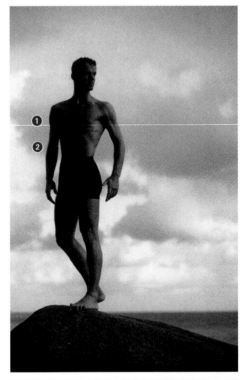

before

after

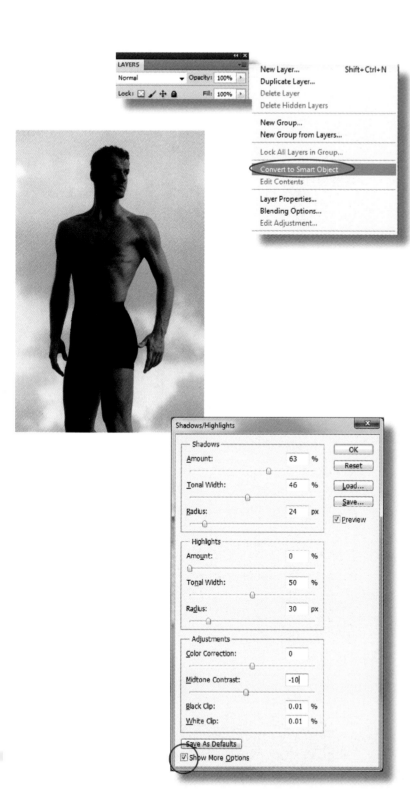

Modulate the body

Modulating a body with light and shadow does not have to be complicated.

Duplicate the background with ⌘/Ctrl+J. Choose CONVERT TO SMART OBJECT from the menu in the Layers panel.

In order to modulate the image, use IMAGE/ADJUSTMENTS/SHADOWS-HIGHLIGHTS to select the Shadows/Highlights dialog box and activate SHOW MORE OPTIONS at the bottom of the panel. However, for Smart Objects this is only possible with CS3 onwards. If you are working with an older version, you should not convert the layer to a Smart Object. You will notice an improvement already in the default setting. With the Amount slider at the top you can lighten the shadows. We set it to 62%. The Tonal Width determines which tones you want to modify. A very low Tonal Width will only lighten very dark areas. We chose a setting of 46%. The Radius affects the contrast of the pixels which can be edited through the Tonal Width. The smaller the Radius, the darker the correction will be and the larger the Radius, the lighter it will be. We set it to 24%. To reduce the contrast in the midtones, we set the Midtone-Contrast to -10%.

Stretch legs

Picture analysis

❶ Stretch both pairs of legs

❷ Maintain image size and proportions

❸ Woman's legs should be more dynamic

In this nostalgic photo, the camera angle had the unfortunate side-effect of shortening the bathing couple's legs. As the dune and the sky appear blurry anyway and do not contain detailed structures, a change of proportion will not be noticeable in these areas. You therefore do not need to be very exact when masking out the legs.

ch1/legs_transform.jpg

before

after

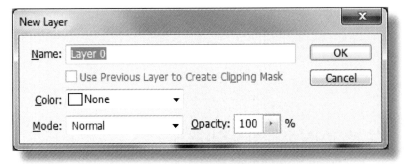

Change workspace

In order to lengthen the legs, you need to add workspace to the bottom edge of the picture. Because the picture size is to remain unchanged, you have to cut off the top edge of the picture.

The simplest solution is to just push the picture up a little bit.

You cannot move the background layer and therefore you need to turn it into a normal layer first. Double-click on the background layer in the Layers panel and confirm with OK in the dialog.

The background layer has now become "Layer 0"; it therefore has all the attributes of a normal layer.

To have better control, reveal the rulers with ⌘ / Ctrl + R and move the picture a few centimeters upwards with the Move tool (V), until you have sufficient space at the bottom for lengthening the legs without cutting off the top of the heads.

Stretch the woman's legs

To have the option of lengthening the woman's and man's legs independently, you edit each pair of legs on a separate layer. Use the Lasso tool (L, Feather 3 pixels) to select the woman's legs and surrounding area.

In order to conceal the transitions between transformed layer and original image as much as possible and therefore save retouching time, you should place the selection in an area without edges and patterns, as in our example picture. Copy the legs onto a new layer with ⌘/Ctrl+J. Name the layer "Woman, legs" and then convert it to a Smart Object.

Now lengthen the legs with the Free Transform tool (⌘/Ctrl+T). Drag the bottom center point of the bounding box downwards about 1 cm.

To give the right leg a bit more dynamic momentum, click on the Warp icon in the Options bar. Drag the top right handle slightly upwards.

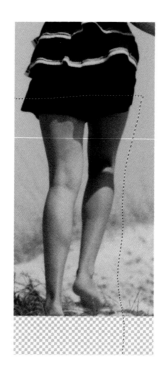

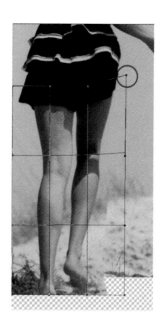

Stretch the man's legs

Proceed in the same way for selecting the man's legs. Guide the top edge of the selection through the two dark stripes in his shorts.

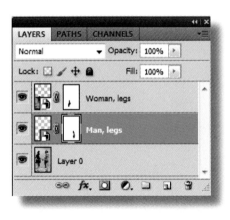

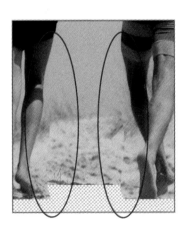

After the transformation, the picture now looks like this. The transitions from the dune still need to be adjusted. Use the Mask icon in the Layers panel to create a layer mask on every layer. Draw over the edges with black and the Brush tool (B , Size 125 pixels, Hardness 0%, Opacity 50%) and adjust the background.

Please note that the layer mask in older Photoshop versions does not change if you alter the layers once more through the transformation. This becomes possible with Photoshop CS4 onwards which has linked layer masks for Smart Objects.

For the last corrections we need to have all layers on a composite layer. Click on all three layers in the Layers panel while holding the Shift-key. This activates all three layers. Merge them by selecting Merge Layers from the menu in the Layers panel (⌘/Ctrl+E). Give this layer a new name to still be able to make further corrections later on.

Now drag the new composite layer downwards to the bottom edge of the picture with the Move tool (V).

Simply use the Clone Stamp tool (S, Size 150 pixels, Hardness 0%, Opacity 100%) to close up the last gap.

The quicker method

If you do not have to stick to exact measurements and can manage without the dynamic momentum of the woman's right leg, you have another option for a quicker solution to this scene. Open the original image, double click on the background layer and confirm the dialog box. You now have a "Layer 0" once again.

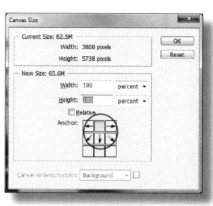

Use IMAGE/CANVAS SIZE to enter a higher value for HEIGHT, in our case 105%. For ANCHOR, click on the top center square and confirm with OK. The expanded area is added at the bottom and is transparent.

Use the Lasso tool ([L], Feather 5 pixels) to select the lower part of the picture. The top border of the selection outline should again go through areas without edges or patterns. Copy the selection to a new layer with [⌘]/[Ctrl]+[J] and push it back to its original position once more.

Use EDIT/FREE TRANSFORM ([⌘]/[Ctrl]+[T]) to drag the lower center handle of the bounding box downwards to the picture edge. Now you do not even need to make any further corrections.

Change body shape with light and shadow

Picture analysis

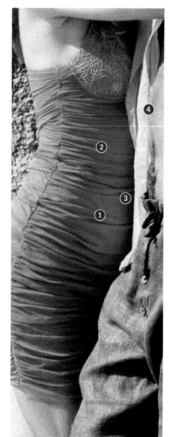

① Darken light reflection

② Enhance contrast in dress wrinkles

③ Insert two wrinkles in fabric

④ Push white shirt slightly to left

This picture makes the woman look pregnant. At first it seems as if we could use the Liquify filter or Warp tool to reduce the abdomen. If the woman was on the picture by herself, this would work. But these functions would also change the man. On closer inspection we notice that the man's white shirt reflects the light. The woman's dress has a strong highlight on the abdomen and therefore appears to be rounded.

ch1/cliff_couple.jpg

before

after

Adjust reflection

In this picture it is a good idea to edit the lights with a neutral layer. Dodge and Burn are not recommended as they affect image pixels directly and therefore change them. First, [Alt]-click on the CREATE A NEW LAYER icon at the bottom of the Layers panel. Select SOFT LIGHT and FILL WITH NEUTRAL COLOR in the dialog and click OK. Then copy the gray layer with [⌘]/[Ctrl]+[J]. In a neutral layer you paint with white in order to lighten an area and black in order to darken it.

To darken the reflection, use black ([D]) and the Brush tool to paint over the light areas ([B], Size 130 pixels, Hardness 40%, Opacity 8%). With this method you are reducing the light reflection on the dress.

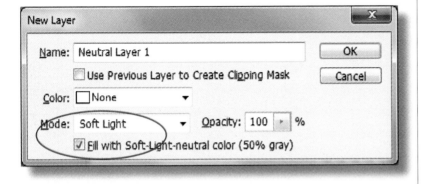

Darken abdomen

Activate the second neutral layer.
That way you won't need to redo
your previous work if you happen to
make a mistake. On this new layer,
darken the abdomen area until it
matches the darkness of the thigh
area.

If the transitions still seem too
hard despite soft brush tips, select
FILTER/BLUR/GAUSSIAN BLUR and
blur the neutral layer with a Radius
of 3 pixels.

You can check the strength of the
Gaussian blur directly in the picture.
The light transitions should not
show any hard edges.

The effect is most noticeable in the
transitions from light to dark within
the picture. To check the neutral
layer, temporarily set the blend
mode to NORMAL. Now you can see
a gray area with dark parts.

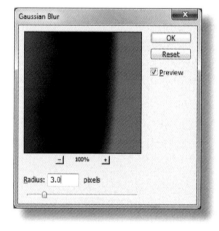

First enlarge the picture to 100%
view by double clicking on the
magnifying glass, otherwise you
will not be able to judge the effect
correctly.

Adapt wrinkles in fabric

The abdomen is now darkened, but the contrast in the wrinkles on the dress is missing. They have to become much darker.

Create a Curves adjustment layer and drag the curve downwards in the first third. It does not matter if you cannot find the best setting straight away. You can always re-open the curve later by double clicking on the layer thumbnail and correct it then.

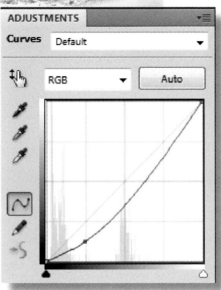

The curve now darkens the whole picture. Click on the layer mask of that layer and fill it with black (⌘/Ctrl+I). Now paint over the shadows in the wrinkles with white and the Brush tool (B) set to a low Opacity of 8%, to darken the shadows even more. The brush tip should be as big as the wrinkle in question and very soft. Alt-click on the layer mask to make it visible. Now you can quickly check your steps. Hide the layer mask again with the Alt-key.

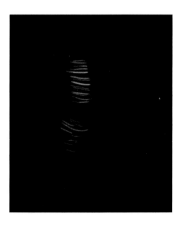

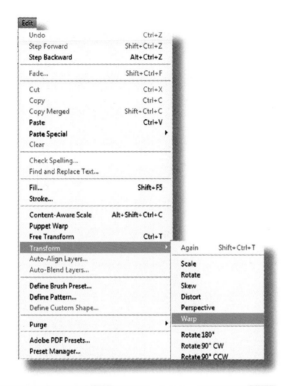

Enhance effect

To perfect the result, you can copy two additional wrinkles into the dress, to make the fabric around the abdomen look less stretched. You can also make the man's shirt fall over the stomach more. Flatten all layers with the command in the Layers panel and save the picture under a new name. This ensures you still have the original file with all layers and can easily make corrections later.

Select a section of the shirt with the Quick Selection tool ([W]) and refine the selection in Mask mode by pressing [Q]. Optimize the selection with black or white. Press [Q] once again and you get a selection. Copy the shirt with [⌘]/[Ctrl]+[J] onto a new layer.

Transform the layer into a smart object with the pop-up menu in the Layers panel. Activate EDIT/TRANSFORM/WARP and use the Warp tool to drag the right side of the shirt to the left, as on the picture. Confirm the transformation and then create a new layer mask by clicking on the Add Layer Mask icon at the bottom of the Layers panel. Finally, use black ([D]) to match the edges of the shirt to the surrounding areas.

Style upper body

Picture analysis

❶ Chest area more muscular

❷ Enhance upper arm muscularity

Bodystyling, the fast way: taut muscles and great upper body with just a few mouse clicks.

ch1/bodystyling.jpg

before

after

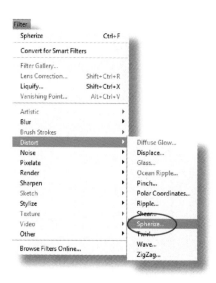

Enlarge upper body

Many people can just dream of getting a more muscular upper body without losing a single drop of sweat. Here you can achieve it with a quick trick.

Copy the background layer with ⌘/Ctrl+J. Use the Lasso tool (L, Feather 20 pixels) to select the area of the upper body that you want to make more muscular. In our example, it is the upper arms and the chest down to the lower ribs. If you make your selection as in the picture, you will not need to adjust the transitions after making your changes.

Give the body more volume with FILTER/DISTORT/SPHERIZE and an Amount of 37% and the Mode NORMAL. That's how quick it can be.

Of course you could also edit each area separately to differentiate and target your alterations more carefully. Make sure to apply the filter to each area only once, otherwise you will create blurs and risk loss of details. Alternatively, transform the body parts to a smart object before making your changes. Then you can apply the filter as many times as you wish.

Refine upper body contours

Picture analysis

❶ Reduce abdomen

A slight correction in the abdomen area has a double effect in this example. The chest now has a more attractive shape and the abdomen seems slimmer.

ch1/deckchair.jpg

before

after

Enlarge breast by reducing abdomen

In order to enlarge a breast it is not always necessary to edit it. In our example it is sufficient to simply make the abdomen slimmer.

First select the abdomen with the Lasso tool and a feathered edge of 5 pixels. Copy the selection to a new layer with ⌘/Ctrl+J. Transform the new layer to a Smart Object via the pop-up menu in the Layers panel.

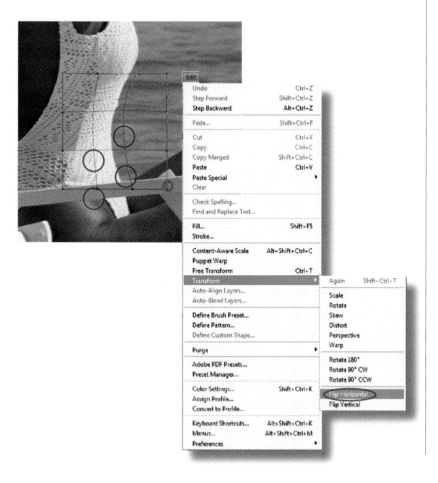

Use EDIT/TRANSFORM/WARP and drag the Warp tool so that the abdomen curves inwards more. You can do this by clicking on any point of the mesh or inside the squares and then dragging them.

Zoom to 100% by double-clicking on the magnifying glass and adapt the edges with a layer mask. Watch out especially for doubled contours and too soft or illogical transitions in the water and the swimsuit.

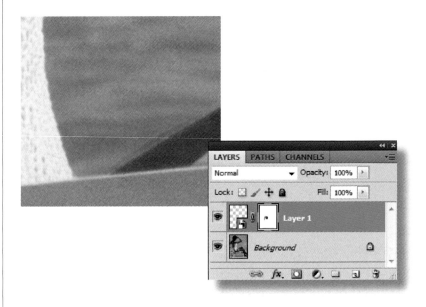

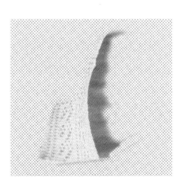

Hide the background layer and you can see what is left of your swimsuit.

A small adjustment has a very noticeable effect.

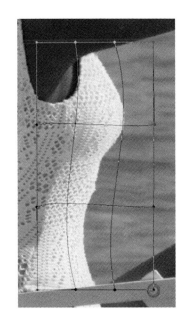

Enhance effect

If you are not satisfied by the result, you can of course enhance the effect even more with the Warp tool.

Use the Lasso tool (⎣L⎦) to select chest and abdomen and convert the selection into a new layer.

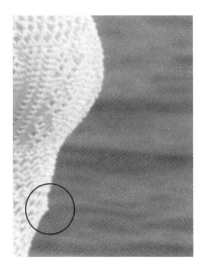

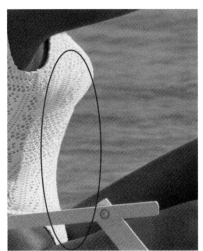

With the Warp tool, create a new shape and retouch the edges with a layer mask. Watch out once more for inconsistent transitions in the background.

Finally, use the Clone Stamp tool to remove the little bulge underneath the breast.

Paint with light and emphasize contours

Picture analysis

❶ Model upper body with light and shadow

The unfortunate lighting conditions and the frontal perspective of this shot cause the upper body contours to be almost lost altogether. We use light and shadow to accentuate the curves.

before

after

ch1/parasol.jpg

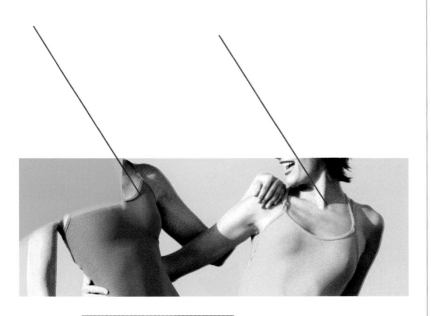

Enhance light and shadow

A closer look at the existing highlights and shadows helps us determine the exact direction of the light source. We have marked it with a red line in the picture.

For greatest possible flexibility, we have created two neutral layers for each model, one for lightening, the other for darkening. Create a neutral layer by Alt -clicking on the CREATE A NEW LAYER icon at the bottom of the Layers panel. In the dialog box, you immediately enter SOFT LIGHT and FILL WITH NEUTRAL COLOR and confirm by clicking on OK. Copy it a further three times by pressing ⌘/ Ctrl + J . Name the layers and create two groups of two layers each to have a better overview. You group two layers by highlighting them while pressing the ⇧ -key and clicking on NEW GROUP FROM LAYERS in the Layers panel.

Use the Brush tool ([B], Size 70 pixels, Hardness 0%, Opacity 8% and white) to paint over all areas you want to brighten. Follow the original brightness distribution and the determined direction of the light. If the light transitions still end up too hard despite the soft brush, you can correct this later. Paint with black ([D]). to darken areas. With a neutral layer you will not achieve the amount of contrast you need. In that case, simply duplicate the layers.

Highlights

Shadows

Highlights

Shadows

To partially undo something you need to paint with 50% Gray at 100% Opacity.

Adapt brightness transitions

As there are two neutral layers for each model, you can now adapt all brightness transitions with the FILTER/BLUR FILTER/GAUSSIAN BLUR. Here you can see the highlights adjusted with a Radius of 10 pixels. Proceed in the same way with the other neutral layers.

Always choose 100% zoom (by double-clicking on the magnifying glass) when sharpening as well as softening to make sure you can see the effect clearly.

Gaussian Blur	
	OK
	Reset
	☑ Preview

‑ 100% +

Radius: 10 pixels

Filter

Last Filter	Ctrl+F
Convert for Smart Filters	
Filter Gallery...	
Lens Correction...	Shift+Ctrl+R
Liquify...	Shift+Ctrl+X
Vanishing Point...	Alt+Ctrl+V
Artistic	▶
Blur	▶
Brush Strokes	▶
Distort	▶
Noise	▶
Pixelate	▶
Render	▶
Sharpen	▶
Sketch	▶
Stylize	▶
Texture	▶
Video	▶
Other	▶
Browse Filters Online...	

- Average
- Blur
- Blur More
- Box Blur...
- Gaussian Blur...
- Lens Blur...
- Motion Blur...
- Radial Blur...
- Shape Blur...
- Smart Blur...
- Surface Blur...

Basic Overview: Workflow

A functioning workflow is largely dependent on the equipment of your work area. This means not only the equipment of computer and monitor, but also the organization of the workspace in Photoshop and the installation of supporting programs.

Hardware

1. Get the most powerful computer for image editing you can afford.

2. Equip your computer with as much RAM as possible. You should have no less than 2 GB, unless you are working only with small images for the internet and do not require any other programs.

3. Get a fast graphics card, especially when using 3D and video files.

4. A large monitor of at least 19 or 21 inches which can be hardware calibrated would be a great advantage.

5. Get a second monitor for the panels. This can be smaller than the main monitor and does not need to be calibratable.

6. A monitor calibration device is available at very low prices (for example http://xrite.com, http://www.basic-color.de/). In a pinch you can also use the computer's own calibration tools. You will find them in the System settings "Monitor" (for Mac) or "Adobe Gamma" (for Windows), they are better than nothing.

7. Set the monitor to a color temperature of 6500 or 5000 degrees Kelvin. Take note of the recommendations in the monitor manufacturer's handbook and set the background of the operating system to a neutral gray.

8. With a graphics tablet by Wacom you can for example regulate the brush size simply by altering the pressure on the stylus. With different pens, a variety of tasks can be completed much better and quicker than with the mouse. For image editing you should choose a tablet that is A4 sized or bigger. Try out different sizes until you find the one best suited to your method of working. This will save your mouse hand a lot of pain.

9. Backup your data regularly, if possible daily, perhaps over night. A 1 terrabyte hard drive and backup programs have become relatively cheap. Look out for such programs as Open Source versions, then they are often even free.

10. Ideally, the walls in your work area should be a neutral gray.

11. Make sure that no windows, light sources or other objects are reflected in your monitor.

12. Calibrate your camera equipment.

Software

1. Take photos in RAW format whenever possible, in order to have the best options for controlling the image.

2. Make sure you always install the latest updates for Photoshop, Camera RAW and all other programs. This way you avoid incompatibilities, speed up the programs and can potentially get new editing functions.

3. Get the free CarbonCopyCloner program for Mac (http://www.bombich.com). It allows you to copy your system and all programs to another hard disk from which you can start, work and in an emergency copy all data back to the original hard disk. All settings and registrations remain intact and you can carry on working as if nothing ever happened. There are similar programs for Windows.

Photoshop set-up

When you open Photoshop for the first time, it appears with the default setting. All panel positions, shortcuts, preferences and color settings are pre-set. This does however not mean that they are all set correctly or sensibly.

One Monitor

1. Position the panels, for example on the second monitor.

2. Choose EDIT/KEYBOARD SHORTCUTS and you can define and save your own keyboard shortcuts.

3. Choose WINDOW/WORKSPACE/NEW WORKSPACE. You can save different workspaces with keyboard shortcuts.

Main monitor

Second monitor

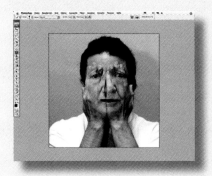

4. With the same menu item, you can access your saved workspaces.

Color settings

To make sure you are working in the right color space and with the correct colors, you need to adapt your color settings to your workflow. For professional work it makes sense to choose the largest possible color space. We work exclusively in Adobe RGB and ProPhoto RGB. Choose EDIT/COLOR SETTINGS and enter individual settings for each purpose. Of course you can save each setting separately for your customers. On the right you can see the color settings for our workflow. If you need to get into the color settings in more detail, we recommend that you read a book about Photoshop basics or Photoshop for photographers. You can find further information about color management on the internet.

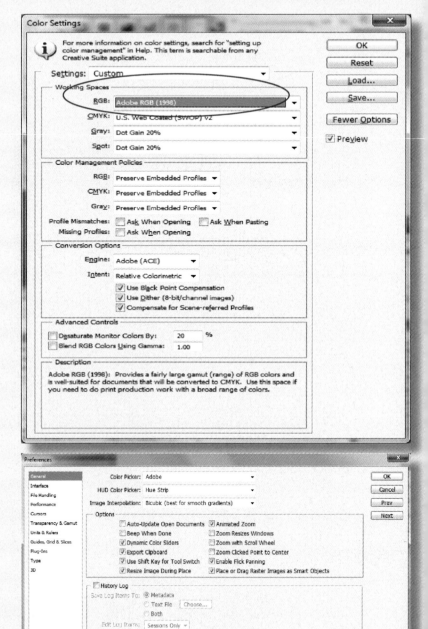

Preferences

In order to be able to work properly, effectively and comfortably you need to change the Preferences in Photoshop. For Mac you will find these in the Photoshop Menu under Mac OSX, for Windows they are in the Edit menu. Here you can choose the displayed cursor shape, how Photoshop handles the different data and how much RAM is assigned. For further information on this topic, refer to the relevant literature, look in the Photoshop Help menu or do a search on the Internet.

The following web pages are very helpful:
http://www.photoshop-weblog.com
http://www.psd-tutorials.com

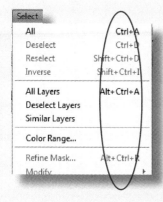

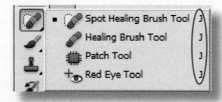

Keyboard shortcuts

With keyboard shortcuts you can speed up your work enormously. Photoshop has several hundreds of them. You can find them next to most menu items and in the Tools panel. Try to remember the shortcut whenever you need to use a tool or command more frequently.

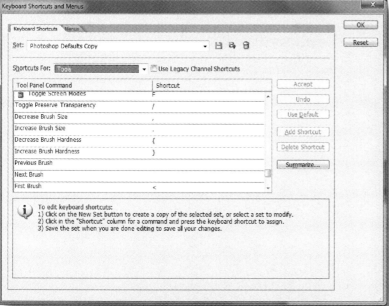

With EDIT/KEYBOARD SHORTCUTS you can specify your own shortcuts. However, bear in mind that they might already be assigned and that you could end up changing predefined shortcuts. We decided to use the keyboard shortcuts "Full stop" and "Comma" for enlarging and reducing brush tips.

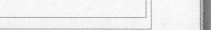

To change the opacity of a tool, simply click on "Opacity" and drag lightly to the right or left, or enter the number 1 to set opacity to 10%. This works with many tools.

Brushes

The brushes are useful tools but often underestimated. Most often they are used with a round shape and some sort of feathered edge. Occasionally, you might change the opacity of the brush and that's it. In the bottom right picture you can see two vertical red lines which were drawn with the Brush tool. The line on the left was drawn with a pressure sensitive stylus, the one on the right with the mouse. The stylus allows working with different sizes and different opacity, without having to change these parameters. Everything is governed by the amount of pressure of the stylus onto the graphics tablet. This allows very effective use of the Painting and Retouching tools which have brushes. A wonderful time-saver. To have access to the panels and settings, you need to activate a Painting or Retouching tool. Most users use the panel from the Options bar to change Size, Sharpness and Shape of the brush tip. With the menu at the top right in the panel you can change the view of the panel and load other brushes. Adobe includes many already on the Photoshop installation DVD, others you can download from the Internet.

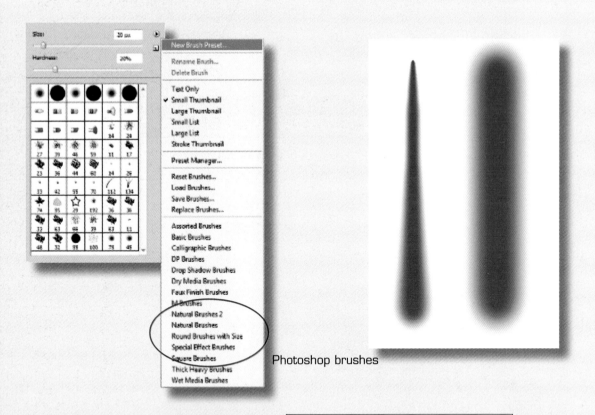

Photoshop brushes

When using additional plug-ins off the internet, read the copyright terms carefully. Some you may use for free, others you can only test before purchasing.

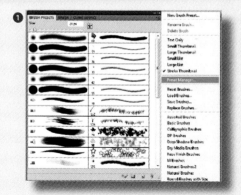

The Brush panel

The Brush panel is even more comprehensive than the brush options from the Options bar. You can access the Brush panel with WINDOW/BRUSH or with the icon in the Options bar.

The BRUSH PRESETS tab (1) shows the effects of each brush. You can also view brushes in the PRESET MANAGER (via panel menu or icon at bottom of Brush Presets tab). The BRUSH tab has a panel subdivided into seven categories (2). If you click on one of them, the Brush Tip Shape dialog window changes (4). Lower down in the panel there are five additional properties (3) which you can activate.

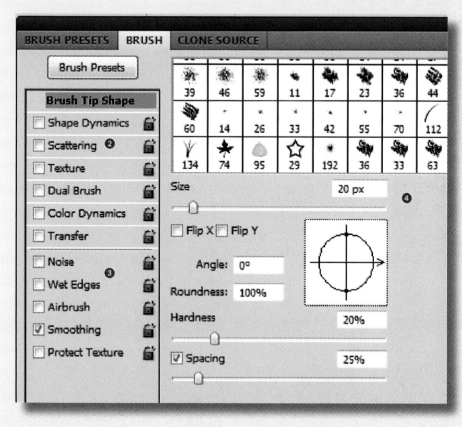

Create custom brush

For certain purposes it might be useful to create your own brush tip. If for example you are editing hair and want to avoid having to paint every single hair, you can create a custom brush which can paint several different and therefore more natural seeming hairs with one single brush stroke. For our example we will create a brush tip which consists of four individual tips. Use FILE/NEW to create a new file with a size of 100 x 100 pixels. Paint with the Brush tool ([B], Size 9 pixels, Hardness 0%, Opacity 100%) to create four differently sized black spots.

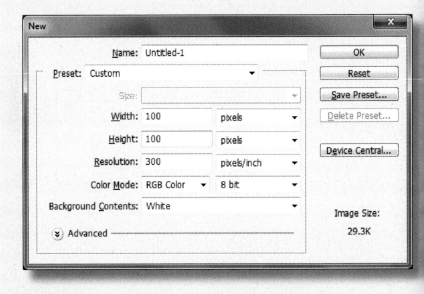

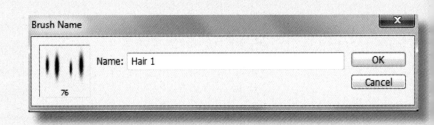

In principle, the brush tip is now finished. To make sure it appears in the Brush panel, save it under EDIT/BRUSH PRESET. We called our new brush tip shape "Hair 1". You can close the picture with the four spots without saving.

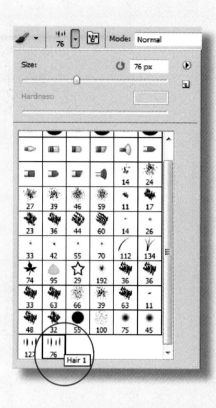

Test the brush tip

When you now open the Brush panel, you will find the brush tip "Hair 1" right at the bottom. In the picture you can see its effect. The brush tips can also consist in different brightness values. If you use a color for creating a brush tip, only the brightness value is adapted. You can also use images or graphics. We restrict our tips to a maximum of 3 MB, otherwise working with them becomes too slow. Make sure to create a new file for the brush tip. To be able to keep the brush tip for later use, save it in the panel menu.

Properties of brush tips for hair

If we wanted to add fine hairs to certain areas of a hairstyle, we would need to paint them in individually and always make sure to get the coloring right.

It is much easier to pull out the additional hairs from the hairstyle using the Smudge tool. To avoid them getting too long, we insert an automatic stop. Choose the Smudge tool, switch to the Brush panel and click on Brush Tip Shape. Now rotate the Angle until the brush tip has the same direction as the hair at the point where you want to edit

To make sure hair does not get too long, activate the Shape Dynamics and set the Control to FADE. Choose a value of 80. In the preview at the bottom of the panel you can see the effects of your settings. Experiment with the different setting options. This way you can find the most effective solution for each individual problem.

Saving tool presets

You can save these properties as well. Activate the Tool Presets panel with WINDOW/TOOL PRESETS. Click on the CREATE NEW TOOL PRESET icon and give it a unambiguous name. Now you always have access to that brush tip with those exact properties. Save the preferences in the panel menu.

Further custom libraries

You can save your own tools and their properties, colors, styles, gradients etc in many panels. Over time you can build up your own custom libraries, mainly through the panel menu. On this picture you can see the menu of the Swatches panel as an example. In the lower rows we created useful colors for skin and hair.

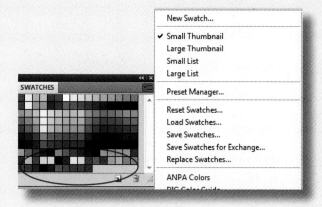

Everything you save in this way is saved in a Presets folder within the Photoshop folder. Backup this Presets folder after important projects on a DVD or with the project itself. This ensures you will still have access to your data later, in case you need to edit that project again one day.

mask-like unattractive flabby long wide oval square pointy triangular individual memorable inconspicu
pointy noble lively attractive vital average common round pinched plain symmetrical asymmetrical r
unattractive mask-like flabby relaxed strained stressed long wide oval square average fine unattrac
pretty interesting lively rough irregular animated lively regular shapeless rigid symmetrical asymmetr
plain lively prominent striking rough regular noble vital mask-like unattractive flabby long wide oval squ
pointy triangular individual memorable inconspicuous attractive vital average common round pinched p

Chapter 2
Facial contours

 How to change facial
properties easily

How to refine facial
contours

 How to adapt head
shape and create
symmetry

How to shape an
elaborate nose

**Basic Overview
Layers**

How to reduce
laugh lines

How to reduce large
noses

How to remove a
double chin

How to correct
distorted images with
lens correction

Change facial proportions

Picture analysis

❶ Enlarge hat

❷ Enlarge eyes

❸ Enlarge mouth

At first you will hardly notice any difference between these two pictures. But if you look more closely you will see that the eyes and mouth are more pronounced in the bottom picture. We changed the proportions of some image details to draw more attention to these areas.

ch2/green_hat.jpg
ch2/curlers.jpg

before

after

Enlarge hat

First we want to give a bigger frame to the eyes and push unfavorable contours more into the background. To that purpose, we need to enlarge the hat without affecting the face. Duplicate the background with ⌘/Ctrl+J and convert this layer to a Smart Object via the menu in the Layers panel.

Use ⌘/Ctrl+T to transform the image horizontally to about 107%. Confirm by pressing the ⏎-key.

Adapt face

Create a layer mask on this layer and paint with black over all areas which you do not want to appear wider. Use the Brush tool (B, Size 80 pixels, Hardness 40%, Opacity 100%). We hid the background in this picture to show how you can better judge the unmasked areas. As you can see, soft transitions are sufficient in the hair and the neck area. Only at the rim of the hat we need to work a bit more precisely. Now show the background again.

Emphasize eyes

We can enhance the effect of the eyes even more by enlarging them a little bit. Select the eyes with the Lasso tool ($\boxed{L}$, Feather 4 pixels). Activate the layer "Background", copy the selected eye section onto a new layer with $\boxed{⌘}$/$\boxed{Ctrl}$+$\boxed{J}$ and convert this layer to a Smart Object. Move the layer upwards in the Layers panel. Press $\boxed{⌘}$/$\boxed{Ctrl}$+$\boxed{T}$ and drag the bounding border 2% to the left and to the right, so you have a total of 104%. Enlarge the transformation border downwards to 104% as well. Confirm with the $\boxed{⏎}$-key. Thanks to the exact selection and the feathered edge, you do not need to make any corrections using a mask.

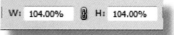

Enlarge mouth

We want to emphasize the mouth as well. Select the mouth and some of the surrounding area with the Lasso tool ($\boxed{L}$) and copy it into a new layer with $\boxed{⌘}$/$\boxed{Ctrl}$+$\boxed{J}$. Convert it into a Smart Object and scale the width of the mouth to 110%. Now press the $\boxed{⏎}$-key.

With this very simple method you can quickly emphasize certain details and direct the attention away from others.

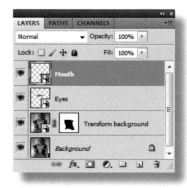

Normal

Scaled horizontally

Scaled horizontally using
Content-Aware Scale

Content-Aware Scale

Content-Aware Scale is similar to
the normal scaling, but the difference
is that there are fewer distortions.
With normal scaling, all details are
simply stretched in one direction.
The result is a very wide face with
distorted eyes, nose and mouth. The
proportions are no longer right. With
Content-Aware Scaling, Photoshop
distinguishes between areas rich in
detail, such as the eyes, and areas that
have little details, such as the skin.
In this case, the skin areas are stret-
ced more than the other areas. Nose,
mouth and eyes remain practically
unchanged.

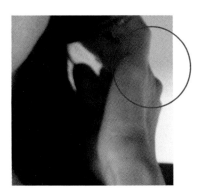

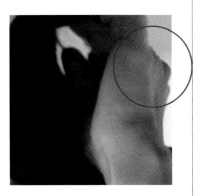

If we scale too strongly, this can
create unwanted distortions even
with Content-Aware Scale, as in our
example on the hand. Fortunately, we
can easily fix this by creating an additional channel.

Create alpha channel to protect image areas

To protect parts of your image with a channel, go to the Channels palette and click on the CREATE NEW CHANNEL icon. Click on the eye icon to show the RGB channel again, but make sure it is not activated. Only the Alpha channel should be activated, as shown here. The image is now covered with red masking color.

Next, use the Brush tool (B) and white to paint over all areas you want to protect from distortion. In our case, we cover eyes, nose, mouth and parts of hands and forearms.

Now activate the RGB channel and hide the Alpha 1 channel. Make sure the Alpha channel is not activated or loaded as selection.

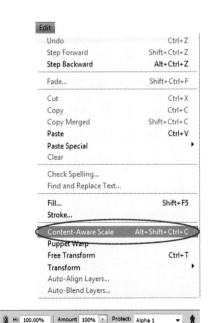

Make hat wider

Go to the Layers palette and duplicate the background with ⌘/Ctrl+J. Choose EDIT/CONTENT-AWARE SCALE.

A normal bounding box appears. Before you start dragging the handles, go to the Options bar and set PROTECT to the Alpha 1 channel. Now drag the left or right handle of the bounding box whilst holding the Alt- and ⇧-key. Your picture will be scaled evenly to the left and right, while the protected areas remain unchanged. Confirm the transformation by pressing the ↵-key. Check your image for artifacts and unwanted distortions at 100% view (by double-clicking on the magnifying glass). To emphasize the eyes or enlarge the mouth, you can proceed as described earlier.

Change proportions with Puppet Warp

Puppet Warp is an ingenious way of changing shapes. It is most often used for repositioning arms or legs on individual layers. But you can use it to change the proportions of entire images, too. First, duplicate the background with ⌘/Ctrl+J. Convert the layer to a Smart Object to make sure you can still change proportions later on without loss of quality.

Choose EDIT/PUPPET WARP to activate the visual mesh. Now you can place pins into the mesh by clicking on it. You can then drag the pins.

If you place not enough pins as in this example, the image will be merely shifted or become overly distorted. The trick is to use the pins to fixate any areas which you want to anchor in place or distort only slightly.

Protect facial shape

To stop the facial shape being changed, you need to place many pins around the face. If you place too many, a warning appears to alert you that this is not possible.

Place some pins into the area around the hat and drag slightly on the image edges (see circles). The hat becomes wider and the surrounding area is adjusted harmoniously.

Adapt face

To change the eyes and mouth you can add pins in the corners of the eyes and the mouth. Then drag the pins apart slightly to adjust the size (see circles). Confirm by pressing the ⏎-key.

As you can see, the editing has caused unpleasant distortions on the right and left cheek.

Reactivate the Puppet Warp mesh. It opens with the same settings you entered last time and you can simply adapt them. Now check the image at 100% view (double-click on the magnifying glass). Retouch any distortions that may still be present.

before

after

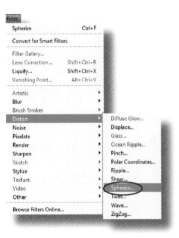

Even quicker

Depending on your motif it may be possible to make someone slimmer even more quickly. Duplicate the background of your original image once more with ⌘/Ctrl+J. Convert the copy to a Smart Object.

Choose Filter/Distort/Spherize. Set the Strength to -39% and the Mode to Normal. Click on Ok and hey presto, the face has become narrow without requiring any further retouching.

Of course, these methods only work so well because the background does not pose any problems. As soon as the background has a detailed pattern, complex corrections of the background may become necessary.

Change head shape and create symmetry

Picture analysis

❶ Make part of face narrower

❷ Change hairstyle

❸ Adapt ears

This male portrait is quite old and no longer corresponds to the model's current look. The picture cannot be reshot in the same way and the customer would therefore like us to update the portrait. His facial features are now somewhat narrower, the hair is cut shorter and in a more rounded style. The customer also wants us to adapt his two unequal seeming ears and would like them closer to the head.

ch2/head_shape.jpg

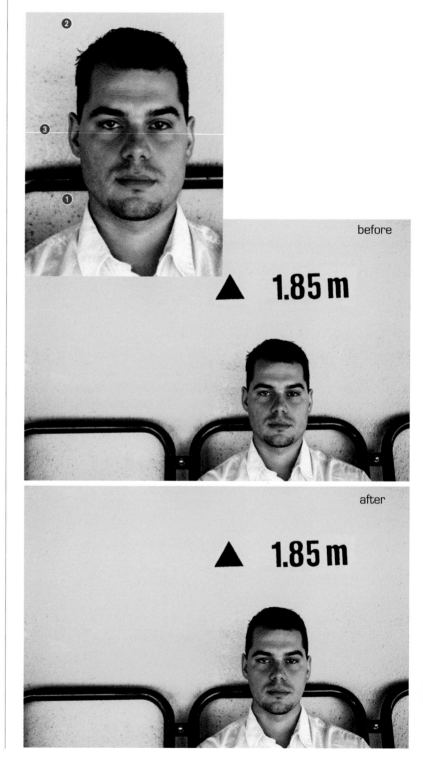

before

▲ 1.85 m

after

▲ 1.85 m

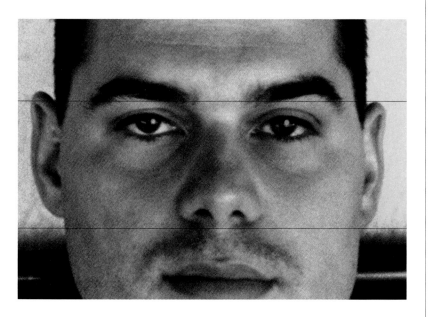

Correct head shape

We will carry out all corrections in one editing step. However, for the ears we will require guide lines. But the guides in Photoshop are not visible in the Liquify filter. Create a new empty layer and use the Single Row Marquee tool to select two single horizontal lines. Fill these with black via EDIT/FILL/USE/BLACK.

Copy the background layer (⬚J). To make sure the Liquify filter does not load the entire image into the editing window, select the head with the Marquee tool (⬚M) and a slight feathered edge of about 5 pixels.

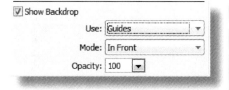

Show guides

Choose the LIQUIFY filter. To show the guides, activate the checkbox SHOW BACKGROUND at the bottom right. Under USE, choose Guides.

Chin and cheeks

Start with the chin line on the right.
Push the cheek line slightly to the
left with the Forward Warp tool (W).
Gradually work your way along the
facial contour to the level of the left ear.
Don't worry about any distortions in the
background, you can correct them later.
Use the settings shown on our picture.

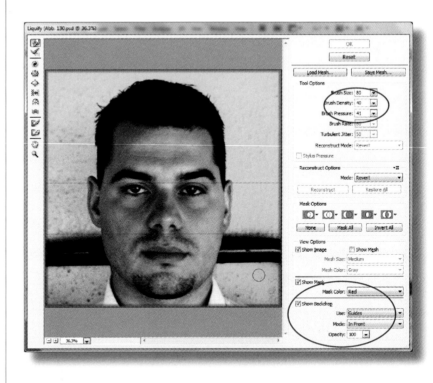

Matching ears

To adapt the ears, zoom to 100%.
Drag the left ear lobe and the upper
part of the ear slightly downwards
with the Forward Warp tool (W).
Then push the entire ear slightly
inwards and give it a rounded shape.
Now match the right ear to the left
one until both ears appear symmetrical.

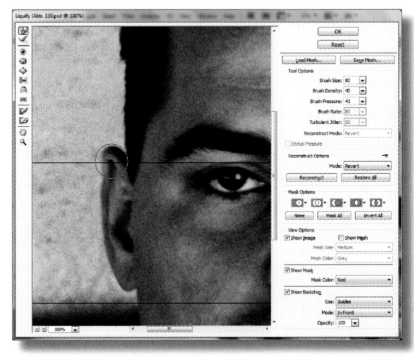

Tool Options

Brush Size: 190 ▾
Brush Density: 40 ▾
Brush Pressure: 41 ▾
Brush Rate: 80 ▾
Turbulent Jitter: 50 ▾
Reconstruct Mode: Revert ▾

Trim haircut

To avoid distorting the wall too much and in order to keep the individual hairs sticking up on the edges, you need a bigger tool tip for the hairdo. Use the values shown here in the dialog box. On a new layer, you can draw a guide line for the hairdo which will give you a better overview. This time, draw the approximate head shape by hand. Push the hairs that are outside of your line slightly inwards. Create a harmonious head shape and then click on OK.

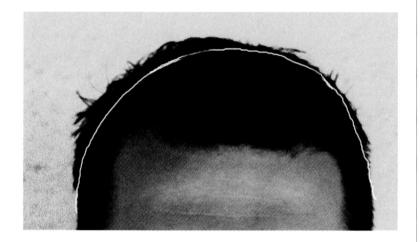

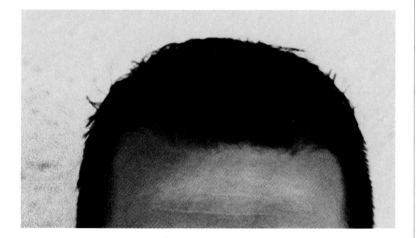

Remove distortions

Due to the Liquify filter, the background has become distorted. This
is especially noticeable with the
metal bar in the background. Use
the Clone Stamp tool to retouch
these areas ($\boxed{S}$, Size 50 pixels,
Hardness 40%, Opacity 100%).

Check the wall closely for any
distortions and blurred areas.
Unfortunately, it is almost impos-
sible to recreate these in print.
Look carefully at your picture to
spot any that may be there.

Creating symmetry quickly

The fastest way of creating symmetry is to flip one half of the face over to form its own mirror image. Select the left half of the face with the Rectangular Marquee tool (M, Feather 0 pixel) and copy the selection to a new layer with ⌘/Ctrl+J.

Flip the layer with EDIT/TRANSFORM/FLIP HORIZONTAL and position it on the right side of the face.

Create a layer mask while pressing the Alt-key. Half of the face is now hidden. Now paint with white and the Brush tool (B) and bring the face back at the faulty intersections.

Hide the background occasionally to be able to judge your retouching more accurately. Make sure that no hard edges are visible.

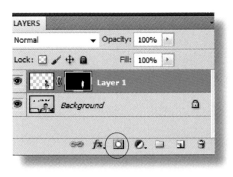

Final adjustments

It is best to make the final adjustments in a composite layer. But the individual layers should be preserved. Activate the top layer, hold the Alt-key and choose MERGE VISIBLE in the Layers menu. The visible layers are merged into one, the original layers are maintained. Now hide all hard transitions in the face with the retouching tools.

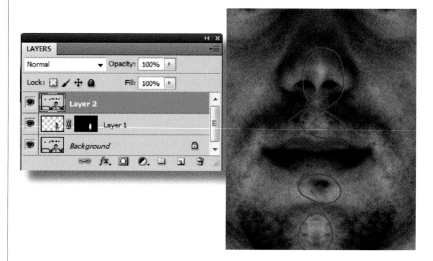

Finally, create a Curves adjustment layer and brighten the face slightly, as shown on this picture. Fill the layer mask with black (⌘/Ctrl+I) and paint with white to brighten the areas which are too dark.

Of course you can now carry on editing the face as described in the first section.

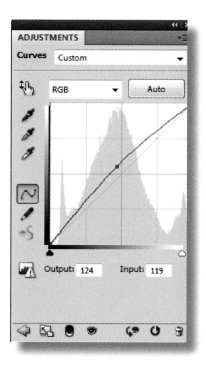

Facial symmetry

It is always surprising just how different the two halves of a face can be. You can see this clearly in these examples. We used the same method to duplicate the right half of the face and flip it over onto the left side around the vertical axis. The astonishing results of this mirroring can be seen here.

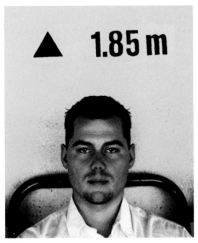

Left side of face flipped

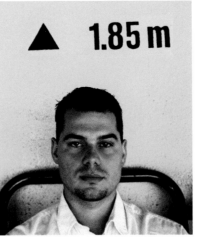

Original

Right side of face flipped

We did the same to a model wearing make-up.
In this case, the differences are hardly noticeable.

Reduce laugh lines

Picture analysis

❶ Reduce laugh lines on chin

❷ Remove double chin

The cordial laughter has created an unflattering double chin in this model. The laugh lines reinforce this impression even more.

before

after

ch2/laugh_lines.jpg

Increase processing speed

If the image has a very large file size and only a certain area needs retouching, it often helps to only work with a section of the image and to re-insert this section later. In our case we only need to change the woman's chin, so we select the area around the chin with the Crop tool ([C]) and confirm by pressing [↵]. Save the new file under a new name.

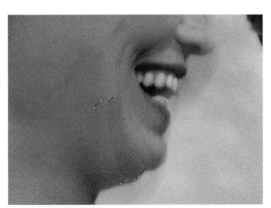

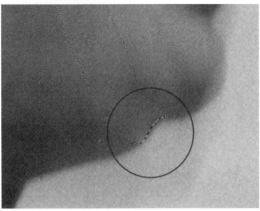

Retouching wrinkles

First remove the offending laugh line around the chin. To do this, copy the background with [⌘]/[Ctrl]+[J]. Now select the laugh line with the Patch tool ([J]) and drag it onto a smooth area of skin.

This tool works best within even areas. If the selection also includes edges, as in our case the lower edge of the throat, we have to drag it onto a similar texture with similar edge characteristics. To that purpose it is important to select both sides of the edge generously and then place edge on edge via the preview window.

Otherwise, it can create unwanted shifts in brightness, as you can see here.

Proceed in the same manner with all other unwanted wrinkles and laugh lines. After the retouching, the face should look something like this.

Make sure that the person still looks natural. A laughing mouth completely without laugh lines appears artificial.

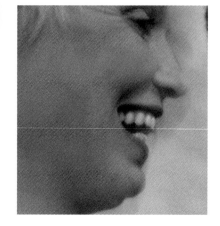

Change chin shape

To give the chin a pretty smooth outline, it is best to stamp in the shape. Create a path with the Pen tool ($\boxed{P}$). Start the path at the lower lip as shown on the picture. This way, the continuation of the path is adapted harmoniously to the areas that are not being changed. Determine your new chin contour with the run of the path (see Basic Overview: Paths, Chapter 7).

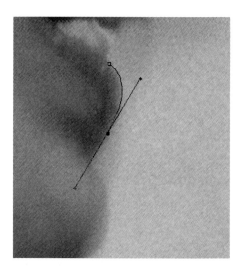

Once the path has the right shape, close it by clicking on the starting point. Save the path via the Paths panel under a new name, for example "Chin".

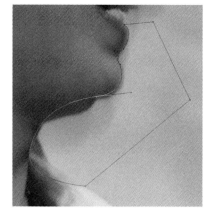

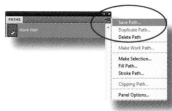

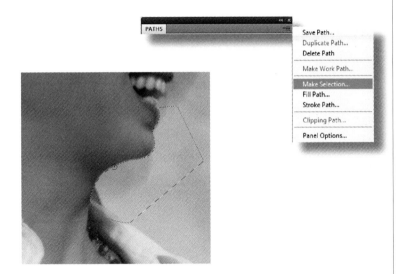

Now load the path as selection via the Paths panel. Enter a Feather Radius of 8 pixels into the dialog. The edge has to be smooth because the original edge is also very flowing. Now remove the double chin with the Clone Stamp tool ([S]).

If the selection border bothers you during retouching, you can make it invisible with [⌘]/[Ctrl]+[H] and visible again with [⌘]/[Ctrl]+[H]. But careful, this does not remove the selection, it only hides it.

Copy and paste retouching into original image

Copy the retouched image with [⌘]/[Ctrl]+[C]. Open the original image and insert the retouched picture with [⌘]/[Ctrl]+[V]. Set the Blend mode to DIFFERENCE. Position the layer in the right place with the Move tool ([V]). The layer becomes black when it is in the right place. Only the changed areas appear light. Set the Blend Mode back to NORMAL (see Basic Overview: Blend Modes, Chapter 4).

Remove double chin

Picture analysis

❶ Remove wrinkles on neck

❷ Narrower neck outline on right and left

❸ Change contour of chin/cheek area on right

❹ Recreate skin texture on neck

❺ Brighten neck, recreate left chin/jaw line

Before we can remedy this double chin, we first have to analyze the way it presents itself. To his purpose it helps to look at the picture "two-dimensionally". The impression of indentations and bulges is created visually by highlights and shadows, or in terms of graphics, by light and dark areas. If we align the brightness of both and create new accents with shadows, we can easily adjust the facial features.

ch2/doublechin.jpg

before

after

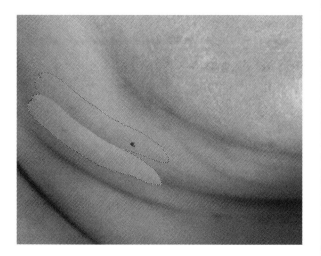

Remove wrinkles

In order to remove the wrinkles, first duplicate the background layer again (⌘ / Ctrl + J) and zoom to 100% by double-clicking on the magnifying glass. Name the layer, for example "Retouch wrinkles".

Select a wrinkle on the neck with the Patch tool (J) and drag the wrinkle onto a smooth area with similar skin texture. Proceed in the same way with all wrinkles. Make sure that you do not retouch too much and end up accidentally removing the chin line. The neck should look something like this after your retouching.

Narrower neck

Choose the Pen tool (P). First create
two exact paths on both sides of the
neck for your new neck contour. Save
the finished paths in the Paths panel.
Give them names, "Neck left" and
"Neck right".

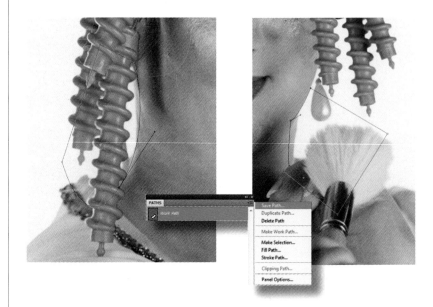

Activate the path "Neck left" in the
Paths panel and transform it into a
selection with a feathered edge of 1
pixel. Duplicate the layer "Retouch
wrinkles" ($\mathcal{H}$/$Ctrl$+J) and
rename it to "Left/Right neck line".
Now remove the neck line with the
Clone Stamp tool (S, Size 20 pixels, Hardness 50%, Opacity 100%).
You can use the area to the left of the
rollers as sample point for the tool.
Proceed in the same way on the right
side.

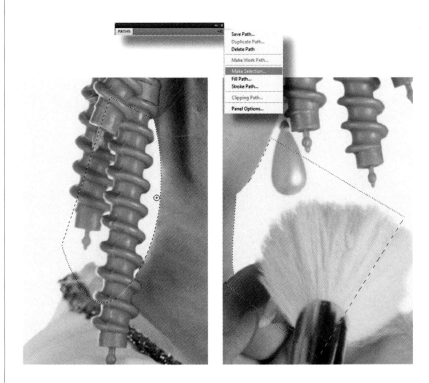

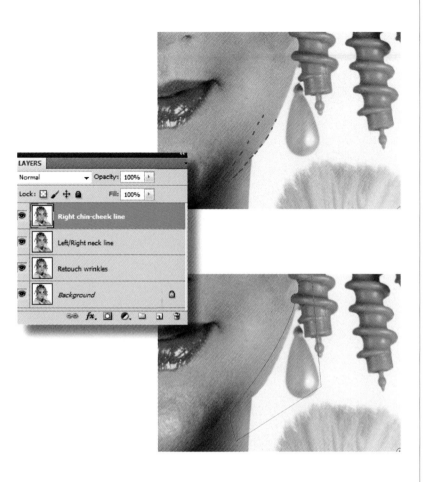

Refine right chin line

After your editing work you can see that chin line and cheek line run parallel and do not meet. We therefore have to align these two lines.

Duplicate the layer "Left/Right neck line" and name the copy "Right chin-cheek line". Create a path with the name "Right cheek" which outlines the new cheek line.

Load the path "Right cheek" again as selection with a feathered edge of 1 pixel and make the cheek narrower with the Clone Stamp tool ([S], Size 20 pixels, Hardness 50%, Opacity 100%).

Now take time to study the result carefully. Which areas are still unsatisfactory? Use the Patch tool (J) and the Healing Brush (J) to retouch the various unpleasing areas, such as strong shadows and bright reflexes.

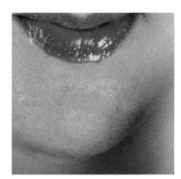

If you over-correct accidentally, you can take each retouching step back with EDIT/FADE. Work on a layer copy to make sure that you can still adjust the overall retouching in its opacity. With a combination of both options you can optimize your retouching.

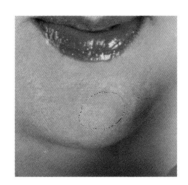

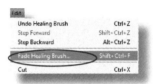

Recreate skin texture

As a consequence of our retouching, the skin texture has suffered greatly. It has become too soft in many places. If you compare the pixellation of the light and dark areas in the original skin texture, you will notice that it is stronger in the dark areas. We will therefore create a selection which is based on the brightness values of the image. The brighter areas will be selected more strongly than the dark ones. For this purpose, we will create a luminosity mask.

Luminosity mask

Duplicate the layer "Right chin-cheek line" and name it "Skin texture". Convert it to a smart object with the Layers panel menu. Change to the Channels panel and click on the RGB composite channels while pressing the ⌘/Ctrl-key. The brightness values are loaded as selection. Click on the ADD LAYER MASK icon at the bottom of the Layers panel. The selection is transformed into a mask. But we only need the mask in the neck area. Use the Pen tool (P) to draw a path around the neck and name it "Neck". Then load the path as a selection with a Feather Radius of 1 pixel. Please note that the top selection border in the last step will also form your left chin-cheek line. Correct the path if necessary.

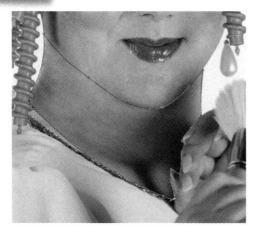

Choose SELECT/INVERSE ($\mathcal{H}$/Ctrl + I). Now the dark areas are selected more strongly. Make sure that the layer mask of the layer "Skin texture" is active. Use EDIT/FILL/USE/BLACK to fill the mask with black except for the neck area.

Click on the Smart Object thumbnail on the layer "Skin texture" and use FILTER/NOISE/ADD NOISE to add noise with a Strength of 4% (see picture).

Mask before filling with black

Mask after filling

To check the mask, you can make it visible by Alt-clicking on the mask thumbnail. You can switch back to the image with the same method.

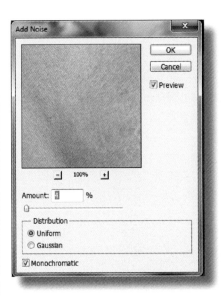

Create chin line on left

The luminosity mask you just created will be needed for adjusting the tonal values as well. Create a Curves adjustment layer in the Layers panel and click on OK without making any changes. Press and hold the Alt-key, then push the mask of the layer "Skin texture" onto the thumbnail of the adjustment layer. The mask is duplicated. Open the Curves dialog by clicking on the layer thumbnail of the curve and drag the center of the curve upwards as on the picture, until a clear chin-jaw-line can be seen.

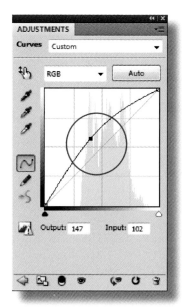

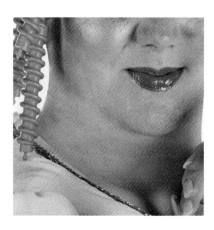

The hard lines created in the process can be eliminated in the mask with the Blur tool (R, Size 60 pixels, Amount 100% and Opacity 100%). The transitions in the mask become softer. You can judge the blur more accurately by switching to image view.

Now check your final result.

Refine nose and chin contours

Picture analysis

❶ Reduce and straighten nose

❷ Slightly reduce chin

Many minor flaws only become noticeable in profile, as in our example. The nose has a slight kink and appears very dominant in this perspective. The pronounced chin also distracts from the otherwise very refined facial features.

before

after

ch2/nose_and_chin.jpg

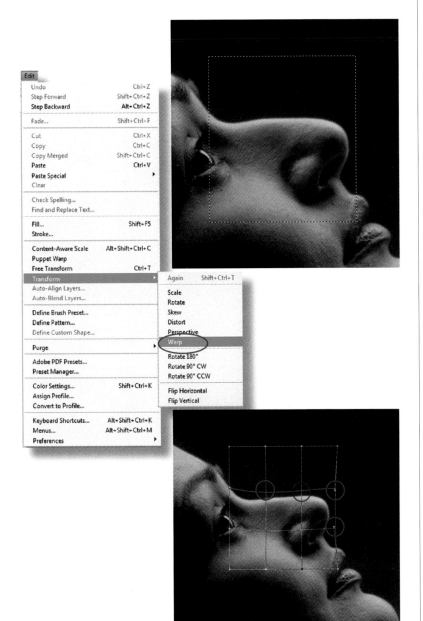

Reduce nose

We want to make the nose smaller and slightly straighten the bridge of the nose. Select the nose as shown on the picture with the Marquee tool ($\boxed{M}$) and a feathered edge of 2 pixels. With $\boxed{\mathbb{H}}$/$\boxed{Ctrl}$+$\boxed{J}$ you can copy this area onto a new layer. Name the layer "Nose" by double-clicking on the layer name and entering the new name. Convert the layer to a Smart Object with the menu in the Layers panel.

Choose EDIT/TRANSFORM/WARP. Drag the four indicated points downwards towards the nose, until you are happy with the new nose shape.

Adapt transitions

In the Layers panel, create a mask for the layer "Nose" and use the Brush tool to remove the edges around the nose (B , Size 35 pixels, Hardness 0%, Opacity 100%). Pay special attention to the lips, the eyes and the skin.

Hide the background layer from time to time to be able to see more clearly which image areas you are removing.

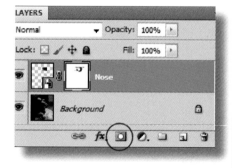

Adapt chin

To make the facial proportions more harmonious, you should reduce the chin a little bit. Select the chin as shown. Copy it again to a new layer with ⌘/ Ctrl + J and transform this layer to a Smart Object.

With the Warp feature you can adapt the chin slightly, simply by clicking in the mesh and dragging slightly to the left. Confirm the transformation.

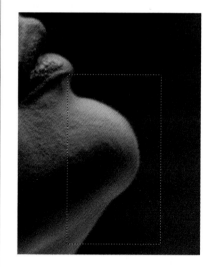

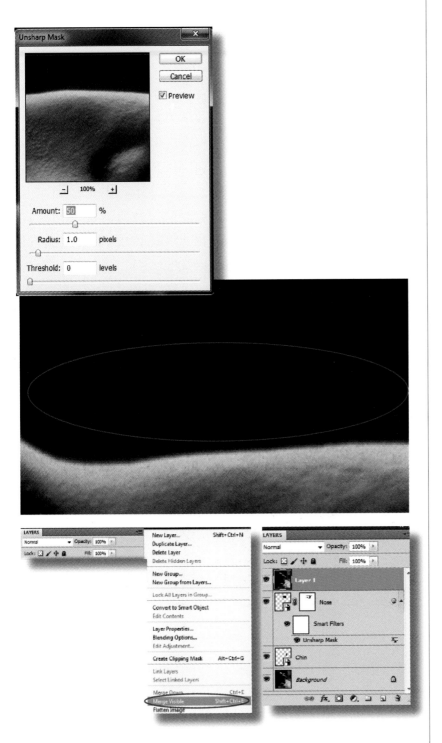

Checking

After retouching you should check each picture carefully. Double-click on the magnifying glass in the Tool bar to see the image at 100%. You will find that the smaller nose has become unsharp due to the distortion. Activate the layer "Nose". Use FILTER/SHARPEN/UNSHARP MASK to sharpen the nose slightly, using the following settings:

Amount 79%
Radius 1 Pixel
Threshold 1

Also look closely at the background near the nose. The structure has become blurred. Unfortunately, this does not show properly on our picture here. Scrutinize the file carefully. Also check the chin and if necessary sharpen some areas.

To simplify the last retouching steps, activate the top layer and choose the menu item MERGE VISIBLE from the Layers panel while pressing the ⌘/Ctrl + Alt + ⇧ keys. A new composite layer is created at the top, containing all layers, which makes editing very simple and effective. Finally, remove the blurred areas in the background with the Clone Stamp tool (S, Size 40 pixels, Hardness 60%, Opacity 100%).

Create witch nose

Picture analysis

❶ Enlarge nose

❷ Recreate texture

To have a make-up artist create a perfectly shaped nose and attach it to our model would cost considerably more than quickly creating it on the computer. It took us just 15 minutes.

before

after

ch2/witch_nose.jpg

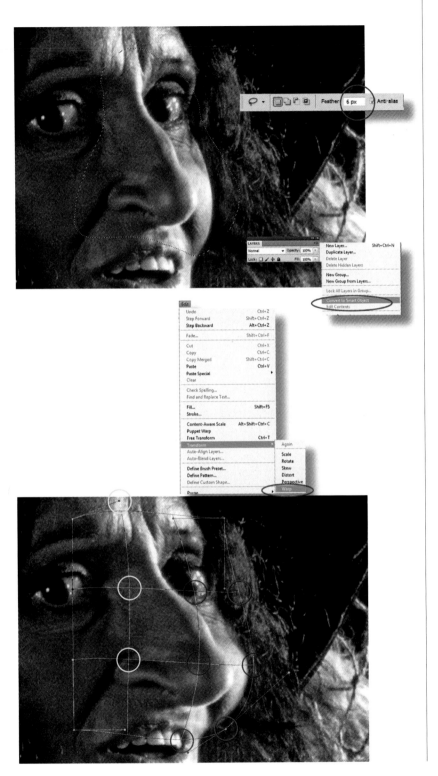

Enlarge nose

Select the nose with the Lasso tool (⌊L⌋, Feather 6 pixels) but do not include the mouth and the eye on the left. Follow approximately the same line as on our picture.

Place the nose onto a separate layer with ⌘/Ctrl+J and choose CONVERT TO SMART OBJECT from the menu in the Layers panel.

Give the nose a new shape with EDIT/TRANSFORM/WARP. Alter the points circled in red by dragging them to the right. The nose will become longer and broader. Then, drag the points marked in yellow back slightly to the left, to the indicated positions. The nostrils and root of the nose are brought back towards their original position. Of course you can also try out other shapes. But make sure not to make the nose too big, or it will become overly blurred. Even in our moderate adjustment we will need to correct the grain-pixel texture of the nose later. Confirm the transformation with the ⏎-key.

Refine transitions

The entire surrounding area to the right of nose was affected and now requires corrections. Create a layer mask in the Layers panel. Use black and the Brush tool (B, Size 30 pixels, Hardness 50%, Opacity 100%) to remove anything that is not part of the nose.

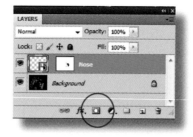

Hide the background by clicking on the eye icon in the Layers panel. The nose should now look something like this. Show the background again.

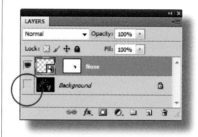

Recreate nose texture

If we look closely at the nose texture at 100% zoom (by double-clicking on the magnifying glass), you will see that is has become very soft. Unfortunately, we cannot simply use a Noise filter, as it does not offer any setting options for grain size, yet we require a rougher texture. In the picture on the right you can see a skin texture through the Noise filter.

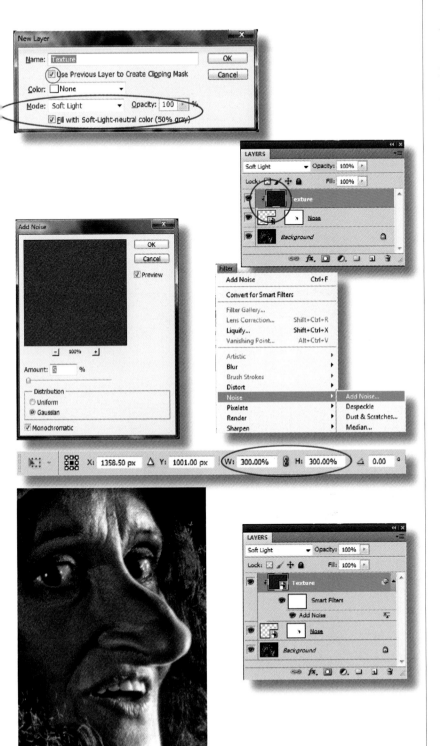

We need to scale the grain to get a suitable texture. Create a new layer by pressing the [Alt]-key while clicking on the CREATE NEW LAYER icon at the bottom of the Layers panel. Name the layer "Texture" in the following dialog and check the box USE PREVIOUS LAYER TO CREATE CLIPPING MASK. Set the Mode to SOFT LIGHT and activate the check box FILL WITH SOFT-LIGHT-NEUTRAL COLOR (50% GRAY). Because of the clipping mask, changes to the layer "Texture" will only be visible on the layer "Nose".

Then convert the layer to a Smart Object. Add noise to the layer with FILTER/NOISE/ADD NOISE (Amount 5%, Gaussian, Monochromatic).

The noise is not enough, therefore increase it with [⌘]/[Ctrl]+[T]. Go to the Options bar and enter 300% for Width and Height. You can try different scales by dragging horizontally over "W" and "H". First activate the button MAINTAIN ASPECT RATIO. In order to see the effect, you first have to confirm each change with the [↵]-key. Compare your grain with the original image structure. Because you are working on a Smart Object, you can change the texture as many times as you like, until you have a perfect result.

Reduce nose

Picture analysis

❶ Reduce nose

The disproportionally big nose distracts from the real eye-catcher of this portrait: the eyes. We therefore want to push the nose a bit more into the background by reducing its size. This will give a better view of the eyes.

ch2/mom_of_karsten.jpg

before

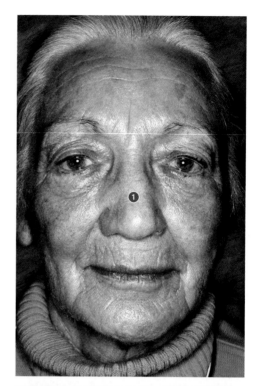

after

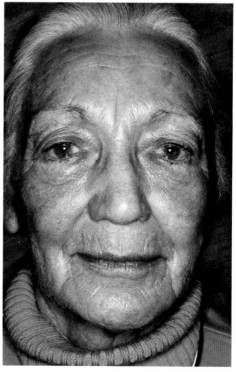

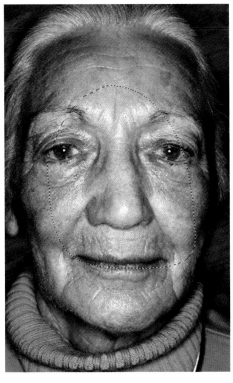

Reduce nose

For reducing the size of the nose, we don't need to do anything complicated.

Copy the background with ⌘/Ctrl+J. In the menu of the Layers panel, click on CONVERT TO SMART OBJECT. Use the Lasso tool (L, Feather 5 pixels) to select the nose and area around it as shown on this picture. For our editing, the nose should about in the center of the selection.

Use FILTER/DISTORT/PINCH to reduce the size of the nose.

Set the Amount of the filter to 11%. Then click OK.

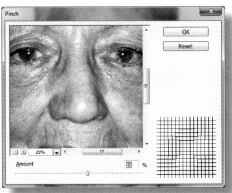

Adapt edges

The Pinch has caused unpleasant double edges around the layer
"Background copy". First, we will
adapt them with a layer mask. Hold
the Alt -key while clicking on the
ADD LAYER MASK icon. The mask
will be displayed in black and the
filter does not take effect. Reveal
the new nose with the Brush tool
(B , Size 200 pixels, Hardness 0%,
Opacity 100%) and white.

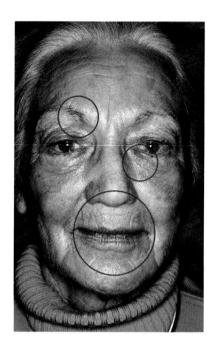

In this manner, you can sort out all
contours on the nostrils and the eyebrows. But this is not possible under
the nose.

To be able to use the retouching
tools in the simplest way possible, it
helps to combine all layers into one.
Activate the layer "Background copy"
and choose MERGE VISIBLE while
holding the Alt - and ⇧ -keys.
Name the new layer, for example
"Composite layer".

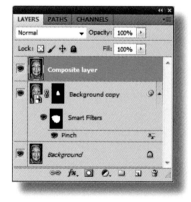

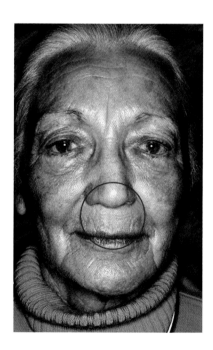

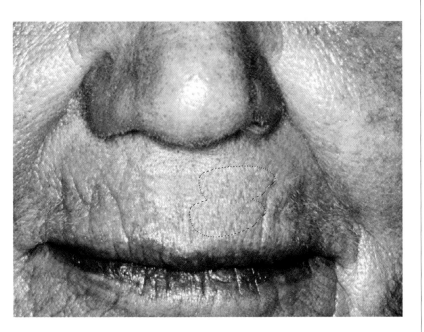

Finally, use the Patch tool ([J]) to remove the duplicated wrinkles and skin patterns which have appeared on the transitions.

Apply lens correction

Picture analysis

❶ Undistort forehead

❷ Correct hands holding chocolate

The extreme wide angle perspective has caused the forehead and the hands to appear very distorted. But how much correction do we need to apply and in what direction? If we were dealing with a architectural image, it would be easy. We would simply correct the perspective distortion by straightening the converging lines. To find out a bit more about the "correct" proportions of the human body, it is worth reading a book about basic portrait drawings or visiting appropriate web sites. In this boy's portrait, we will resort to a fundamental truth about facial proportions: the eyes are in the middle of the head.

ch2/boy_with_chocolate.jpg
ch2/two_girls.jpg

before

after

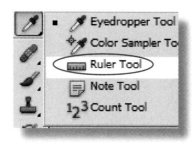

Analyze facial proportions

First create three horizontal guides which will help us measure different distances with the Ruler tool (I). The first guide has to be at the level of the eyes, the second is level with the chin and the third level with the crown. The boy's mouth is slightly open, we therefore move the bottom guide up a little bit. For the top guide, you just have to guess where the crown of the head is, under the hair and cap.

The following process of measuring the face will be shown using Photoshop Extended; these functions are not included with the lower priced standard version. With Extended, we can save and compare the measurements. Choose the panel for the measurement logs with WINDOW/ MEASUREMENT LOG.

Measurements

In the Measurement Log dialog, click on RECORD MEASUREMENTS. Use the Ruler tool ([I]) to measure the distance between top and middle line, and between middle and bottom line. To get an accurate straight line, press and hold the [⇧]-key. You can see the difference between the two distances in the Length values.

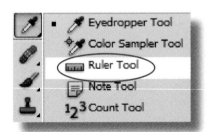

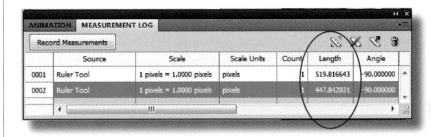

Your version of Photoshop may not have the Measurement Log function. In that case, you just need to make a note of the values in the Info panel and then compare them.

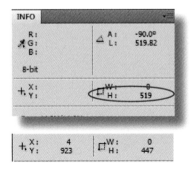

Correct distortion

To correct the distortion, duplicate the background with [⌘]/[Ctrl]+[J]. Name this layer "Head". Convert the layer to a Smart Object, that is very important. Unfortunately, we cannot enter our measurements in the command FILTER/LENS CORRECTION.

We therefore have to try out different measurements, then measure the changes again and approach the final result little by little. Without conversion to a Smart Object, you would have to start over again and again. After some experimentation, we came to the following optimum result: Set the slider REMOVE DISTORTION to a value of -16, this makes the body proportions appear more harmonious. The distorted forehead still seems to stretch towards the camera. Set the VERTICAL PERSPECTIVE to +27. The image is tilted slightly backwards from the center axis. Click on OK.

Check distances

To check the distances once more, you need the three guides again. Then measure the distances between them.

The first values were:

519.8 pixels to 447.8 pixels

and now:
495.8 pixels to 489.8 pixels

The two distances have become much closer. They are not exactly equal, the inaccuracy when placing the guides is too high. Also, the eyes are not always exactly in the middle between chin and crown in every person. That rule is just a rough guideline.

ANIMATION	MEASUREMENT LOG					
	Source	Scale	Scale Units	Count	Length	Angle
0001	Ruler Tool	1 pixels = 1.0000 pixels	pixels	1	519.816643	-90.000000
0002	Ruler Tool	1 pixels = 1.0000 pixels	pixels	1	447.842031	-90.000000
0003	Ruler Tool	1 pixels = 1.0000 pixels	pixels	1	495.825106	-90.000000
0004	Ruler Tool	1 pixels = 1.0000 pixels	pixels	1	489.827221	-90.000000

The head is still too big. To correct this, go to Lens Correction once again. Set the Scale to 90%. Confirm by clicking OK.

The head now has the correct proportions, but the hands with the chocolate are still too large.

Adjust hands and chocolate

To adjust the hands, first hide the layer "Head". We will edit the hands on a separate layer. Copy the background with ⌘ / Ctrl + J and convert it to a Smart Object. We call this layer "Hands".

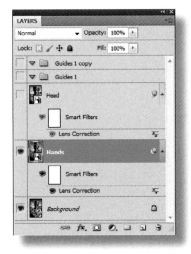

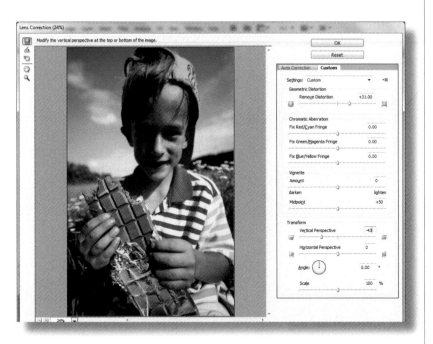

Activate the filter LENS CORRECTION once again. Experiment with different values for REMOVE DISTORTION and VERTICAL PERSPECTIVE, just as before. As the hands are at the edges of the picture, they appear too large in proportion, as did the forehead. We will make them smaller with a pincushion correction. The best value which lets the size ratios appear harmonious is +31. Confirm by clicking OK.

Adjust head and hands

To adjust both layers to one another, show the layer "Head" again and create a layer mask by holding the Alt-key and clicking on the CREATE LAYER MASK icon. The mask becomes black and the layer "Head" no longer has any effect. Use white and the Brush tool (B, Size 70 pixels, Hardness 40%, Opacity 100%) to bring back the head.

In order to see more easily what the mask reveals, we have hidden the lower layers in the picture on the right. The transitions on the body and the lateral head contours are perfect. In the area above the head, we need to make some adjustments. Save the picture with all layers. To be able to retouch errors better we need all layers except for the background layer merged into one. Highlight all layers, except for the background layer, by holding the ⌘/Ctrl-key and clicking into the space next to the thumbnail, then press ⌘/Ctrl+E. Confirm the dialog DELETE HIDDEN LAYERS?. This only refers to the hidden guides which we no longer need. Save the picture under a new name.

Add missing image areas

Due to our corrections, some image areas are missing at the sides and the bottom of the picture. If you hide the background layer, you can see these very clearly. For retouching it is important to work on a composite layer. Activate the top layer and press ⌘/Ctrl+⇧+Alt+E. A new layer appears at the top of the Layers panel. Add the missing areas with the Clone Stamp tool (S).

Perfect sky

Use the Patch tool ([J]) to adjust the color of the dark area of sky above the boy's head. Highlight the area at the top left with the Patch tool ([J]), as shown on the left, and drag it down and to the right. When you release the graphics pen or mouse button, the upper part of the sky is replaced and the colors and brightness values are adjusted. Proceed in the same way with the other areas. Finally, check the entire picture carefully, especially in all corrected transitions.

Combinations with slightly overlapping selections are also possible.

Analyze distortion

This picture was also taken with a wide-angle lens. It shows much stronger distortion than the boy's portrait. If we tilt the picture backwards through the horizontal axis, to reduce the first woman's dominant forehead, the chin will be overly distorted. If we use a pincushion correction, it has a negative impact on the woman at the back. We therefore need to find a compromise. For now we will concentrate only on the woman in the foreground and work in small steps.

Reduce distortion

Choose the Lens Correction filter and drag the Remove Distortion slider to the right, to about +53. The picture curves inwards, the faces become smaller towards the center of the image and take on a more natural shape. The negative consequences are that the picture is now very small and the woman in the background appears larger, but also more distorted.

Use Scale to enlarge the picture to 148%. You can see the intermediate result (before scaling) on the picture on the right.

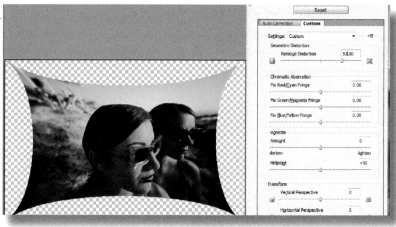

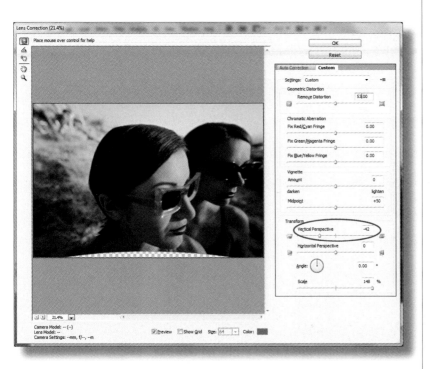

To move the head of the woman in the foreground a bit more away from the edge of the picture, we need to tilt the bottom part of the picture slightly backwards from the horizontal. We need to find a compromise to make sure the forehead does not become too dominant. We chose the setting shown here (-42).

The correction had a negative impact on the woman in the background. She now tilts too much to the right, the frame of her glasses nearly touch the edge of the picture and seem very distorted. We will fix this with the Warp function. You need to experiment a lot, because Photoshop unfortunately does not show the lens correction. You are starting from the original picture. When you confirm the warp with ⏎-key, it will be applied.

Choose EDIT/TRANSFORM/WARP. Drag the top right corner to the left, to make the woman look less inclined to the right. Click on OK. If the result seems to jar with the lens correction, choose Warp again and keep correcting.

Add missing image areas

The various corrections have caused some errors. The pixellation or graininess has become blurred due to the distortion. If you hide the background, you can see missing image areas at the bottom of the picture. Add them with the Clone Stamp tool (⌊S⌋) on a composite layer. Activate the top layer and press ⌊⌘⌋/⌊Ctrl⌋+⌊⇧⌋+⌊Alt⌋+⌊E⌋.

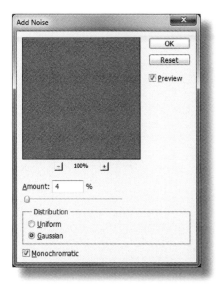

Add noise

Create a neutral layer at the top of the Layers panel, by filling a new layer with 50% gray and setting the Blend Mode to Soft Light (see Basic Overview: Blend Modes, Chapter 4). Convert this layer to a Smart Object, to be able to change the filter's Amount at a later stage if necessary. Use Filter/Noise/Add Noise to add a Noise of about 4%.

With a layer mask you can restrict the noise to the areas of the picture which have suffered too much from our editing work.

Basic Overview: Layers

The Layers panel is the linchpin of Photoshop. Layers are just like those good old bits of paper that we used to cut up and make into a collage when we were children, except they offer many more possibilities. We can change the size and shape of layers, vary their colors and tonality, choose different transitions, the so-called blend modes, move them, crop their content with masks and change their transparency. With layers, you build up a picture step by step and can maintain control over your image editing. If at all possible, you should never work on the original background layer, but instead copy it before you start editing. That way, you can always access the original image again without making any changes to it.

Layer mode

With the layer mode you determine how an image is calculated in contrast and color against the one below it.

Layer opacity

Reduces visibility down to 0%

Reduces visibility of image pixels down to 0%, but layer effects remain visible.

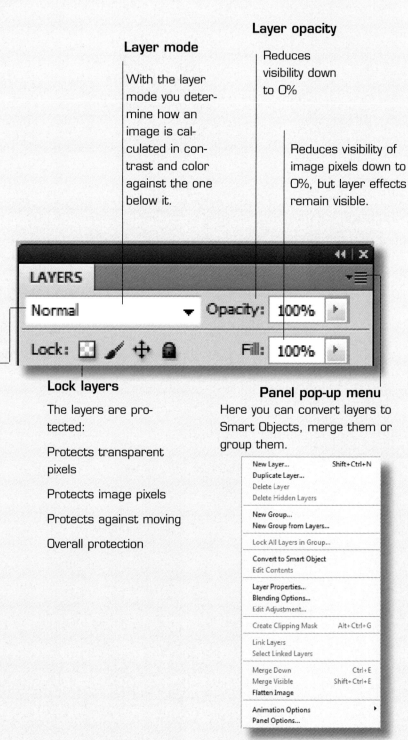

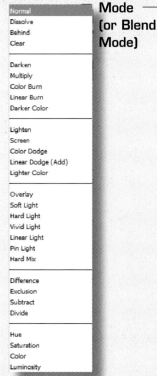

Mode (or Blend Mode)

Lock layers

The layers are protected:

Protects transparent pixels

Protects image pixels

Protects against moving

Overall protection

Panel pop-up menu

Here you can convert layers to Smart Objects, merge them or group them.

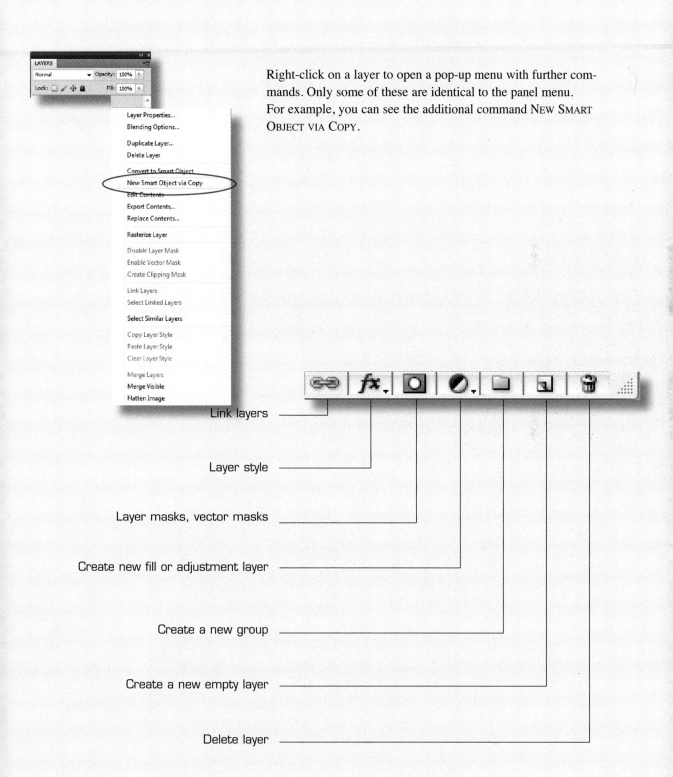

Right-click on a layer to open a pop-up menu with further commands. Only some of these are identical to the panel menu. For example, you can see the additional command NEW SMART OBJECT VIA COPY.

LAYERS

Normal   Opacity: 100%

Lock: Fill: 100%

Layer Properties...
Blending Options...

Duplicate Layer...
Delete Layer

Convert to Smart Object
New Smart Object via Copy
Edit Contents
Export Contents...
Replace Contents...

Rasterize Layer

Disable Layer Mask
Enable Vector Mask
Create Clipping Mask

Link Layers
Select Linked Layers

Select Similar Layers

Copy Layer Style
Paste Layer Style
Clear Layer Style

Merge Layers
Merge Visible
Flatten Image

Link layers

Layer style

Layer masks, vector masks

Create new fill or adjustment layer

Create a new group

Create a new empty layer

Delete layer

The layer symbols

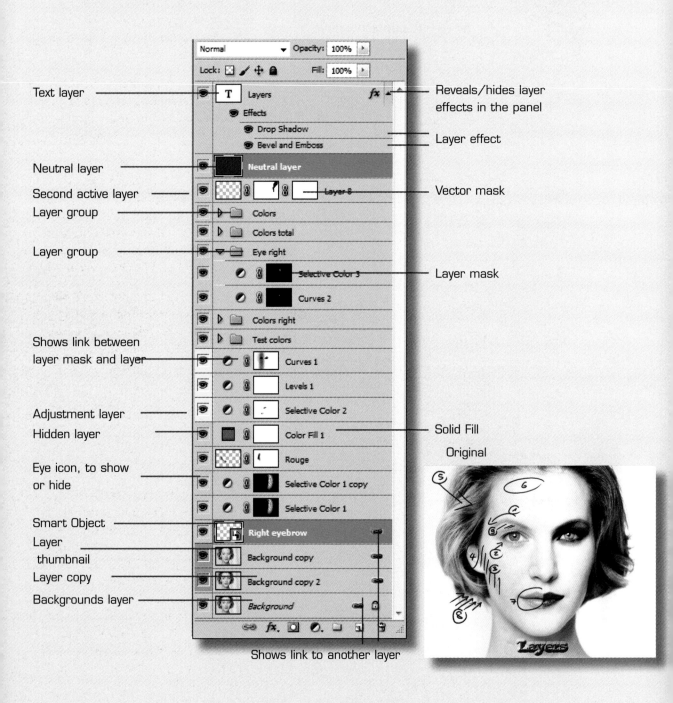

Text layer

Reveals/hides layer effects in the panel

Layer effect

Neutral layer

Second active layer

Vector mask

Layer group

Layer group

Layer mask

Shows link between layer mask and layer

Adjustment layer

Hidden layer

Solid Fill

Original

Eye icon, to show or hide

Smart Object

Layer thumbnail

Layer copy

Backgrounds layer

Shows link to another layer

Panel contents:

Normal   Opacity: 100%

Lock: ☒ ✏ ✛ 🔒   Fill: 100%

T Layers   *fx* ▲

👁 Effects

👁 Drop Shadow

👁 Bevel and Emboss

Neutral layer

Layer 8

Colors

Colors total

Eye right

Selective Color 3

Curves 2

Colors right

Test colors

Curves 1

Levels 1

Selective Color 2

Color Fill 1

Rouge

Selective Color 1 copy

Selective Color 1

Right eyebrow

Background copy

Background copy 2

Background

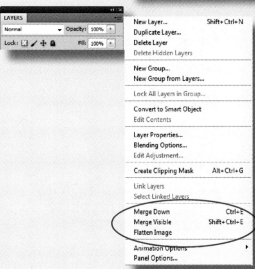

The layer mask

The layer mask conceals parts of a layer. You create a layer mask by clicking on the ADD LAYER MASK icon at the bottom of the Layers panel.

The layer mask is white at first. You can use the painting tools and black to hide all areas of the image layer that are not required. You can make them visible again with white.

If you press and hold the [Alt]-key while creating a layer mask, the mask is black straight away and the layer becomes invisible in the picture. Now you can use the painting tools and white to reveal the areas you want.

Make sure that the mask icon is outlined in bold while you are editing the mask. This indicates that you are indeed working in the mask.

Merge layers

Sometimes it becomes necessary to merge layers. This can be done in several ways. You can merge a layer with the one below it (MERGE DOWN) or activate several layers and merge all of them. You can merge all visible layers, or merge all visible layers into the background while discarding hidden layers (FLATTEN IMAGE). Keep in mind that every layer increases the file size and therefore slows down processing.

Load layer mask as a selection

Press and hold the ⌘/Ctrl+X-keys and click on the layer mask thumbnail in the Layers panel. The corresponding mask is loaded as selection.

Deactivate layer mask

⇧-click on the mask thumbnail in the Layers panel. The mask is disabled, the layer becomes completely visible. Click again while pressing the ⇧-key to enable the mask.

Copy a layer mask

Click on a layer mask in the Layers panel. Hold the Alt-key and drag the mask to another layer. This replaces an existing mask. If you drag the mask without the Alt-key, it is not copied but moved onto the target layer.

Display a layer mask

Hold the Alt-key and click on a layer mask in the Layers panel. This displays the grayscale mask. Return to image view by Alt-clicking again.

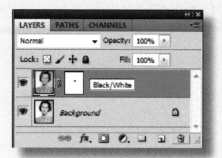

Name a layer

Double-click on the layer name. You can enter a different name if you wish. Make use of this function to maintain a better overview of your document.

Create clipping mask

A clipping mask ensures that the enabled layer only affects the layer immediately below it, not any others that are further down in the stack. If you press the Alt-key when creating an adjustment layer, the dialog box USE PREVIOUS LAYER TO CREATE CLIPPING MASK appears. Check the box and confirm by clicking on OK. The adjustment layer is indented in the Layers panel. You can remove the clipping mask by placing the cursor on the boundary between two layers and Alt-clicking on it. Repeat the same step to recreate the clipping mask.

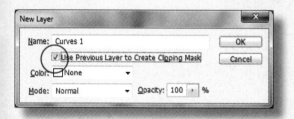

Group layers

To stop the Layers panel getting too long, you can combine layers into groups. Activate the various layers with the ⇧-key and choose NEW GROUP FROM LAYERS in the pop-up menu in the Layers panel. Name the group and click on OK.

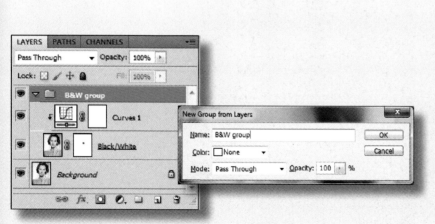

shiny expressive glowing attractive pretty brown bright make-up natural dark lively mysterious big small ti
dull brilliant reddened over-worked blue radiant awake effective mystical damp clear open closed almond-sha
blinking happy enigmatic green swollen pronounced winking striking interesting curious striking wide inquisi
dull oval curious bored fascinating shiny expressive glowing attractive pretty alert brown bright make
natural dark lively beautiful mysterious big small tired dull brilliant reddened over-worked blue radiant aw
effective mystical damp clear open closed almond-shaped blinking happy enigmatic green swollen pronoun
winking striking interesting curious striking wide inquisitive dull oval curious bored fascinating beaut

Chapter 3

Eyes

 How to emphasize
eyes with make-up
effects

How to sharpen eyes in
case of camera shake

 How to open up and
brighten blinking eyes

How to remove
reflections on glasses

**Basic Overview:
Channels**

 How to remove a
hooded eyelid

How to make eyes look
clear and intensify or
change eye color

 How to sharpen important
details in case of shallow
depth of field

How to remove red eye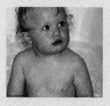

How to make tired eyes
look fresh

Emphasize eyes with make-up effects

Picture analysis

1. Thicken and reshape eyebrows
2. Thicken eyelashes
3. Apply eye shadow
4. Improve complexion
5. Apply rouge and lipstick

We will show you how to use colors, pens and brushes to make eyes more expressive. The computer gives you a whole range of options, from discreet daytime make-up to spectacular gala make-up.

ch3/makeup_fx.jpg

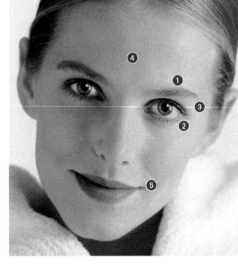

before

after

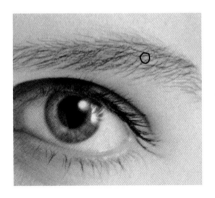

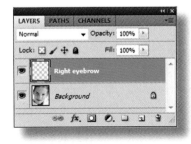

Thicken eyebrows

If you compare the bright side of the face (on the right) to the shady side (on the left), the eyebrows and the lower eyelashes look much thinner and irregular. To thicken the brows, we need to paint color in the direction of the hairs with a fine tool. The Pencil tool ([⇧]+[B]) serves this purpose well. Create a new empty layer in the Layers panel. Name this layer "Right eyebrow". Now paint small black hairs with the Pencil tool ([B], Size 3 pixels, Hardness 0%, Opacity 100%). The brows now appear too dark, therefore reduce the layer opacity to about 60%.

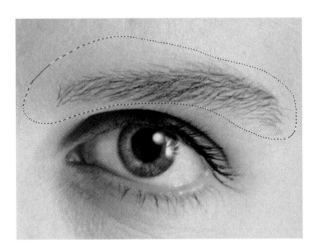

Shape eyebrows

Next, we want to give the eyebrows a nice shape and move them upwards a bit. This opens the eyes more and allows us more options for accentuating the eyes with color. We need to place the eyebrow onto a separate layer. Create a new layer and press Alt while choosing MERGE VISIBLE. Eyebrow layer and background layer are merged into the new layer. Name it "Merged layer". Use the Lasso tool ([L], Feather 3 pixels) to select the eyebrow and copy it to another layer with [⌘]/[Ctrl]+[J].

Transform this layer to a SMART OBJECT using the menu in the Layers panel and name it "Right eyebrow merged". Hide the layer and remove the original eyebrow on the layer below, using the retouching tools. Now switch back to the layer "Right eyebrow merged" and choose EDIT/ TRANSFORM/WARP. Give the eyebrow a nice shape and make it slightly narrower. Then, reposition it and hide the transitions with a layer mask.

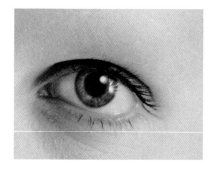

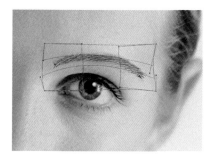

Eyebrow variant

Often it can be helpful to try out the effect of different eyebrow shapes. The left eyebrow is much thicker, therefore we can select that one, give it a pleasing shape and use it for both sides. This saves us the trouble of having to replace individual tiny hairs and ensures the highest degree of symmetry.

First use the Clone Stamp tool (⎡S⎤) to remove any little hairs that break ranks. Select the eyebrow, copy it with ⎡⌘⎤/⎡Ctrl⎤+⎡J⎤ and experiment with different shapes with the Warp tool. Then remove the two original eyebrows with the retouching tools.

When repositioning the brows, make sure they are symmetrical.

Painting eyelashes

We will create the eyelashes using a slightly different method. Create a CURVES adjustment layer. Darken the image strongly and then fill the layer mask with black. The effect is canceled out. Now paint with white and the Brush tool (B, Size 3 pixels, Hardness 0%, Opacity 20%), not only retracing the existing eyelashes, but adding new ones as well. Add some extra tiny spots at the root of the little hairs, to make them look even fuller. In the same step, you can lengthen individual eyelashes on the top lash-line.

On the left, you can see the mask of the Curve. This method has the advantage that you can change the intensity of the eyelashes any time with the Curve.

Improve complexion

Before applying color accents, we will improve the complexion with a new SELECTIVE COLOR adjustment layer. Create the adjustment layer and reduce the Magenta portion of the Reds by about -35%. Click on OK.

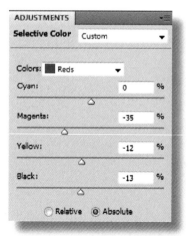

Eye shadow

Create another CURVES adjustment layer for applying eye shadow. First darken the composite picture in the RGB channel, only paying attention to the area around the eyes. Then switch to one of the color channels and adapt it until you have found a pleasing color. For the terracotta shade in our example we dragged the curves for Blue and Green Channel upwards. Then press ⌘/Ctrl+I. The layer mask turns black. Reveal the make-up with the Brush tool (B, Size 70 pixels, Hardness 0%, Opacity 5%) and white. Often a mere touch of color is sufficient to create more lustrous eyes. Apply the color from the movable part of the lid towards the eyebrows and ensure very soft transitions.

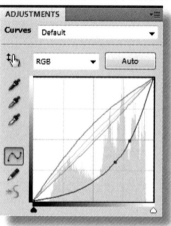

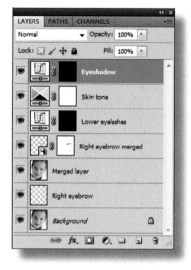

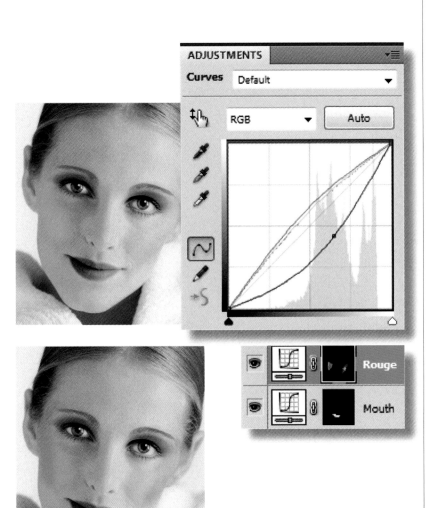

Play around with colors and experiment with different effects. If you need more ideas, you can get make-up tips from magazines, books or on the internet.

Color lips

Next to the accentuated eyes, the lips should not seem too drab. We use a CURVES adjustment layer to darken the lips in the RGB channel. Lift the curves for the individual colors. We intensified the Blues and Greens as well. Make the layer mask black with (⌘/Ctrl+I) and reveal the lips with white.

Apply rouge

Rouge works like an artificial shadow, it shapes and adds youthful fresh-ness to the face. For a natural look we choose an appropriate lip color. Copy the Curve "Mouth" (⌘/Ctrl+J) and name it "Rouge". Fill the layer mask with black once again. Use the Brush tool (B, Size 200 pixels, Hardness 0%, Opacity 5%) to lightly bring out the rouge from the cheek bones to the hairline. Rouge makes round faces look narrower. For angular faces, a mere touch of color around the jaw bones is usually enough.

With these techniques you can now try out an endless variety of make-up effects.

Open blinking eyes

Picture analysis

❶ Enlarge eyes

❷ Correct color cast in white of eyes

❸ Brighten white of eyes

Every photographer has encountered this problem: the more intense the illumination, the more reject photos with partially or completely closed eyes you are likely to end up with. This happened in our example. The picture was taken in bright daylight, the white walls act as reflectors and increase the brightness even more.

ch3/blinking_eyes.jpg

before

after

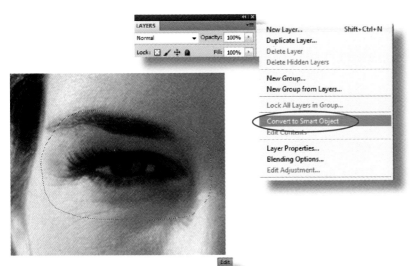

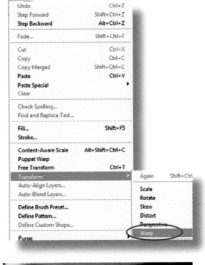

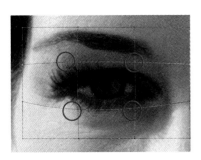

Enlarge eyes

To enlarge the first eye, select it with the Lasso tool (⌐L⌐, Feather 5 pixels). Copy the eye onto another layer with ⌘/Ctrl+J and select CONVERT TO SMART OBJECT from the pop-up menu in the Layers panel. Now you can change the eye shape any time without loss of quality. This is very important in our case, as we want to enlarge and adapt the second eye as well, which makes additional corrections necessary.

Choose EDIT/TRANSFORM and then the WARP function. Drag the center crosspoints slightly outwards. The eye becomes larger. Confirm by pressing the Enter key.

Show the rulers with ⌘/Ctrl+R. Drag out two horizontal guides and position them at the top and bottom edge of the enlarged eye.

Do the same with the second eye. Use the guides and the other eye to help you. Create a layer mask for each eye layer by clicking on the ADD LAYER MASK icon at the bottom of the Layers panel. Correct the transitions with black (D) and the Brush tool (B).

To make it clearer, we have hidden the background image.

After making your changes, you can see if the eye has the right shape. Both eyes have the right size, but they still seem to squint. This is due to the slightly hooded eyelid in each eye. We can change this with the Liquify filter.

However, this filter cannot be applied to a Smart Object. You can of course rasterize the Smart Object with the menu in the Layers panel, but then you lose the original settings of the Warp dialog.

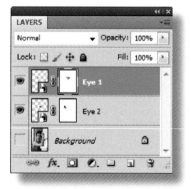

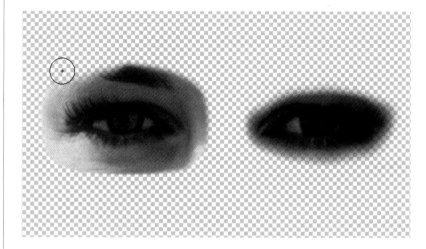

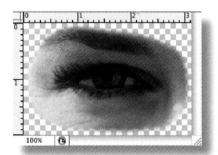

Double-click on the SMART OBJECT thumbnail in the Layers panel and confirm the displayed warning with OK. This opens an independent file with the name "Layer 1", with the contents of the layer "Eye 1". You can now edit this picture like any other.

After editing, the file must be saved in the same place. Press ⌘/Ctrl+S and close the picture. The changes appear immediately in the layer "Eye 1".

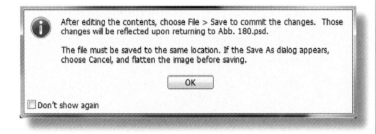

After editing the contents, choose File > Save to commit the changes. Those changes will be reflected upon returning to Abb. 180.psd.

The file must be saved to the same location. If the Save As dialog appears, choose Cancel, and flatten the image before saving.

OK

☐ Don't show again

Correct hooded eyelid

Copy the layer "1" with
⌘/Ctrl+J. Choose Filter/Liquify
to edit the hooded eyelid with the
Forward Warp tool (W). Try our settings first, as shown in the picture.
Place the center of the tool tip just
below the hooded lid and push it
upwards a tiny bit. It's best to just
click up with the mouse or even better
with a graphics tablet, as if you wanted to tap something gently. This stops
the pixels getting too smudged.

Then click on Ok, save the picture
with ⌘/Ctrl+S and close it. You
can see the changes straight away
in the picture. Do the same with the
other eye.

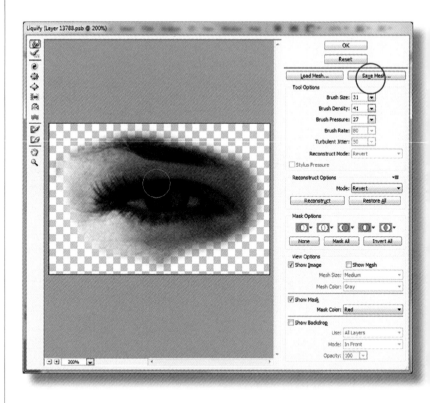

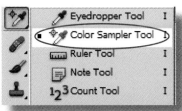

Color correcting eyes

Blinking eyes always have another disadvantage: they are badly illuminated and appear much too dark. The yellow reflections from the walls add a color cast. In order to remove it from the whites of the eyes, we will create two sampling points in the whites of the eye with the Color Sampler tool.

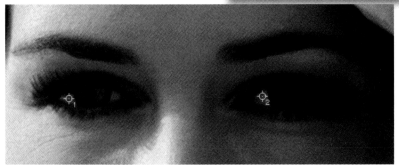

The Info panel now displays the values of the sampling points 1 and 2, and you can see that there is a definite red tint: the values for Red are considerably higher than those for Green and Blue.

Create a SELECTIVE COLOR adjustment layer by clicking on the CREATE NEW ADJUSTMENT LAYER icon at the bottom of the Layers panel.

The SELECTIVE COLOR dialog opens and a second column of values appears in the Info panel: the original color values are displayed on the left, the color values after the adjustment is made on the right

First correct the REDS. Enter the following values.

CYAN: +91
MAGENTA: −100
YELLOW: −100
Black: 0
METHOD: ABSOLUTE

The colors red and green now have become closer, just not yet the blue. Remember, gray is a mixture of equal parts of all three colors.

In the SELECTIVE COLOR window, choose NEUTRALS under COLORS. Enter the following values.

CYAN: 0
MAGENTA: 0
YELLOW: −8
BLACK: 0
METHOD: ABSOLUTE

The white of the eyes at sampling point 1 now is a nearly neutral gray, sampling point 2 still has a slight yellow tint. This can be caused by the skin reflection and is therefore acceptable.

The color correction is applied to the whole picture.

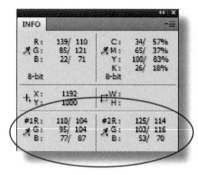

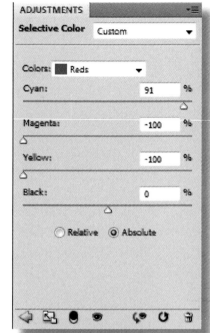

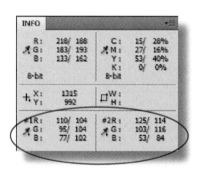

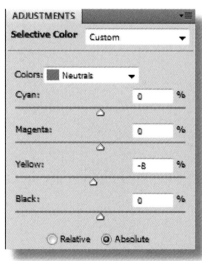

To make sure the color correction only affects the eyes, click on the layer mask in the panel and press ⌘/Ctrl+I. The layer mask turns black. The correction is no longer displayed. Use white and the Brush tool (B, Size 8 pixels, Hardness 0%, Opacity 100%) to paint over the eyes.

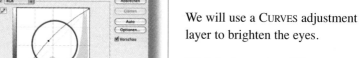

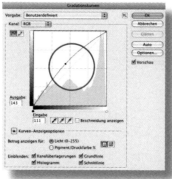

Solid Color...
Gradient...
Pattern...

Brightness/Contrast...
Levels...
Curves...
Exposure...

Brighten eyes

We will use a CURVES adjustment layer to brighten the eyes.

Click in the center of the curve and drag it upwards a little. This also affects the whole picture. Do the same to the layer mask as you did with the SELECTIVE COLOR, to make sure only the eyes are affected.

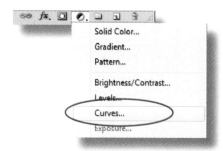

Adapt eye size and hooded eyelid

Picture analysis

❶ Enlarge left eye

❷ Lift hooded eyelids

A hooded eyelid is if the movable part of the lid is hardly visible. The most common tip by makeup-artists: apply dark eyeshadow in the crease of the lid, a light tone on the lid and under the eyebrows. With the computer we have even more options. Just by lifting the lids we can make the eyes appear bigger, more expressive and more alert.

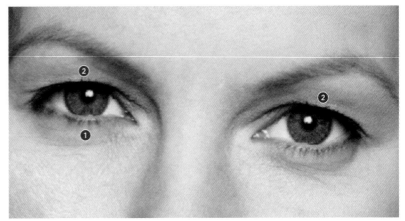

before

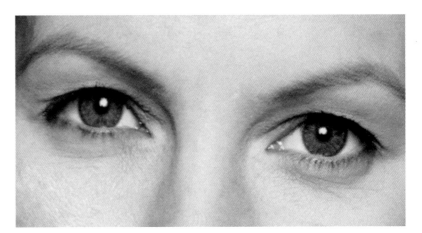

after

ch3/hooded_lid.jpg

Enlarge eye

To make the left eye the same size as the right eye, we need three guides. Photoshop only offers horizontal or vertical lines, so we need to do it differently. Click on the CREATE NEW LAYER icon in the Layers panel.

Create a selection with the SINGLE ROW MARQUEE TOOL, and fill it with black or any other color using EDIT/FILL.

Press ⌘/Ctrl+T to rotate the guide so that it goes through both pupils.

Copy this guide twice with ⌘/Ctrl+J and position the two copies at the top and bottom lash line of the right eye.

Use the Rectangular Marquee tool to select the left eye and surrounding area and copy it to a new layer with ⌘/Ctrl+J. Scale the eye with ⌘/Ctrl+T. Use the guides for reference, but also listen to your own aesthetic sense regarding the harmony of the proportions.

To adjust the eye boundaries, create a layer mask with the icon at the bottom of the Layers panel. Remove the unwanted areas with black (⟨D⟩) and the Brush tool (⟨B⟩).

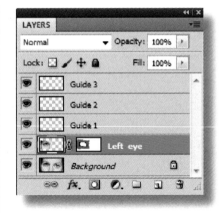

Hide all other layers to check the eye.

Now click on the background in the Layers panel and copy it with ⟨⌘⟩/⟨Ctrl⟩+⟨J⟩. Activate the layer "Left eye" and press ⟨⌘⟩/⟨Ctrl⟩+⟨E⟩. to merge it into the background. Save the image.

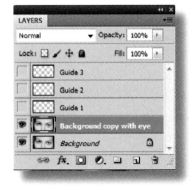

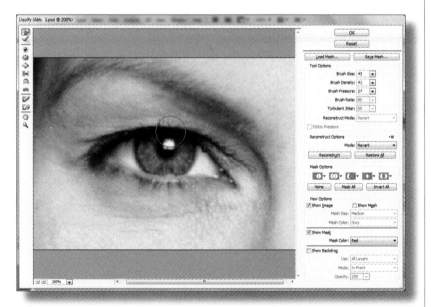

Lift hooded eyelid

Now we want to lift the top lids
a bit to open the eyes more.
Copy the background layer with
⌘/Ctrl+J. Select the left eye
with the Rectangular Marquee (M).
Choose FILTER/LIQUIFY and drag the
lid slightly upwards with the Forward
Warp tool (W), as shown on the picture. Give the lid a nice curved shape.
Then edit the lid of the right eye in
the same manner.

This small correction has not changed
the pupil shape, therefore no further
correction is required.

As second step, you can increase the
effect. Add optical emphasis to the
area beneath the eyebrows by applying light makeup to that patch of skin
(see also workshop "Emphasize eyes
with make-up effects", Chapter 3).

Sharpen in case of shallow depth of field

Picture analysis

❶ Sharpen eyes

With long focal lengths and small apertures, the depth of field is often not sufficient. Especially with non-static close-ups of two people, the plane of focus is not necessarily on all pairs of eyes. Partial sharpening can help.

before

after

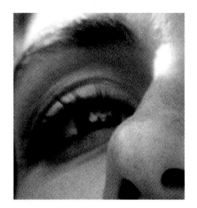 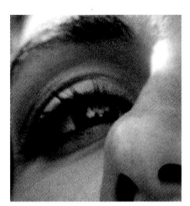

ch3/sharpen_eyes.jpg

Sharpening important image areas

In this example, the plane of focus falls on the woman's lips and the man's right eye. We will sharpen these areas even more, to increase the impression of sharpness. But mainly we want to sharpen the man's left eye and the woman's eyes. We do not need to and in fact should not sharpen the man's lips. They do not have any detail and we would only be sharpening the film's structure or noise structure, which would add unpleasant structure to the image.

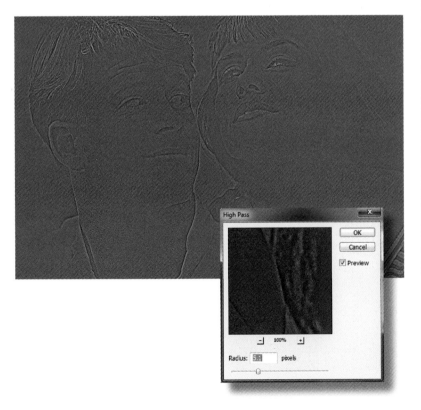

Copy the background with ⌘/Ctrl+J and convert it to a SMART OBJECT in the Layers panel menu. Call the layer "Sharpening". Choose the High Pass filter with FILTER/OTHER/HIGH PASS. We chose this filter because it adds nicer emphasis to the edges than the UNSHARP MASK filter. To get the right setting, set the Radius to 0.1 pixels, the image turns gray. Now slowly drag the slider to the right and the contours will emerge gradually. At a Radius of 5.1 pixels, the eye details are optimally adjusted. Click on OK.

The entire layer is still gray with contours shining through. Set the layer mode to SOFT LIGHT. The gray will disappear and you now have a sharpened image.

Reduce sharpening

To sharpen only individual areas, create a layer mask by holding the Alt-key whilst clicking on the ADD LAYER MASK icon. The black mask covers the sharpening. Now use white and the Brush tool (B, Size 9 pixels, Hardness 60%, Opacity 40%, Flow 100%) to partially bring out sharp contours. Do not paint too broadly, use small brush tips to retrace individual details carefully.

Hold the Alt-key and click on the layer mask to display the mask. Here you can see what our mask looks like. Click once more on the layer mask whilst holding the Alt-key, and you can see the picture again.

Increase sharpening

To increase the sharpening, right-click on the layer "Sharpening" and choose NEW SMART OBJECT VIA COPY to make sure you have two independent layers.

You can of course continue editing this copy in the mask, if you feel that the sharpening has become too much in certain places. If you think the sharpening as a whole is too strong, reduce the layer's Opacity.

After sharpening, always check the

image at 100% view by double clicking on the magnifying glass. This is the only way to judge the image as a whole. Oversharpening shows in color shifts and the colorful pixellation of image areas, such as on this picture. For the purposes of demonstrating oversharpening, we exaggerated our sharpening (see also Basic Overview "Sharpen", Chapter 6).

Neutralize and brighten whites of eyes

Picture analysis

❶ Remove yellow tint from whites of eyes

❷ Brighter eyes

Eyes only appear really expressive and beautiful if the whites do not show any discoloration. In this picture, we can see tiny red blood vessels in the eyes and the dim artificial light causes an extreme yellow tint. We will show you two methods with which you can turn tired, reddened eyes into expressive and bright eyes.

ch3/eye_whites.jpg

before

after

Correct whites of eyes

To eliminate the color tints, create a new BLACK&WHITE adjustment layer using the icon in the Layers panel. The whole picture turns black and white.

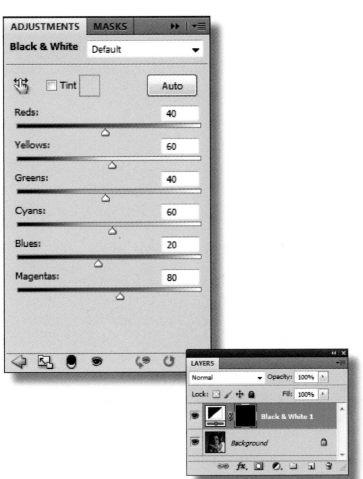

We only want to decolorize the eyes and not the entire image, therefore press ⌘/Ctrl + I.

The layer mask turns black and the layer setting is no longer visible. Now use the Brush tool (B, Size 15 pixels, Hardness 0%, Opacity 100%) and white to bring back the correction in the whites of the eyes.

Fine-tuning

For fine-tuning, activate the layer "Black & White 1" and go to the Adjustments panel which shows the Black & White adjustment. The color tint in the whites of the eyes consists of red and yellow. You therefore need to experiment with the Red and Yellow sliders. Drag them to the left to make the areas containing those colors darker, drag them to the right to make them lighter. We set the Reds to 105% and the Yellows to 51%.

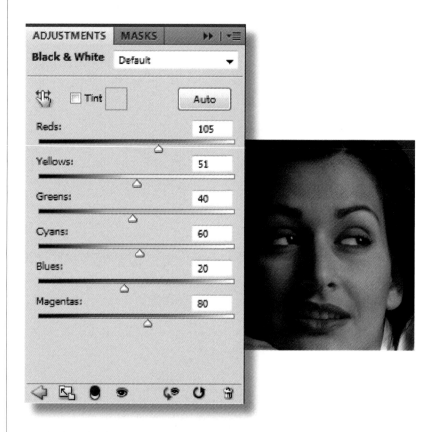

Second method

A particular correction method may work with one picture but not necessarily with another. This alternative method is more time-consuming, but also more reliable and should achieve the same result.

Create four sampling points with the Color Sampler (I), as shown on the picture. To sample only the color in the eyes, set the Color Sampler tool in the Options bar to SAMPLE SIZE 5 BY 5 AVERAGE. The Info panel F8 expands downwards, displaying the values of the four sampling points.

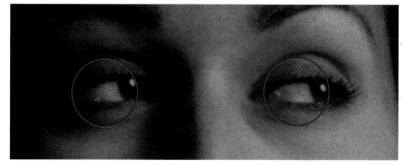

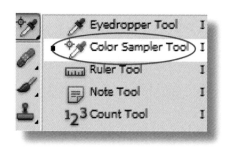

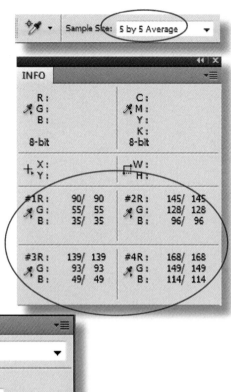

Here you can see that the red content is especially high in all four sampling points. We need to have all three colors at approximately the same value to produce neutral gray.

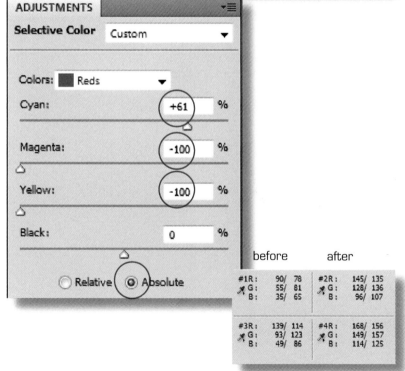

Create a SELECTIVE COLOR adjustment layer and activate the Method ABSOLUTE. The Info panel displays two values, BEFORE and AFTER. We need to set the target values so that all have approximately the same value. It does not matter how high or low the value is.

To reduce red, increase the complementary color CYAN in the REDS and reduce MAGENTA and YELLOW. Red consists of Magenta and Yellow.

The blue content is still too low. Switch to the YELLOWS and reduce YELLOW. Yellow complements blue, therefore the blue is increased.

There is still a slight color tint which you will not be able to remove with this selective color correction. Create a second Selective Color adjustment layer and reduce the YELLOW value in the NEUTRALS very slightly. Now all colors have nearly the same value. The acceptable tolerance is about 5%.

These corrections once again affect the whole picture. We already created a mask for the eyes in the previous adjustment layer. We can use it again for this adjustment layer. Hold the Alt -key and click on the mask of the layer "Selective Color 1". Drag the mask onto the layer above it. Confirm the REPLACE LAYER MASK dialog with Yes. The correction now affects only the eyes.

Two different methods and the same result. With other images or tasks it may well be that only one of these methods will work. You should always try to use the simplest one.

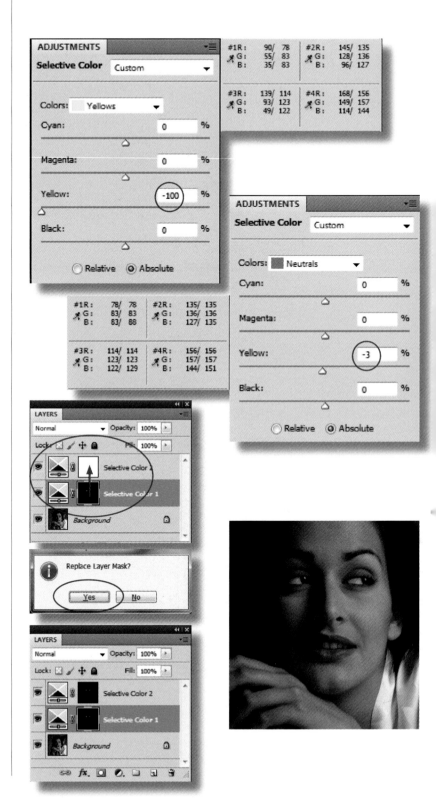

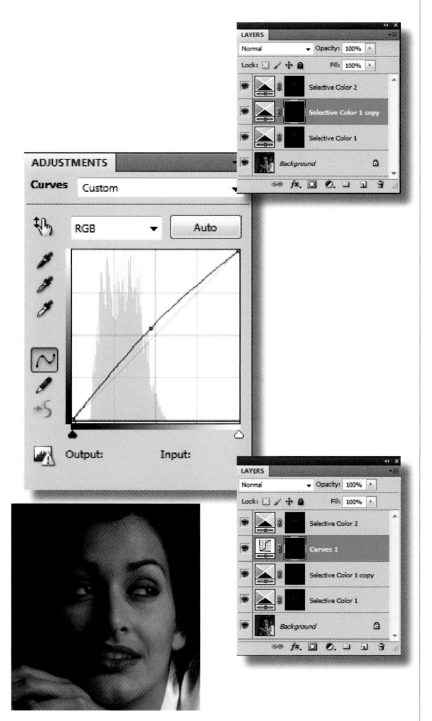

Whiter and brighter teeth

Often you can use the same adjustment layers to brighten the teeth at the same time. In this example, we did it separately to make it clearer. Simply copy the "Selective Color 1" with ⌘/Ctrl+J and fill the layer mask with black. Paint with white to reveal the teeth again. In this case, the color correction is too strong for the teeth. Reduce the layer opacity to about 55%. For brightening, create a Curve adjustment layer and drag the center of the curve slightly upwards. The whole picture is now brighter. To apply the brightening only to the teeth, hold the Alt-key and drag the layer mask of the layer "Selective Color 1 copy" to the layer "Curves 1". Then confirm that you want to replace the mask. Now the curve only affects the teeth.

Sharpen in case of motion blur

Picture analysis

❶ Reduce motion blur

❷ Sharpen image

One of the greatest challenges in children's portraits is sharpness. There should at least be a basic level of sharpness in expressive image areas, such as the eyes. That is not easy to achieve with children who gesture wildly and continuously jump around all over the place. But before you chuck an apparently unsharp picture in the bin, it is worth double-clicking on the magnifying glass to check the image at 100% view.

From CS4 onwards with OpenGL graphics card, zooming to 100% view is not as important any more.

ch3/blurred_eyes.jpg

before

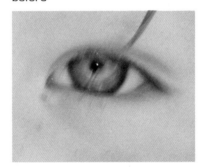 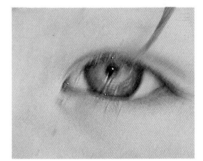

after

Detect motion blur

Since Photoshop CS2, we have the SMART SHARPEN command. This function allows removing motion blur. First we need to set the direction of movement. To determine it exactly, it is best to measure it. If you have already displayed the Smart Sharpen filter, click on CANCEL.

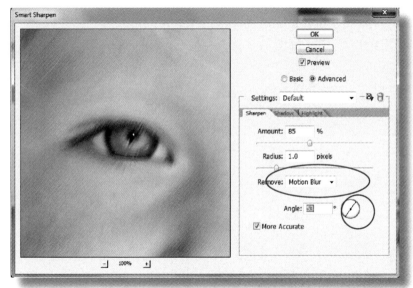

Zoom far into the picture: Click on the bottom left corner of the Navigator and enter a magnification of 600%. Confirm with the ⏎-key.

Measure angles

Find a spot in the picture where you can see the direction of movement clearly. Here, we chose the left eye. Choose the Ruler tool in the Tools panel. Click in the picture and draw a line from bottom left to top right through the motion blur. The Options bar now displays the Angle A: 56.3 degrees. Do not draw the line from top right to bottom left, as this would give the wrong angle measurement for our purposes.

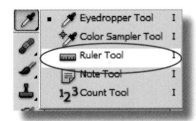

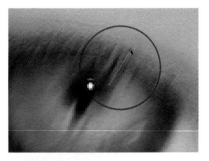

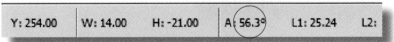

Duplicate the background with ⌘/Ctrl+J. Convert this layer to a Smart Object with FILTER/CONVERT FOR SMART FILTERS. We called the layer "Smart Sharpen".

There is, incidentally, no difference between choosing CONVERT FOR SMART FILTERS or using the pop-up menu in the Layers panel to convert a layer to a Smart Object.

Activate the Sharpen filter with FILTER/SHARPEN/SMART SHARPEN.

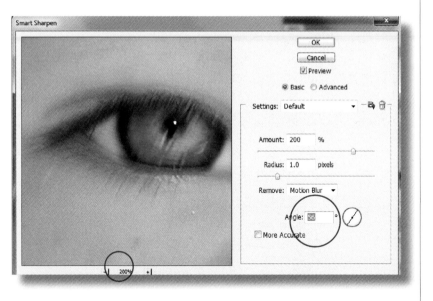

Reduce motion blur

Set the zoom in the filter preview to 200% to allow better assessment. Set the REMOVE box to Motion Blur. In the ANGLE dialog, enter the 56.3 degrees we measured. Photoshop will round down the value to 56 degrees when you click on other sliders. You will not notice the difference of 0.1% in the picture. Set the Radius to 1 pixel and experiment with the Amount. We found a value of 200% best. Activate the MORE ACCURATE button; the contrast increases slightly. Once you have found the right setting, click on OK. The motion blur is now largely fixed. But the image is still not quite sharp enough. We need to apply sharpening to the image as a whole. The High Pass filter works well here, as it has a strong effect.

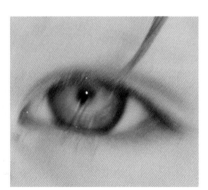

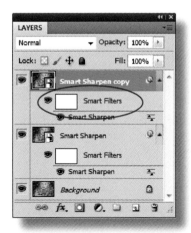

Simple sharpening

First, duplicate the layer "Smart Sharpen" by pressing ⌘/Ctrl+J or right-clicking on the layer and choosing NEW SMART OBJECT VIA COPY in the menu. This also duplicates the filter. However, we do not want to double the effect. Click on the Smart filter in the copy and drag it to the dust bin. The filter is canceled. Name this layer "High Pass".

Choose FILTER/OTHER/HIGH PASS.

As soon as you apply the filter, the image turns all gray. Set the preview window to 100%. Now you need to find a radius which depicts the small, fine lines lighter. Areas should show uniform gray as much as possible. With a Radius of 1.8 pixels we can see eye, eyelashes and hair slightly lighter. This low setting is sufficient. Click on Ok.

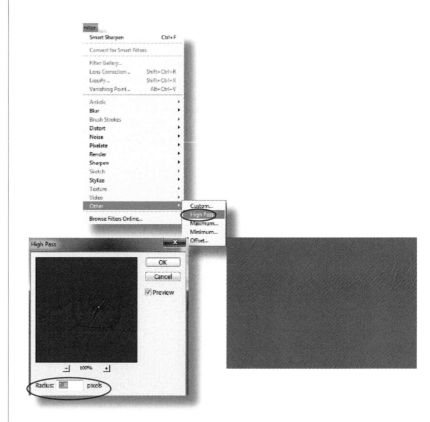

To be able to see our image again without gray fog, set the layer's blend mode to LINEAR LIGHT. The image is now much sharper. But the skin has suffered. It now shows little skin irritations and red blood vessels. We will therefore partially remove the sharpening. Activate the layers "High Pass" and "Smart Sharpen" whilst pressing the Shift key.

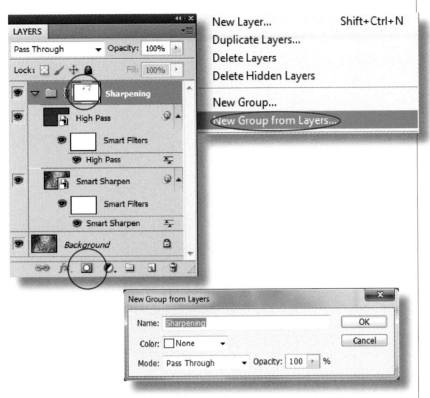

Partial sharpening

In the pop-up menu of the Layers panel, click on NEW GROUP FROM LAYERS. Name the group "Sharpening" and click on OK. You can create a layer mask for this group, just as with a normal layer, by clicking on the ADD LAYER MASK icon at the bottom of the Layers panel. Paint with black ([D]) over all areas that you do not want to sharpen, especially the cheeks and forehead. With this mask, you remove both sharpenings.

Use the Brush tool ([B], Size 80 pixels, Hardness 0%, Opacity 20%).

If you inspect the image closely, you will note that there are contour edges around some of the hairs. These are caused by the High Pass filter. If you click on the filter mask, you will see that you cannot make any changes here, due to the blend mode LINEAR LIGHT. Instead, create a normal layer mask on the "High Pass" layer and use it to remove the excessive sharpening by painting over the hairs with black. The sharpening effect of the Smart Sharpen remains.

Remove reflections from glasses

Picture analysis

① Remove light reflection from glasses

Editing reflections on glasses can cost a disproportionate amount of time and therefore money. During the photo shoot you should therefore take at least one photo in the same position without glasses.

ch3/glasses_reflect_1.jpg
ch3/glasses_reflect_2.jpg

before

after

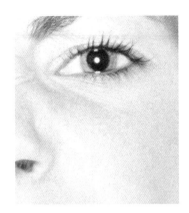

Insert eye

In order to remove the reflection on the glasses, we need to patch the eye. We can copy the right half of the eye and try adapting it. Or we can find a suitable picture of the eye without glasses, copy it and paste it into our picture.

Open both images and select the right eye in the picture "glasses_reflect_2. psd" with the Lasso tool ([L]). Copy it with [⌘]/[Ctrl]+[C]. Click on the original picture "glasses_reflect_1. psd" and insert the eye with [⌘]/[Ctrl]+[V]. Convert it to a SMART OBJECT via the panel menu. You can now close the file "glasses_reflect_2. psd".

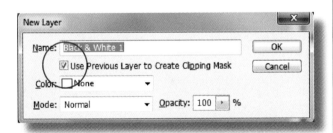

The inserted eye is still in color, but we need it in black and white. Create a new BLACK&WHITE adjustment layer by holding the Alt-key and clicking the icon in the Layers panel. Tick the box USE PREVIOUS LAYER TO CREATE CLIPPING MASK. Confirm the dialog with OK.

The layer "Black&White 1" is displayed indented in the Layers panel. It now affects only the layer "Eye", even if you reposition or transform this layer.

To retouch the reflection on the glasses, hide the layer "Eye" again for now. Click on the background and duplicate it with ⌘/Ctrl+J. Remove the light reflection with the retouching tools.

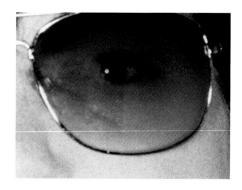

Show the layer "Eye" again and set the blend mode to MULTIPLY. Reduce the opacity until you can clearly see the layer beneath. Place pupil on pupil with the Move tool (V).

Size and orientation do not exactly match the original yet. Rotate and scale the eye with ⌘/Ctrl+T. We enlarged the Width to 102.9%, the Height to 113.8% and rotated the eye by -4.6 degrees. Work with the transformation box, then the values in the display change in parallel.

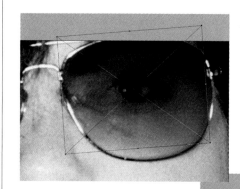

The eye now curves too strongly at the top.

Use EDIT/TRANSFORM/WARP to pull the upper eye lid slightly downwards.

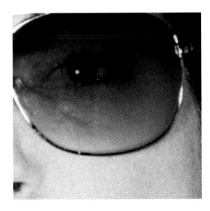

Use a layer mask to adapt the edges. Click on the icon at the bottom of the Layers panel and use black ([D]) and the Brush tool ([B], Size 80 pixels, Hardness 0%, Opacity 40%) to paint over the areas bordering the eye.

Fine-tuning

We want to bring out the shape of the eye more. Remember how you created a BLACK&WHITE adjustment layer at the beginning, without changing any settings. Click on the layer "Black&White 1" in the Layers panel. The Adjustments dialog reappears. Change the Reds and Yellows whilst watching the left side of the upper eye lid. If you drag the sliders to the left, the lid gains contrast and the contours become more modulated.

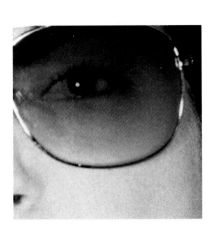

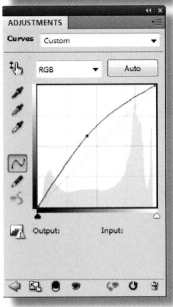

Lighten glasses

To finish, lighten the whole image with a CURVES adjustment layer. Use the layer mask to limit the effect to the glasses.

Make eyes look clear

Picture analysis

❶ Remove catchlight from eye

❷ Create new reflection

❸ Blacken pupil

❹ Make eyes clearer

❺ Match eye color to ice lolly color

The eyes look rather watery due to the eyes' different planes of focus. Also, the pupil is obscured by the catchlight, which does not make the eyes look very clear.

before

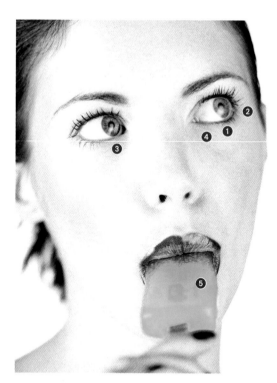

after

ch3/icelolly_lady.jpg

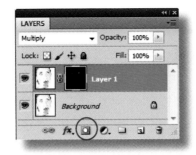

Remove catchlight from eye

To remove the reflection from the eye, we will first darken it slightly. Copy the background layer with ⌘/Ctrl+J and set the blend mode to Multiply. Hold the Alt-key and click on the Add Layer Mask icon at the bottom of the Layers panel. Now paint over the pupils with white (D) . They become slightly darker. Also paint over the roots of the upper eye lashes. This frames the iris nicely and emphasizes the entire picture.

Use the Lasso tool (L, Feather 3 pixels) to select an area on the iris without catchlight. Copy this area to another layer with ⌘/Ctrl+J and select Convert to Smart Object in the pop-up menu of the Layers panel.

Drag this part onto the iris reflection and rotate it with ⌘/Ctrl+T until all areas are covered up. Confirm the transformation with the ⏎-key.

The edges still do not overlap entirely. Create a layer mask and adapt the transitions with black ([D]) and the Brush tool ([B], Size 20 pixels, Hardness 0%, Opacity 100%). Proceed in the same way with the other eye. A few minor edges will remain imperfect. We will correct these later with different tools.

The pupil is still too light. To darken it, create a new empty layer at the top of the Layers panel. Paint over the pupils with the Brush tool and black ([B], Size 20 pixels, Hardness 0%, Opacity 100%). Then reduce the layer's opacity to about 63%, to adapt the black to the lightness of the original pupil. Try out different settings and watch closely which opacity gives you the best results. Save the image with all layers.

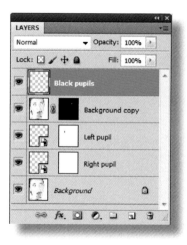

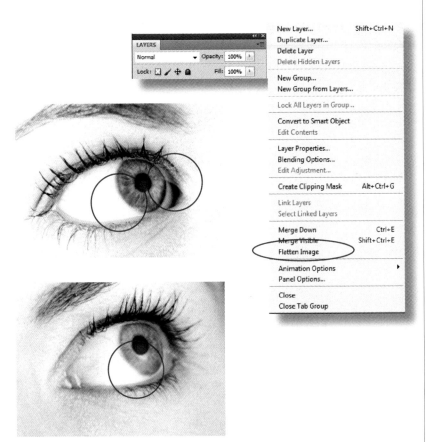

New Layer...	Shift+Ctrl+N
Duplicate Layer...	
Delete Layer	
Delete Hidden Layers	
New Group...	
New Group from Layers...	
Lock All Layers in Group...	
Convert to Smart Object	
Edit Contents	
Layer Properties...	
Blending Options...	
Edit Adjustment...	
Create Clipping Mask	Alt+Ctrl+G
Link Layers	
Select Linked Layers	
Merge Down	Ctrl+E
Merge Visible	Shift+Ctrl+E
Flatten Image	
Animation Options	▶
Panel Options...	
Close	
Close Tab Group	

Fine retouching

For fine retouching the iris border and the structures within the iris, it is best to work on one single layer. Choose FLATTEN IMAGE from the pop-up menu in the Layers panel. Copy the background with ⌘/Ctrl+J, name this layer "Fine retouching" and save the picture as "icelolly_lady_2. psd".

Both eyes still show small flaws. Double-click on the magnifying glass to zoom to 100%. Use the Clone Stamp tool (S) and the Healing Brush tool to fix missing structures and unwanted edges. Vary the size and opacity of the tool tips.

Change eye color

In a normal portrait, we would now be done with the eye retouching. But in our example, we also want to match the eye color to the color of the ice lolly.

Create a new BLACK&WHITE adjustment layer with the CREATE NEW FILL OR ADJUSTMENT LAYER icon in the Layers panel. In earlier versions of Photoshop, click on the option HUE and adjust the Hue slider until the color of the ice lolly appears in the preview window on the right, that is at about 179 degrees. In the new version of Photoshop, you check the TINT box, then click on the color swatch to activate the COLOR PICKER. Enter 179 degrees for Hue and click on OK. The whole picture now takes on that color.

Press ⌘/Ctrl+I and the layer mask turns black. The coloration disappears. Use the Brush tool (B) and white to paint over the iris. The color reappears. If you think it is too strong, reduce the layer's Opacity accordingly.

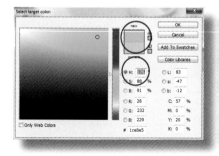

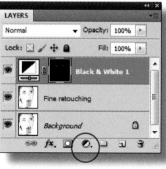

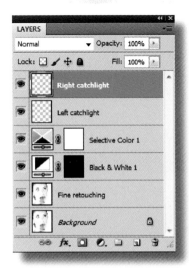

The eye color now matches that of the ice lolly. You can therefore finish the fine-tuning quickly. Create a SELECTIVE COLOR adjustment layer at the top and experiment a little bit. We decided to use the following values.

Colors:	CYANS
CYAN:	–43%
MAGENTA:	–5%
YELLOW:	–62%
BLACK:	+9%
METHOD:	ABSOLUTE

This way you can adjust the color quickly and efficiently, without requiring further masks.

Create reflection in eye

It helps to have a catchlight in the iris, to achieve bright, shiny eyes. To create the reflections in the eyes, first create a new empty layer in the Layers panel. Paint a catchlight into the iris with the Brush tool and white ([B], Size 10 pixels, Hardness 0%, Opacity 100%). If you find the catchlight too hard, use FILTER/BLUR/GAUSSIAN BLUR with a Radius of 6.8 pixels. If the reflection is still too hard, apply the filter again with [⌘]/[Ctrl]+[F]. Proceed in the same way with the second eye. You can try out various positions and sizes for the reflection. The effect can be very different. Save the picture when you are finished.

Possible variations

The possible options for further editing are limited only by the boundaries of your own imagination. We want to draw more attention to the eyes and the ice lolly. We will therefore push all other details into the background using desaturation. Flatten all layers again. Create a HUE/SATURATION adjustment layer.

First adjust the REDS and YELLOWS sliders as shown here. You now have a black and white picture with a few color accents.

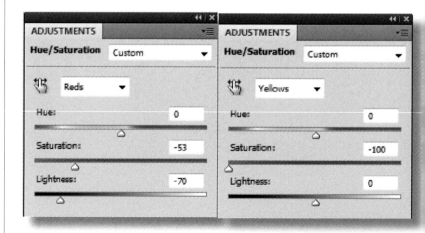

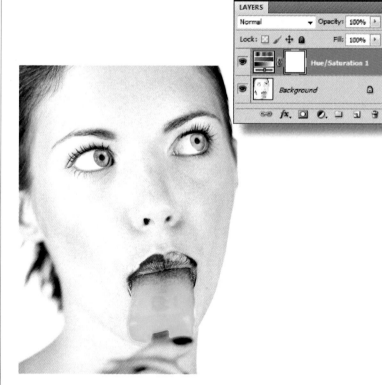

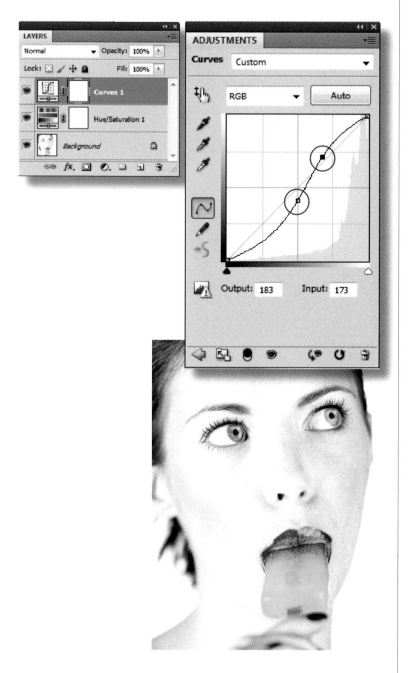

Create another CURVES adjustment
layer at the top of the Layers panel
and increase the contrast slightly. To
that purpose, drag the highlights part
of the curve upwards and the shadows
part of the curve downwards. Try out
other settings as well.

Remove red eye

Picture analysis

❶ Remove red eyes

The red eye effect is a frequently occurring problem despite modern camera equipment. It is caused by a frontal photographic flash, for example by compact cameras. The light from the flash is reflected by the retina and the pupil appears red on the picture. Fortunately, red-eye is very easy to correct.

ch3/redeyes.jpg

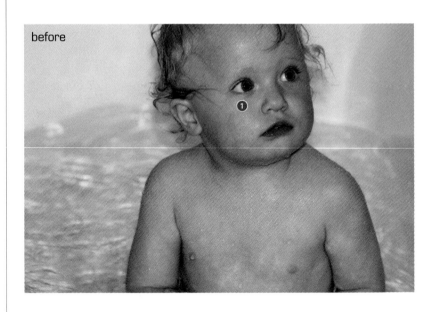

before

after

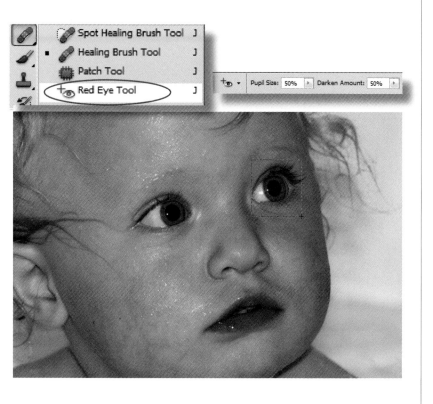

Remove red eye

Choose the Red Eye tool ($\boxed{\text{J}}$) and simply click in the red pupil. The red immediately disappears. Alternatively, you can use the tool to draw a rectangle around the eye, in case Photoshop does not recognize the eye properly. This happens very rarely. We set the Pupil Size to 50% in the Options bar at the top. If the red continues slightly into the iris as well, you need to increase this value. Reduce the value if the iris is now larger than the original. With Darken Amount you regulate the darkness of the pupil. We left it at 50%.

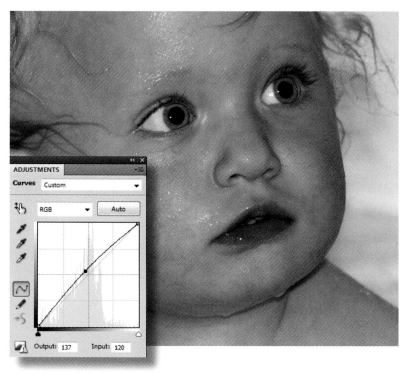

If you now think that the separation between pupil and iris is worse, you can correct it with a CURVES adjustment layer. Brighten the iris and the white of the eye. Use a layer mask to brighten only these areas.

Basic Overview: Channels

The channels contain information about color and brightness of a picture. Additional channels can be created from saved selections or help us create them. Large color spaces such as LAB and RGB cannot be rendered completely in the smaller print color space CMYK. That is also the reason why you will not see any difference between the colored pictures on the right.

A picture and its channels

A black and white picture contains one gray channel.

An RGB picture contains the fundamental colors red, green and blue. When mixed together, they make yellow, magenta and cyan. All pictures on the book DVD are in RGB.

A CMYK image consists of the fundamental colors cyan, magenta, yellow and black. When mixed together, they make red, green and blue. We need this color space in some chapters to create selections.

A LAB image consists of the lightness channel, the a-channel, which is responsible for red-green, and the b-channel, which is responsible for blue-yellow. We need this color space, for example, to sharpen an image without color shifts.

The Channels panel

Composite channel
Shows all color information.

Color channels
These contain the color information, in this case for an RGB picture.

Filter mask
of an active layer with smart filter

Alpha channels
pixel-based masks, such as saved selections

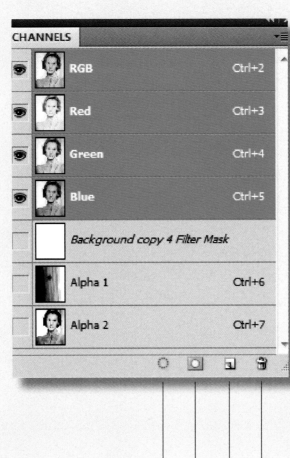

Panel menu

Load channel as selection
Drag a channel onto this icon.

Save selection as channel
Click on this icon after creating a selection.

Create new channel
Click on the icon to create a new empty channel.

Delete selected channel
Drag a channel onto the icon to delete it.

Load color channels as selection

The corresponding brightness values of the color are loaded as selection if you hold the ⌘/Ctrl+X-key while clicking on the layer thumbnail of a color channel or the composite channel in the Channels panel.

Save and load selection

You can save an existing selection by clicking on the SAVE SELECTION AS CHANNEL icon (1). The new channel is called Alpha 1. You can load a saved selection by dragging a channel onto the LOAD CHANNEL AS SELECTION icon (2), or with the menu item LOAD SELECTION.

Edit channel

You can edit a single channel in the same way as any black-and-white image. Activate the channel by clicking on it. Now you can correct the channel with the Brush tool, the Gradient tool, filters or with IMAGE/EDIT. Then load it as a selection. To edit the image again, click on the RGB composite channel at the top.

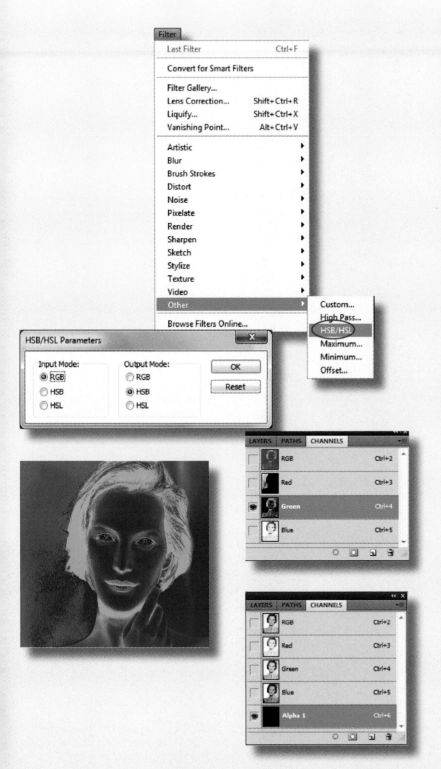

Saturation mask

The saturation mask is based on the color saturation values of an image. The color saturation is loaded as selection. Saturated areas allow stronger editing than unsaturated ones.

The filter HSB/HSL is no longer part of the default installation of Photoshop. You need to download it from the Adobe website.

Apply the HSB/HSL filter to a copy of your image. In the parameters, set Input Mode to RGB, Output Mode to HSB. The image now appears in strange colors. We now need the green channel, as it contains the gray-scale of the color saturation.

To do this, we first need to copy it into the clipboard (Duplicate Channel, Destination: New; Load Channel as Selection; Copy) and then paste into a new alpha channel of the original image.

Reactivate the RGB composite channel and make it visible again. The Alpha 1 channel should no longer be active or visible. Load the new channel with SELECT/LOAD SELECTION.

During the next editing steps we decide to use, such as an adjustment layer, only the most saturated colors are altered. In our example on the right, we reduced the overall saturation with HUE/SATURATION.

Luminosity mask

The luminosity mask is based on the brightness distribution within an image. This is loaded as selection. Brighter areas allow stronger editing than darker ones. To edit darker areas more strongly, invert the selection with ⌘/Ctrl+I.

If you ⌘/Ctrl-click on the layer thumbnail of the RGB channel in the Channels panel, the brightness values are loaded.

Now you can edit this selection just like any other selection.

Additionally, you can save the selection as channel and edit it like a grayscale image or place it onto another layer with ⌘/Ctrl+J.

In this example, we used the luminosity mask and a Curve to darken the bright areas. The shadows are hardly affected.

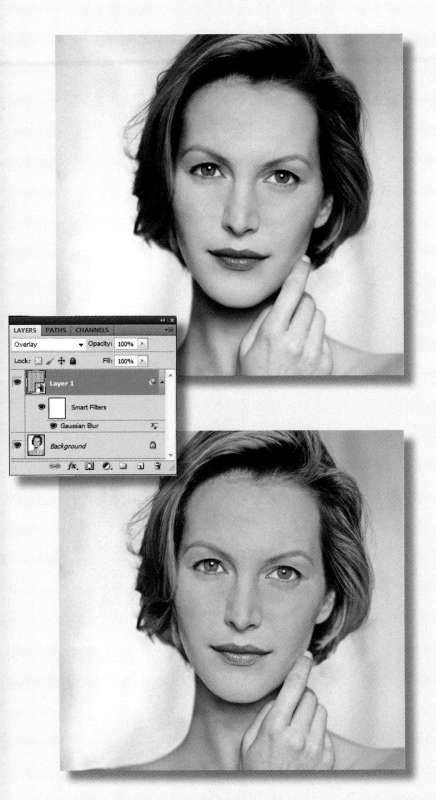

Contrast mask

With a contrast mask, you can
quickly balance extreme contrasts in an image. This method
has the disadvantage of causing
color shifts, as you can see in our
example.

Always work on the copy of your
background and choose the blend
mode OVERLAY. With IMAGE/ADJUST/
INVERT you turn the layer into a negative.

Convert it into a SMART OBJECT. Use
the Gaussian Blur to soften it. The
Radius can vary greatly, depending on
image and resolution. Try out different Amounts.

Now correct the color shift.

Chapter 4
Mouth

 How to use artificial
lip gloss to create vivid
lips

How to make lips smile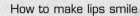

 How to make thin lips
seem fuller

**Basic Overview
Blend modes**

How to correct teeth

 How to improve an
unsatisfactory mouth on
your photo and whiten
teeth

How to bring color to
pale lips

Apply lip gloss

Picture analysis

❶ Apply lip gloss

Shiny lip gloss adds volume to lips and makes the mouth appear more vivid. With the Plastic Wrap effect, you can easily create artificial lip gloss.

ch4/lip_gloss.jpg

before

after

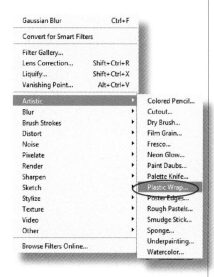

Improve lip contour

The light reflection at the bottom lip edge is a bit too strong and the lip loses contour. To fix this, copy the background with ⌘/Ctrl+J and set the blend mode to MULTIPLY. The whole picture is darkened. To make sure only the lip is affected, hold the Alt-key and create a layer mask. The effect is canceled. Paint with the Brush tool (B), low Opacity and white over the lip areas that you want to darken.

Create lip gloss

For the lip gloss we use the Plastic Wrap filter. Copy the background again and place it at the top of the Layers panel. Convert the layer to a SMART OBJECT. Choose FILTER/ ARTISTIC/PLASTIC WRAP. As with all filters, you need to watch the view size. You should set it to 100% to ensure that you can judge the effect accurately. Think about what you want the lips to look like. Would you like a little bit of shine or a lot, should the details of the lips remain visible and how hard or soft do you want the transitions between the shiny and less shiny areas to be? Try out different combinations. Click on OK when you are happy with the result.

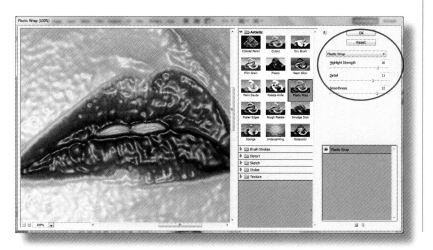

Create a black layer mask again and reveal the lip gloss by painting over it with white and the Brush tool ([B]). Do not paint over the lip contours.

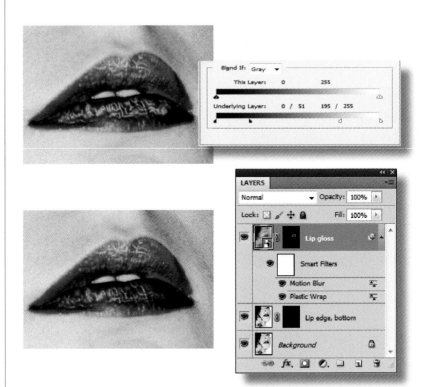

The lip gloss is still too dominant and too hard. Double-click on the empty area to the right of the "Lip gloss" thumbnail to open the Blending Options dialog. We want to intensify the dark and light areas of the original lips slightly. Adjust the sliders of UNDERLYING LAYER. We chose the following settings:

0/51   195/255

> To separate the triangle sliders, press and hold the [Alt]-key while dragging (see Basic Overview "Special Layer Techniques", Chapter 5).

Now we want to soften the lip gloss a bit more. Choose FILTER/BLUR/MOTION BLUR.

To create a longish reflection, we set the ANGLE to roughly horizontal. Set the DISTANCE slider first all the way to the left and then gradually drag it to the right. Keep watching the change in the lip gloss. When you have found a setting that you are happy with, note down the value and drag the slider further to the right. Quite often you will get other interesting effects. We chose 430 pixels.

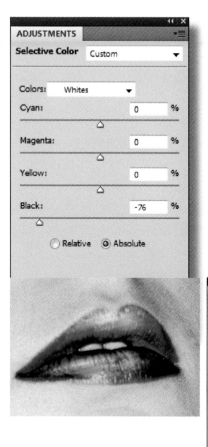

Increase sheen

The lip gloss now has the right shape, but the sheen has suffered during editing. We use a SELECTIVE COLOR adjustment layer to reduce the black in the Whites by 76% and in the Neutrals by 46%.

With a layer mask you can restrict the correction to the lips. Press ⌘/Ctrl+I to turn the layer mask black and make the effect invisible. Now use the Brush tool (B) and white to reveal the effect in certain areas.

Another example

The PLASTIC WRAP filter can react very differently, we therefore want to show you another example. For these makeup-free lips we found a very attractive and natural sheen at these settings:

20/15/15.

In this instance, no further editing was necessary, apart from limiting the filter to the lips via a mask.

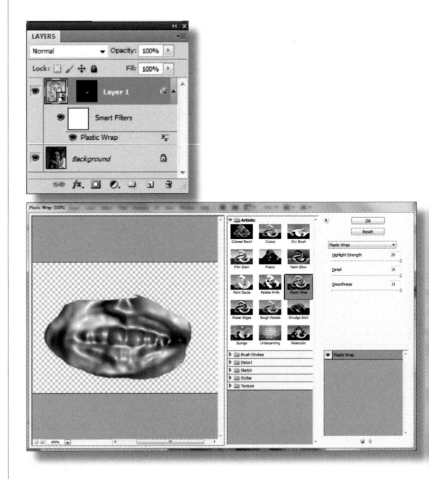

before

after

Full lips

Picture analysis

❶ Fuller upper lip

A pretty smile often makes the lips look very thin because they are tensed and stretched. This effect is even more noticeable with red lipstick.

ch4/full_lips.jpg

Larger upper lip

The woman's upper lip appears too
thin. The perspective is very frontal,
therefore we can simply transform the
upper lip to enlarge it.

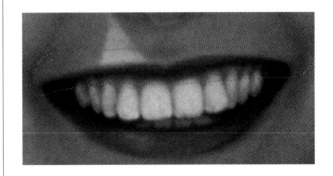

Select the upper lip and surrounding
area with the Lasso tool (L , Feather
4 pixels). Copy the selection with
⌘ / Ctrl + J to a new layer and
call it "Upper lip". Convert the layer
to a SMART OBJECT in the menu of the
Layers panel.

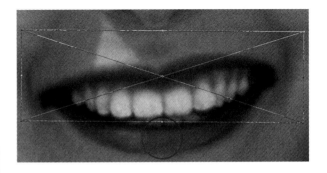

Press ⌘ / Ctrl + T to display the
transformation box. Drag the bottom center handle of the bounding
box downwards. In this example,
the upper lip was enlarged to 150%.
Rotate the upper lip very slightly
clockwise, about 0.5 degrees. Watch
the values displayed in the Options
bar.

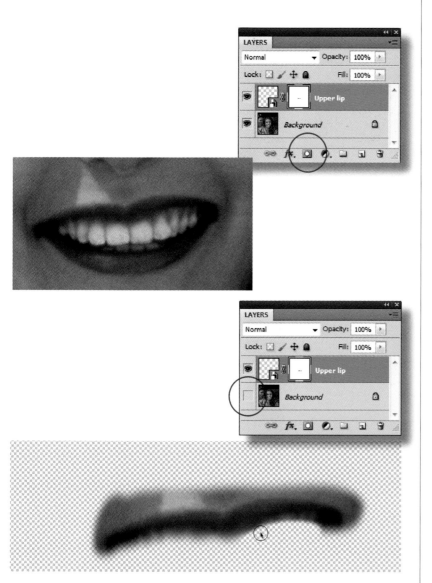

Adjust upper lip

The generous selection around the upper lip at the beginning of our editing has caused changes to the surrounding areas such as skin, gums and teeth. On the transition between upper lip and skin this has the positive effect that the transitions already look rather good. The teeth on the other hand have suffered. Due to the transformation, the teeth are now obscured by lip and gums at the top.

To improve the tooth area, you need to create a layer mask by clicking on the ADD LAYER MASK icon at the bottom of the Layers panel. For better assessment, hide the "Background" layer by clicking on the eye icon next to the layer's thumbnail. Use the Brush tool (B , Size 25 pixels, Hardness 20%, Opacity 100%) and paint with black to hide the upper row of teeth. Then show the background again.

You should not slavishly restrict yourself to the tool settings we suggest in this book. Try out different settings and keep testing and experimenting until you get the best possible result.

Mouth correction

Picture analysis

❶ Cover gums

❷ Correct tooth line slightly

❸ Whiten teeth

The happy laughter shows large areas of gums, which seems somewhat unattractive. In this case, it is not possible to enlarge the upper lip in order to cover the gums. The facial proportions would change too much. Stretching the teeth upwards does not give a satisfactory result either. The best option is moving the teeth upwards a fraction, thereby enlarging the mouth opening slightly.

ch4/gums.jpg

before

after

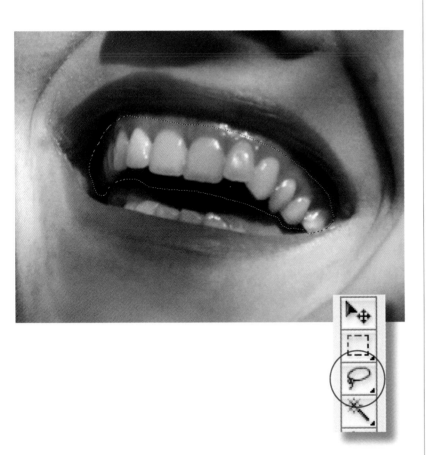

Select teeth

Select the upper row of teeth with the Lasso tool (L, Feather 4 pixels) as shown on the picture. Copy the selection to another layer with ⌘/Ctrl+J. Click on CONVERT TO SMART OBJECT in the pop-up menu of the Layers panel. We named the layer "Teeth".

To be able to work better, hide the layer "Teeth", activate the background layer and click on the CREATE NEW LAYER icon in the Layers panel. We named the new layer "Mouth cavity".

Remove original teeth

Because we want to reposition the upper row of teeth, we first need to remove the original teeth so they are not in the way. Activate the Eyedropper and set the Sample Size in the Options bar to 5x5 pixels. The default setting of 1 pixel is not enough for defining a color. To darken the oral cavity, choose the Brush tool (B, Size 25 pixels, Hardness 50%, Opacity 100%). Move the cursor to the dark areas of the mouth, press the Alt-key and click once. The cursor turns into an eyedropper and samples the dark color.

Now cover the upper teeth and the gums. The picture now looks rather creepy, best not to show anyone. Show the layer "Teeth" again and activate this layer.

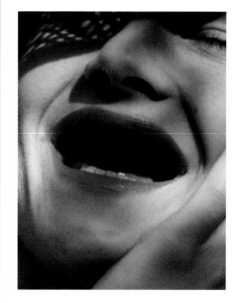

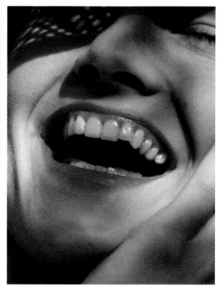

Reposition teeth

Next, position the teeth with the Move tool (V). The position does not need to be exactly right yet. The upper lip now seems rather thin. Create a layer mask by clicking on the mask icon at the bottom of the Layers panel and reveal the upper lip by painting with the Brush tool (B) and black (D).

As you can see, the position of the teeth is still not quite right after revealing the upper lip. Click once on the smart object thumbnail, to switch from the mask to the teeth. Now use the Move tool (V) to move the teeth downwards until you are happy with the position.

Up to Photoshop CS3, a Smart Object did not have a Chain icon and therefore no link to the mask. You could therefore move the teeth independently of the mask. The teeth would consequently always be moved "under" the lip. From Photoshop CS4 onwards, you simply need to deactivate the Chain icon by clicking on it.

Straighten teeth and adjust length

It is easier not to work on a smart object for retouching and cleaning the individual teeth, because a smart object cannot be simply retouched (see Basic Overview "Special Layer Techniques", Chapter 5). As we have not yet scaled the picture in any way nor changed the pixels, we now choose LAYER/SMART OBJECTS/ RASTERIZE in order to rasterize the layer. You could also Ctrl-click/ right-click on the layer and choose RASTERIZE LAYER in the resulting dialog.

To be able to see the teeth fully for retouching, hide the layer mask on the layer "Teeth" by holding the ⇧-key and clicking on the layer mask thumbnail. The mask is hidden.

Use the Lasso tool (L, Feather 1 pixel) to select a tooth that needs improving and refine the selection in Mask mode (Q). To return to the selection, press Q. again. Copy the tooth with ⌘/Ctrl+J position it at the top of the Layers panel. Name it "Tooth 1".

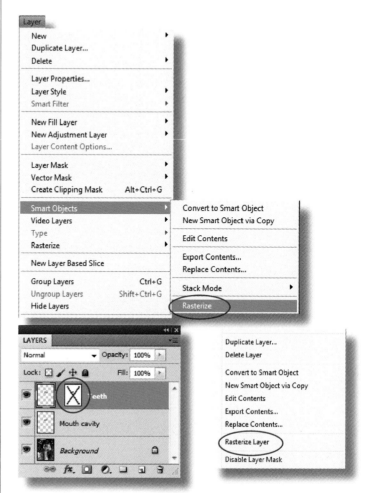

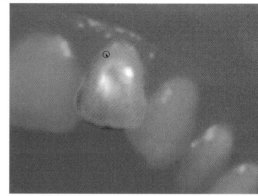

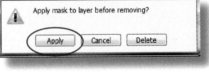

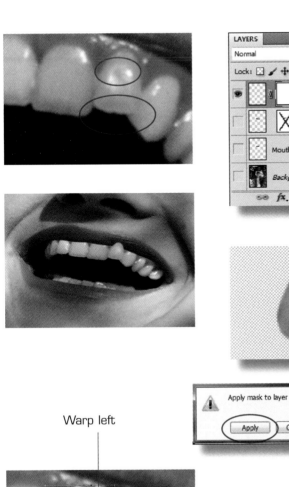

Warp left

Warp right

Remove any grooves from the tooth, reduce the reflections and use the Clone Stamp tool (S, Size 8 pixels, Hardness 70%, Opacity 100%) to give it a new shape. The new shape may not fit in completely with the other teeth. Remove these areas with a layer mask. Use black (D) and the Brush tool (B, Size 5 pixels, Hardness 40%, Opacity 100%) to remove the tooth outline which may overlap other teeth. Hide the other layers occasionally to make it easier. Once the tooth is perfect, you can drag the mask of the layer "Tooth 1" to the recycle bin. Click on APPLY in the resulting dialog. Transform the tooth to a SMART OBJECT. Show the other layers again.

Use EDIT/TRANSFORM/WARP to improve the tooth shape. Make sure that the right part of the tooth gets warped slightly to the left. The tooth next to it on the right seems to be beneath it, but should be next to it. Proceed in the same manner with the other teeth that you feel need improving.

Now the new teeth partially stick out over the upper lip. Hold the ⇧-key and activate all tooth layers, then select NEW GROUP FROM LAYERS in the menu of the Layers panel. Name the group and create a layer mask on it. Use black (D) and the Brush tool (B) to remove the teeth that stick out.

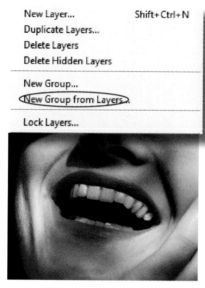

Adapt teeth

To adapt all teeth in one step, we create an empty layer at the top of the Layers panel. It may be that this new layer is automatically placed into the group, in that case just drag the new layer on top of the group. With the Clone Stamp tool (S, Size 15 pixels, Hardness 30%, Opacity 100%) you now adapt the shape of the lower edges of the teeth. First you need to activate SAMPLE: ALL LAYERS in the Options bar. Now all layers that are underneath that layer are included. This way you can also edit the lower row of teeth. We also used a neutral layer to darken the back right area of the mouth cavity (see Basic Overview "Special Layer Techniques", Chapter 5).

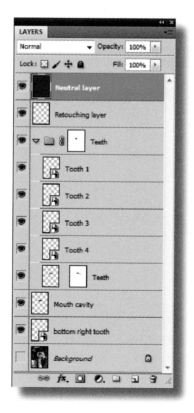

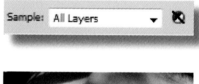

If you look really closely you will note that the dark mouth cavity is too even. This is due to the Brush tool with which we darkened these areas at the beginning.

We need a bit of noise in there. Click on the layer "Mouth cavity" and activate the button LOCK TRANSPARENT PIXELS in the Layers panel. This ensures that the following filter is only applied to the painted area.

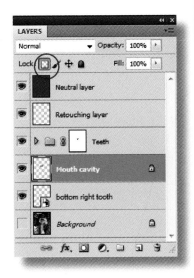

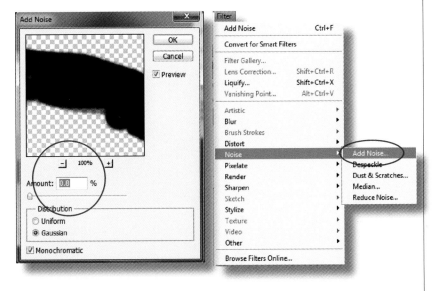

Choose FILTER/NOISE/ADD NOISE. Set the Amount to 0.8%. That is very little, but important for a high-quality print, because completely unstructured areas would immediately show and look wrong. Now save the image.

You should get into the habit of saving the picture very often with ⌘/Ctrl+S to make sure important steps of your work do not get lost.

Whiten teeth

To make whitening the teeth as easy
as possible, we need to have them
on a single layer. Drag the layer
"Mouth cavity" directly on top of the
background. Now activate the layer
"bottom right tooth", the layer group
"Teeth" and the layer "Retouching",
while holding the ⇧-key. Then
press ⌘/Ctrl+E.

All activated areas are merged
into the top layer, i.e. the layer
"Retouching layer". We will rename
this layer "Teeth". First save the picture under a new name to make sure
you have saved the previous file with
all layers. You never know what a
customer may want you to change
later on, and this saves you having to
repeat all editing steps all over again.

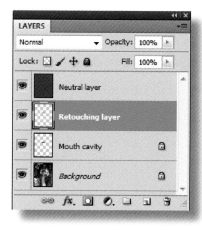

Select the Color Sampler tool (I)
and create a sampling point on one
of the front teeth. The values are displayed at the bottom of the Info panel.
The teeth clearly have a red-yellow
cast.

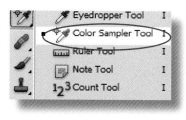

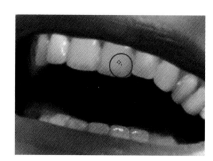

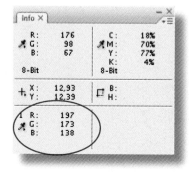

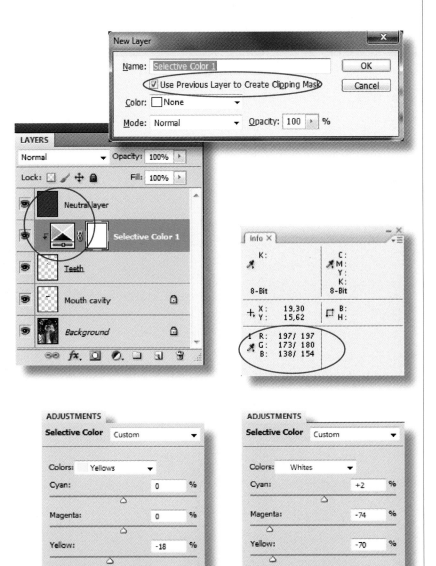

We will use a SELECTIVE COLOR for color correction. Activate the SELECTIVE COLOR via the CREATE NEW ADJUSTMENT LAYER icon while holding the Alt -key. Check the button USE PREVIOUS LAYER TO CREATE CLIPPING MASK. The adjustment layer is created as clipping mask and therefore only affects the layer "Teeth". The layer is shown indented and with a down arrow in the Layers panel.

The Info panel now shows you two values when you place the sampling point: the before value and the after value (on the right). Set the following parameters:

Colors: WHITES
CYAN   +2
MAGENTA   −74
YELLOW   −70
BLACK   0

Colors: YELLOWS
CYAN   0
MAGENTA   0
YELLOW   −18
BLACK   0

The color values in the Info panel approach each other. If all three color values were equal, we would get gray. A slight color cast is therefore necessary. But one tooth is still too yellow.

To correct the yellow tooth, set another sampling point on this tooth. This sampling point 2 indicates that Blue is very low. Blue is the complement of Yellow, therefore we get a yellow cast. Activate the SELECTIVE COLOR again while holding the [Alt]-key, name it "Yellow tooth" and check the box CREATE CLIPPING MASK FROM PREVIOUS.

Set the following color values:

Colors: REDS
CYAN   0
MAGENTA   −40
YELLOW   −41
BLACK   0

Colors: YELLOWS
CYAN   −47
MAGENTA   −100
YELLOW   −100
BLACK   0

Then fill the layer mask with black with [⌘]/[Ctrl]+[I]. The correction now no longer affects the picture. Use the Brush tool ([B], Size 20 pixels, Hardness 0%, Opacity 10%) and white to bring out the correction on the relevant tooth again.

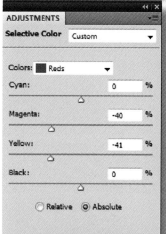

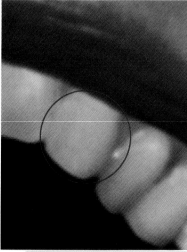

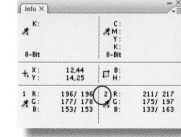

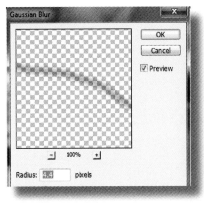

Create shadow

Now all that is missing is a little shadow on the teeth and the upper lip. Create an empty layer at the top and use the Brush tool to paint a little narrow line on the teeth, along the lips. Set the Layer Opacity to about 50% and choose the GAUSSIAN BLUR from the Filter menu. We set the Radius to 4 pixels. If you are not happy with the shadow's intensity, simply adjust the Layer Opacity. Save the picture. Merge all layers in the layers panel into the background with FLATTEN IMAGE. To finish, retouch any small flaws you may still find and then save the result under a new name.

Smile, please!

Picture analysis

❶ Make mouth appear friendlier

Often it is only a minute detail that turns a serious facial expression into a smiling one. In this case, it's the corners of the mouth which curve downwards. If we draw a line between upper and lower lip, you can see it very clearly. The mouth also seems somewhat pressed together. You can make the mouth look more relaxed by enlarging its width slightly.

ch4/smile.jpg

before

after

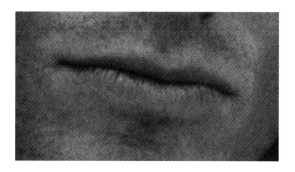

Select mouth

For editing it is better to have the mouth on another layer. Select the mouth and surrounding area with the Lasso tool (⌴) and a feathered edge of 5 pixels.

Copy the mouth onto another layer with ⌘ / Ctrl +J and name the layer "Mouth".

The original mouth on the background is no longer needed. It could get in the way during editing, therefore we should remove it. Show the background again and copy it. Hide the layer "Mouth" and remove the mouth with the retouching tools, such as the Clone Stamp.

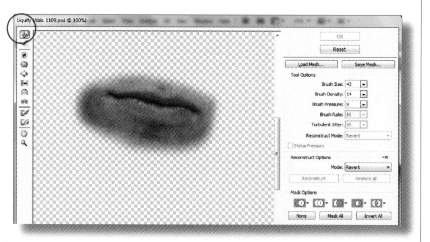

Adapt left corner of mouth

Show the layer "Mouth" again and copy it with ⌘ / Ctrl +J. Hide the layer "Mouth" and work on the copy. Choose FILTER/LIQUIFY. Use the Forward Warp tool (W, Brush Size 43, Brush Density 14 and Brush Pressure 9) to push the left corner of the mouth and a small part of the lips slightly upwards. Do not make the changes too noticeable. Already you can see a slight blur, but we can correct it later. Click on Ok.

Adapt right corner of the mouth

We will replace the right corner of the mouth with the left one. This widens the mouth slightly, because the right corner of the mouth appears somewhat shortened due to the perspective from the slight rotation of the head. Use the Rectangular Marquee (M, Feather 0 pixels) to select the corner of the mouth, copy it to a new layer with ⌘/Ctrl+J and convert it into a SMART OBJECT.

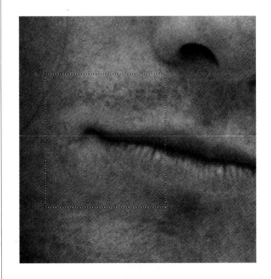

For positioning, reduce the layer Opacity until you can see the bottom corner of the mouth clearly. First flip the layer horizontally. With ⌘/Ctrl+T you activate the Free Transform bounding box. To be able to rotate the new corner of the mouth into the correct position, drag the reference point onto the spot marked in red or click on the little squares in the Options bar. Now rotate the box slightly, using the left corner of the mouth as a guide. Press the ↵-key and set the layer Opacity back to 100%.

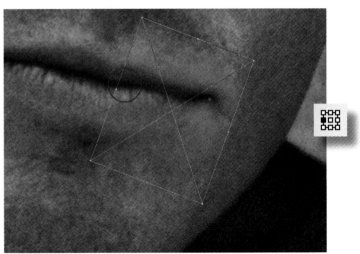

Now create a layer mask on the layer "Right mouth corner", remove the link between mask and layer and adapt the new mouth shape to the surrounding skin. Depending on the amount of skin you previously selected for the layer "Mouth copy", you need to create a layer mask there as well, in order to adjust the skin transitions.

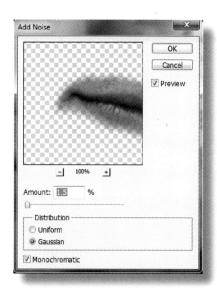

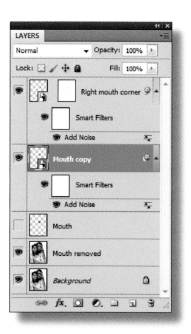

"Sharpen" mouth corners

The slight blur in the mouth corners can be removed with a Noise filter. Convert the layer "Mouth copy" to a SMART OBJECT as well. Choose FILTER/NOISE/ADD NOISE, set the Amount to 1.5%, Distribution to GAUSSIAN and activate MONOCHROMATIC. Click on OK.

You can apply the same settings to "Right mouth corner" by clicking on the sublayer "Add noise" and Alt -dragging it onto the layer.

The corners of the mouth now have structure again and no longer appear blurry.

Correct teeth

Picture analysis

❶ Lengthen left canine

❷ Adjust length of upper teeth

❸ Make teeth rounder

Beautiful teeth adorn the face naturally, just as much as eyes or mouth. They therefore deserve the same amount of attention to detail. In our picture, we would like to correct the upper row of teeth, as the unfavorable perspective of the shot makes the teeth look very jagged and irregular.

ch4/fix_teeth.jpg

before

after

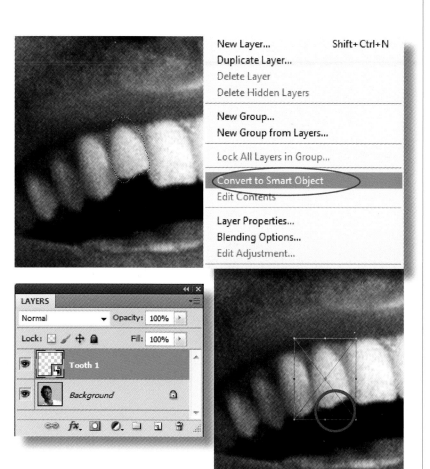

Lengthen left canine tooth

To correct the left canine tooth, select it with the Lasso tool (L, Feather 1 pixel). Copy it onto a new layer with ⌘/Ctrl+J. Choose CONVERT TO SMART OBJECT from the pop-up menu in the Layers panel and name it "Tooth 1".

With ⌘/Ctrl+T you transform the the tooth by dragging it downwards until it has approximately the same length as the other teeth.

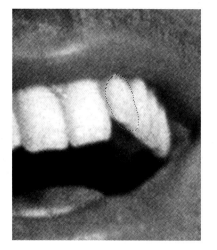

Adjust right row of teeth

Select the right canine tooth with the Lasso tool and place it on its own layer with ⌘/Ctrl+J. Name the layer "Tooth 2".

Now copy this layer again with ⌘/Ctrl+J. Name the new layer "Tooth 3". Convert these layers into a SMART OBJECT one by one. Hide the top layer.

Activate the layer "Tooth 2" and position the tooth. Scale the tooth lengthwise with ⌘/Ctrl+T until it matches the rest of the row nicely.

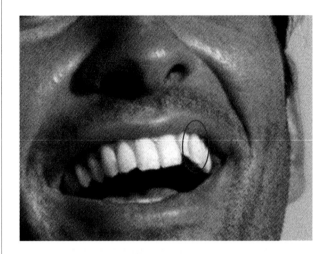

Now show the layer "Tooth 3" again and do the same with this layer. Position this tooth to the right of the right front tooth.

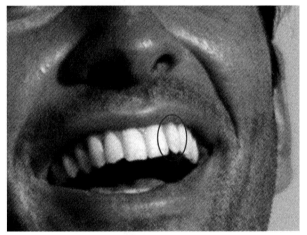

The teeth are already looking much better, but the tooth edges are still too irregular.

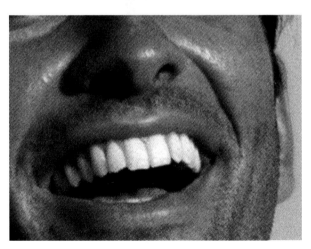

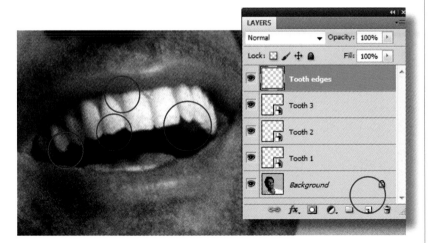

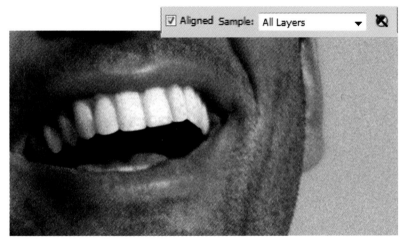

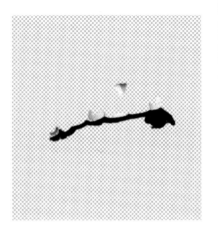

Make tooth edges rounder

For fine retouching, we will use the Clone Stamp tool. For utmost flexibility we will not flatten the layers yet.

First use the icon at the bottom of the Layers panel to create a new layer at the top of the Layers panel. Name this new layer "Tooth edges".

Now switch to the Clone Stamp tool ([S], Size 10 pixels, Hardness 40%, Opacity 100%). In the tool's Options bar, choose the setting SAMPLE: ALL LAYERS. The retouching is applied to the new layer and you can make changes any time without affecting the original picture. Make the tooth edges a little bit rounder. Also edit the gaps between the teeth and remove the inappropriate light reflection on the molar on the right.

If you hide and show the other layers from time to time, you can judge the effect of your retouching.

Of course you can also lighten the teeth and adapt the color, as described in the Chapter "Mouth correction".

Emphasize lips

Picture analysis

❶ Decolorize picture

❷ Add lipstick

If the model's eyes only show
a hint of make-up, you can add
glamorous emphasis to the mouth
by applying luscious red lipstick.
We increased this effect even more
by reducing the overall amount of
Reds and Yellows in the picture.

ch4/red_lips.jpg

before

after

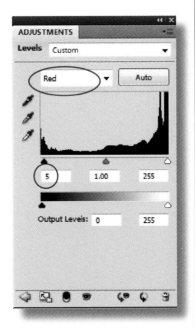

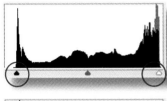

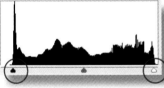

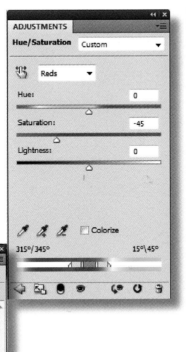

Tonal correction

First we will optimize the tonal values using a LEVELS adjustment layer. We adjust the settings in the individual Red-, Green- and Blue-channels, not the composite channel. Drag the sliders for shadows and highlights back to the beginning of the histogram. The lips are already showing more and a slight color cast has also been eliminated.

Pastel shades

The color environment is still too strong. With a HUE/SATURATION adjustment layer, we will give it some pastel shades. The skin tones are red and yellow. Reduce the saturation in the Reds to –45 and in the Yellows to –71. The correction is now too much. Change this by simply reducing the layer Opacity to 82%. The skin now has a nice, subtle hue and gives our mouth a pretty frame.

Increase shine

First we will increase the shine on top and bottom lip.

Copy the layer "Background" with ⌘/Ctrl+J then drag it to the top of the Layers panel and name it "Lighten". Set the blend mode to SCREEN. The whole picture becomes lighter. To make sure this is only applied to a few areas of the lips, create a black layer mask by holding the Alt-key while clicking on the ADD LAYER MASK icon. Now use white and the Brush tool (B, Size 20 pixels, Hardness 0%, Opacity 10%) to reveal the light areas on the lips. The lip contours should not be made brighter, otherwise three-dimensionality will be lost.

Darken lips

Duplicate the layer "Background" again, position it at the top and set the blend mode to MULTIPLY. Name the layer "Darken". The picture as a whole becomes darker. Cover everything with a black layer mask and reveal the lips again. To increase the effect, copy the layer with ⌘/Ctrl+J. Reduce the Opacity of this layer to about 50%.

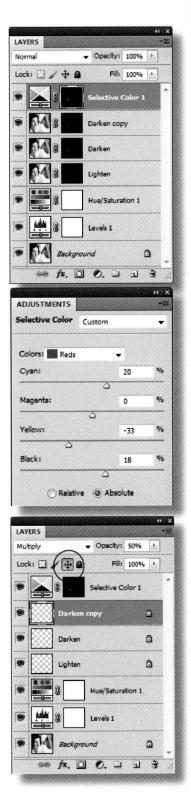

Change lip color

The color of the lips is still too exaggerated and could perhaps be a bit darker. Click on CREATE NEW FILL OR ADJUSTMENT LAYER and then on SELECTIVE COLOR. For the colors, choose REDS. Darkening one color can be achieved by increasing BLACK and the complementary color. By increasing CYAN, the red's intensity is lowered. The tone already seems much more noble. To increase this effect, we reduce the YELLOW in the REDS. You can see our settings on the left. The method RELATIVE means that the colors present within a color will be changed. If a color is not present, it can be neither reduced nor increased. Click on the ABSOLUTE button. The method ABSOLUTE does not refer to present colors, but adds new colors. Try switching between the methods RELATIVE and ABSOLUTE, then you will see the difference clearly.

Due to the many image layers, the file size is now almost 70MB. But we only need the revealed lips from each layer. The file will become smaller if we delete the masks of these image layers. Click on the layer mask and drag it to the dustbin. Confirm the dialog that appears with APPLY. You can protect the layers from being moved by clicking on the LOCK POSITION button at the top of the Layers panel. The file size is now smaller.

Basic Overview: Blend modes

The blend mode, also referred to as layer mode or blending mode, determines how the pixels of a layer and therefore its color and lightness information are calculated with the layers underneath it. You can apply blend modes to any kind of layer, except for the background. In practical exercises, you are most likely to encounter the following most common blend modes:

Multiply

Has a darkening effect and is especially useful for adding detail to areas which are too light.

Screen

Has the opposite effect to Multiply. Lightens all tonal values and lowers the contrast.

Soft Light

Increases the contrast, but not with 50% gray. It hides 50% gray, therefore this blend mode is especially useful for neutral layers, the High Pass filter and the Add Noise filter.

Hue

Combines the color values of the active layer with the luminance of the one below, but not with grayscale. Very well suited for coloring or re-coloring while maintaining the original luminance values.

Color

Combines the color values of the active layer with the luminance values, the hue and saturation of the underlying layer. Well suited for coloring or re-coloring image areas as the colors are rendered more strongly. Also useful for coloring grayscale images.

Difference

Has a comparing function and is useful for precise overlaying of almost identical image areas. Identical image areas are displayed as black, different ones as light edges.

Luminosity

Adopts the color values of the layer below and uses the luminance values of the active layer. Very effective for any kind of contrast change to stop the colors being affected.

However, simply describing the physical effect of the various modes does not give you an impression of the visual effect, which can be very surprising and therefore hard to plan for. We are going to demonstrate the various effects of several blend modes on an example picture.

Photo Filter Cooling Filter (80)

with varying filter settings and different blend modes

Duplicated background

with different blend modes

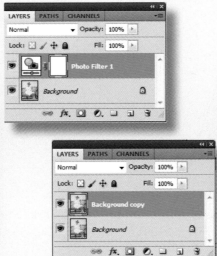

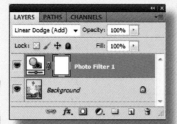

LAYERS | PATHS | CHANNELS
Exclusion ▾ Opacity: 100% ▸
Lock: ☒ ✐ ✛ 🔒 Fill: 100% ▸
👁 Photo Filter 1
👁 Background 🔒
🔗 fx. ◉ ⊘. ▢ ▢ 🗑

LAYERS | PATHS | CHANNELS
Vivid Light ▾ Opacity: 100% ▸
Lock: ☒ ✐ ✛ 🔒 Fill: 100% ▸
👁 Background copy
👁 Background 🔒
🔗 fx. ◉ ⊘. ▢ ▢ 🗑

LAYERS | PATHS | CHANNELS
Soft Light ▾ Opacity: 100% ▸
Lock: ☒ ✐ ✛ 🔒 Fill: 100% ▸
👁 Photo Filter 1
👁 Background 🔒
🔗 fx. ◉ ⊘. ▢ ▢ 🗑

LAYERS | PATHS | CHANNELS
Soft Light ▾ Opacity: 100% ▸
Lock: ☒ ✐ ✛ 🔒 Fill: 100% ▸
👁 Background copy
👁 Background 🔒
🔗 fx. ◉ ⊘. ▢ ▢ 🗑

LAYERS | PATHS | CHANNELS
Hue ▾ Opacity: 100% ▸
Lock: ☒ ✐ ✛ 🔒 Fill: 100% ▸
👁 Curves 1
👁 Layer 1
👁 Background 🔒
🔗 fx. ◉ ⊘. ▢ ▢ 🗑

Of course you can keep experimenting by changing the layer opacity or combining image areas by using masks. There are no limits to your imagination.

Chapter 5
Skin

fresh tanned pale wrinkly smooth shiny matte chapped relaxed beautiful rosy silky pastel-shaded yo
old soft dimply wrinkled impure rough stretched tender taught uneven fine yellow pure saggy healthy
burned flawless reddened sore sallow smooth glowing matte cracked soft beautiful rosy silky pastel-sha
young old smooth pale pasty spotty shiny dimply matte chapped soft attractive rosy silky tender young

How to improve skin
texture and skin tone

How to change the
skin tone and color
other areas

How to achieve
flawless complexion

How to use various
blurs

How to correct
color casts in
the skin

How to reduce light
reflections and over-
exposure to certain
areas
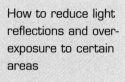

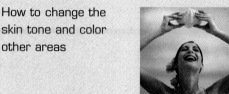
How to brighten
and smooth away
skin indentations

**Basic Overview
Special Layer
Techniques**

How to create beauti-
ful skin by blurring and
increasing contrast

How to eliminate glare

How to add oomph to
a badly lit portrait with
the White Skin effect

How to create an
even skin tone

How to adapt strong
skin contrasts

How to create beautiful
skin tone by decolorizing

How to make a face
look younger

Improve skin texture and skin tone

Picture analysis

Woman:

❶ Remove skin impurities and dimples

❷ Smooth away wrinkles

❸ Improve make-up

❹ Make skin silkier, maintaining skin texture

❺ Remove offending little hairs

Man:

❻ Remove skin impurities

❼ Trim large beard stubble

❽ Reduce wrinkles slightly

❾ Remove hairs from between eyes

❿ Remove little blood vessels

The biggest problem in this example is posed by the variety of different skin textures due to the many irregularities, different skin types and different planes of focus. The skin should not become softer, only smoother, we therefore cannot simply work with a Blur. We are going to need to carry out elaborate manual retouching.

ch5/couple.jpg

before

after

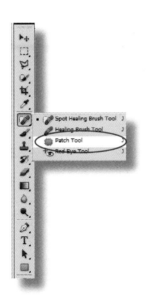

Remove skin impurities

First use the Patch tool ($\boxed{J}$) to remove all larger skin impurities, small blood vessels and irregularities. Always make sure you drag the selection to a pure skin area which also shows the same skin texture.

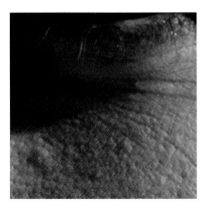

A

B

In Picture A, the selection of the nose was dragged onto the man's cheek. The resulting error in the skin texture on the nose is clearly visible in Picture B. In that case, you need to select smaller areas and find a similar skin texture, for example in the area surrounding the nose.

Also remove wrinkles, any hairs that go in the wrong direction, and small hairs on ears and nose. Use smaller selections and gradually work your way towards the desired result.

For removing smaller hairs from the ears, use the Clone Stamp tool (S, Size 15 pixels, Hardness 50%, Opacity 100%).

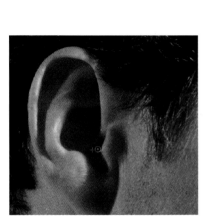

Once you are finished with the rough retouching, use the Spot Healing Brush tool to remove smaller impurities (J, Size 20 pixels, Hardness 50%).

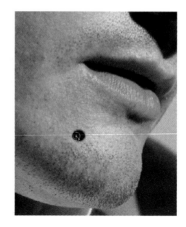

Remove hairs from upper lip

The tiny hairs at the woman's mouth pose a challenge. First remove the most noticeable hairs with the Patch tool (J).

Create skin pattern

Editing the very fine tinier hairs with the normal retouching tools does not give a satisfactory result. A better option is painting a new skin texture on top of the tiny hairs.

Duplicate your retouching layer by dragging it on the CREATE A NEW LAYER icon. Name this layer "Pattern".

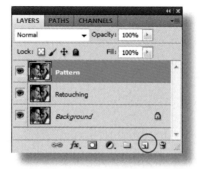

Generate a new skin pattern with FILTER/PATTERN MAKER. Use the Rectangular Marquee tool ($\boxed{M}$) to select a part of the upper lip. You should only select light skin areas. First set the parameters as shown on this picture.

With newer versions of Photoshop, Pattern Maker is no longer included and you need to download the Pattern Maker filter as optional plug-in from the Adobe download web page.

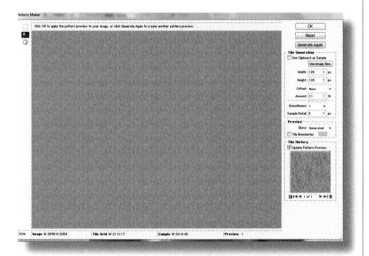

Click on GENERATE. You can of course keep on changing the pattern with the settings on the right-hand side until you are happy with it. Then click on OK. The pattern is applied to the whole picture.

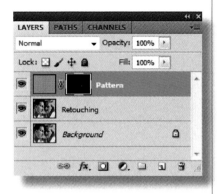

To get the pattern to the right areas, hold the $\boxed{Alt}$-key and click on the ADD LAYER MASK icon at the bottom of the Layers panel. A black mask is added. The pattern becomes invisible. Now use the Brush tool ($\boxed{B}$, Size 24 pixels, Hardness 30%, Opacity 40%) to paint over the little hairs near the lip.

Hide the two bottom layers to be able to judge the skin texture better. Show the layers again and lower the Opacity of the pattern layer to 70% to allow some of the original texture to shine through.

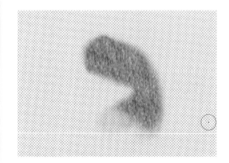

Adapt brightness

The pattern has not only obscured the hairs but also the shady areas above the lip. Hold the Alt-key and create a Curve using the NEW FILL OR ADJUSTMENT LAYER icon. Activate the option USE PREVIOUS LAYER TO CREATE CLIPPING MASK and confirm with OK. Now the Curve only applies to the layer "Pattern".

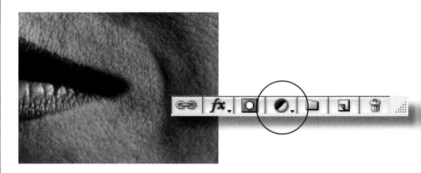

Drag the highlights and shadows of the curve slightly downwards while watching the changes in the skin texture. Not only the brightness values but also the color values are changed. To stop this happening, set the Mode to LUMINOSITY.

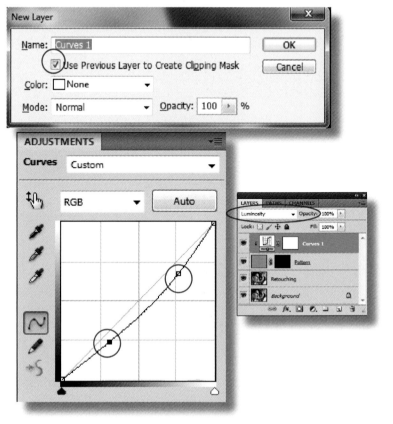

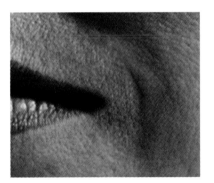

Darken only until the pattern and the surrounding skin areas have identical brightness values.

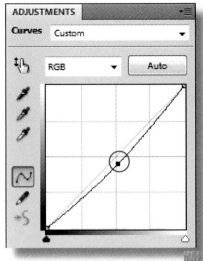

The upper lip now has the right brightness. To darken the corners of the mouth further, create another Curve while holding the ⌈Alt⌋-key and using the option CLIPPING MASK. Drag slightly downwards from the center. Now set the layer mask back to LUMINOSITY.

Use the layer mask to adapt the brightness on the transition areas. This is especially important at the top lip because otherwise it will turn too dark. This is the first part of a skin retouching and depending on how you are planning to use the picture, you may be finished now. Save the picture with all layers.

Silky skin

The skin is now much smoother and more even, but the large pores in the skin still show. In the next editing step, we will smooth the skin texture even more, without making it look artificial or overly "ironed-out" flat.

Hold the ⇧-key and activate all layers except the background layer, then press ⌘/Ctrl+E. The activated layers are merged into one composite layer. We name this layer "Retouched". Choose CONVERT TO SMART OBJECT in the menu of the Layers panel. Save the picture under a new name. Copy the layer "Retouched" with ⌘/Ctrl+J and name it "Silk 1".

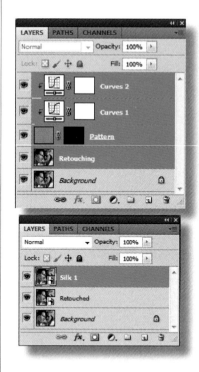

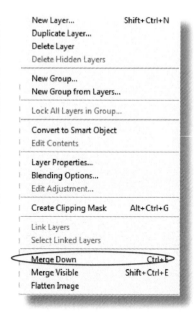

Surface Blur

Use FILTER/BLUR/SURFACE BLUR to blur the skin. Set the RADIUS to 15 pixels and the THRESHOLD to 112 levels. Only watch the skin when changing the settings, the other image areas are not important for now. Click on OK.

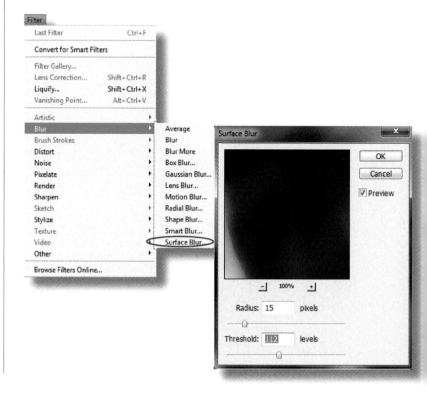

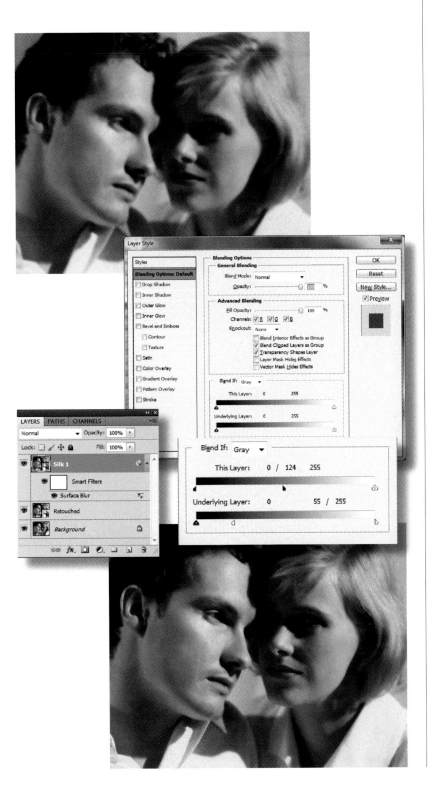

The entire picture is now blurred. However, we want the shadows in the picture to have their original richness of detail. The highlights should also be more pronounced. To retrieve all these effects with a layer mask would cost a lot of time and effort.

Retrieve details

To bring back the mentioned details, double-click on an empty area in the layer "Silk 1". The Blending Options appear. For our purpose, the lower area is most relevant. The sliders under THIS LAYER hide brightness areas and we will then see the original picture in those areas. The sliders under UNDERLYING LAYER show brightness areas and therefore the original structures in the underlying layers. To split the triangular sliders apart, Alt -click on one half of the slider handle and drag it. Set the sliders to the settings shown here.

THIS LAYER
0/124 255

UNDERLYING LAYER
0 55/255

Alt-click on the ADD LAYER MASK icon. Then paint with the Brush tool (B, Size 100 pixels, Hardness 20%, Opacity 30%) and white in the black mask and reveal the silky skin again. Occasionally hide the lower layers to be able to judge your editing work on the mask more easily.

On this mask, you can paint over the hair as well. It will only be blurred very slightly, as these brightness values were previously hidden in the Blending Options.

Of course you could also use this procedure for each face independently. That takes more time, but provides more flexibility. By double-clicking on the layer you can activate the hidden brightness areas any time and change the settings. By converting the layer to a SMART OBJECT, you can also change and adapt the Blur filter as many times as you like, until you are happy with the result.

Adapt colors

The skin is now perfect, but the faces still have a few reddened areas. We will soon fix that. Click on SELECT/COLOR RANGE.

Set Select to REDS. Click on OK.

Create a SELECTIVE COLOR adjustment layer. Because of the selection you have already created, the adjustment layer automatically has a layer mask.

Set the Colors to REDS and drag the MAGENTA slider a little bit to the left. The red areas become desaturated. Keep watching the changes in the picture and stop when you are happy with the skin tone. If the woman's lips should appear too colorless, paint with black in the mask to bring out the lips again.

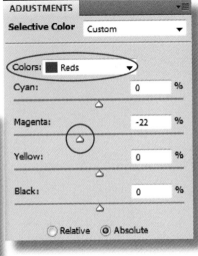

The skin tone is still a bit too yellow. Use a second SELECTIVE COLOR (see picture) to reduce the yellow slightly, until the skin tone looks more natural.

Finally, we lighten the eyes with a CURVES adjustment layer. Fill the layer mask with black and use the Brush tool ([B]) to reveal the brightness in the eyes again.

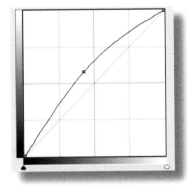

Porcelain skin

Picture analysis

1. Remove impurities
2. Soften face
3. Soften neck and neckline
4. Soften hand
5. Change skin color

In today's beauty and health advertising, a super-perfect skin is expected, achieved through the means of digital retouching. The same applies for any form of depiction of famous personalities, stars and starlets. Our model has a naturally beautiful, smooth skin. Normally, further retouching would not be necessary. But the so-called porcelain skin or doll's skin effect can be applied to any face. In addition to an absolutely even complexion, it also adds a somewhat doll-like, slightly artificial touch. The amount to which this effect is applied can of course be adjusted and is a matter of personal taste.

ch5/porcelain_skin.jpg

before

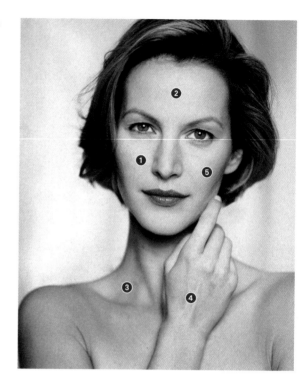

after

Preliminary retouching

For a first basic cleansing of the skin, copy the background layer with ⌘/Ctrl+J and name it "Retouching". Zoom into the picture to 200% with ⌘/Ctrl+ so that you can see several skin impurities, skin flakes and little make-up lumps.

Click on the Spot Healing Brush tool (J) and then on the little arrow in the Options bar to open the menu. If you are working with a graphics tablet, make sure SIZE (in the Options bar) is set to PEN PRESSURE. Your brush tip is now adjusted in size depending on the pressure exercised on the pen. Now you do not need to keep using the keyboard to change the brush size and will be able to work more efficiently. First remove irregularities on cheeks and forehead.

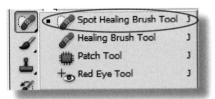

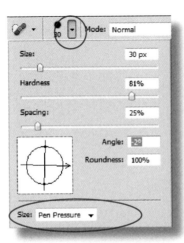

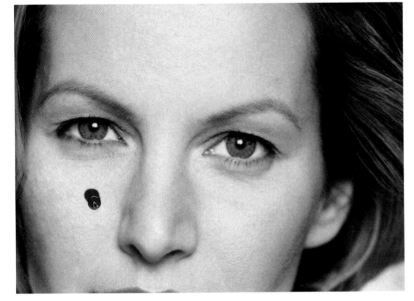

Many users forget that you can change the shape of the brush tip. For the wrinkles under the right eye, an elliptical brush tip is better. The retouching transitions will be more exact. Try out various different settings.

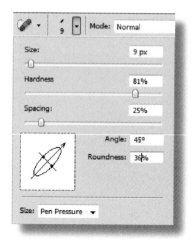

To make sure the retouching integrates well into the picture, you should always drag the tool into the same direction as the wrinkles, direction of hair growth etc. If these are curved, follow the curves with the tool as well.

This tool works really well on skin areas. But on strong edges, such as hairs or lips, it can create unwanted textures. Switch to the Patch tool (J). Select a flawed area and then drag that selection to a clean area with similar texture. Retouch the whole face.

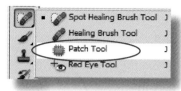

Don't forget the neck, the neckline, the shoulders and the hand. When you are done, your picture should look similar to the one on the right.

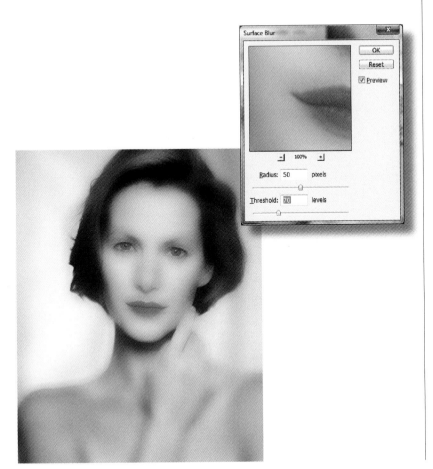

Soften face

In this portrait, we are confronted with at least three different skin textures: the face, shoulders and neckline, as well as hand and arm. We need to give them different degrees of blur.

Let's start with the face. Duplicate the layer "Retouching" and convert it to a SMART OBJECT to make sure you can reuse the following filter any time. Name the layer "Blur 1". Choose FILTER/BLUR/SURFACE BLUR. When choosing the filter settings, only pay attention to the skin. Everything else is irrelevant. The setting we chose, Radius 50 pixels and Threshold 70 levels, seems rather high at first. But remember that you can change the setting any time. Click OK.

Retrieve details

The whole picture is blurred. Hairs, eyes, lips and upper body should however remain unaffected. Of course you could use a Smart Filter mask to reveal the details, but this would be a lot of work. In our case, it is easier to retrieve the fine details with the layer style.

Simply double-click on the empty space on the right of the "Surface Blur 1" layer thumbnail. This opens the LAYER STYLE dialog. For our purpose, the bottom of the dialog is important. Drag the top black slider to the right to hide the dark tonal values, if you drag the white slider to the left, you make the light tones disappear. The bottom sliders make the corresponding tonal values of the underlying layer "Retouching" show in the composite picture. To split the sliders, drag them while holding the Alt -key. Set the following parameters.

BLEND IF: GRAY
THIS LAYER:
41/139   233/255
UNDERLYING LAYER:
0   235/255

The hair and hair roots become sharper again (see Basic Overview "Special Layer Techniques", Chapter 5).

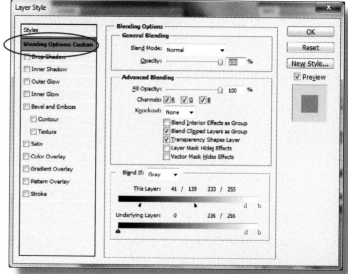

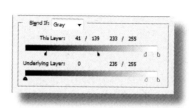

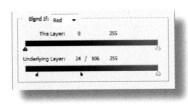

To retrieve even more details, you can adjust not only all the tonal values, but also those of individual colors. Choose them under Blend if. When you change the following settings, keep a close eye on hair, eyelashes and lips.

Blend if: Red
This layer:
0   255
Underlying Layer:
24/106   255

Blend if: Green
This layer:
0/198   255
Underlying Layer:
0/93   250/255

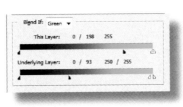

Many important details are now sharp again. But the eyes and lip as well as hair still appear as if covered by a slight haze. Remove this with a mask. Click on the Smart Filter mask and use black and the Brush tool ([B], Size 30 pixels, Hardness 20%, Opacity 30%) to remove the blurry haze. This blur is only meant for the face. Also cover all other areas by setting the tool's Opacity to 100%. Rename the layer "Surface blur face".

Soften shoulder and neckline

We do not need to repeat all these steps for the shoulders and neckline. Duplicate the layer "Surface blur face". To make it an independent layer, without reference to the source layer, copy it with LAYER/SMART OBJECT/NEW SMART OBJECT VIA COPY. Name the layer "Surface blur neckline".

Now we cannot use the Smart Filter mask of this layer to remove the blur from the face and lift it onto the body. Try it, but it won't work. You therefore need to click on the Smart Filter mask and fill it with white via EDIT/FILL/USE/WHITE. Click on the layer "Surface blur neckline" and create a layer mask by holding the [Alt]-key and clicking on the icon at the bottom of the Layers panel. The mask turns black and you can use white to reveal neck and neckline.

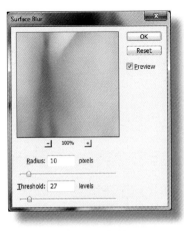

The blur is much too strong. To adapt it, double-click on the name of the filter "Surface blur" in the layer "Surface blur neckline". The Filter dialog appears again. We reduced the RADIUS to 17 pixels and THRESHOLD to 58 levels. You can experiment with different settings.

Soften hand

Proceed in the same way with the hand. Here we used a RADIUS of 10 pixels and a THRESHOLD of 27 levels.

The hand still looks rather artificial, therefore double-click on a free area in the layer "Surface blur hand" to activate the Blending Options dialog.

You can set, for example, the following values:

BLEND IF: GRAY
THIS LAYER:
41/151   233/255
UNDERLYING LAYER:
0   192/255

The skin texture emerges faintly.

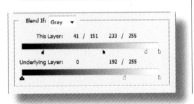

You now have three independent layers. You can perfect the results for each with the filter options, the layer opacity and the layer style. We find that the face has become too soft. We therefore decide to reduce the Opacity of the layer "Surface blur face" to 80%. Save your picture with all layers.

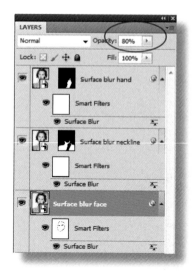

Change skin color

The skin texture is now alright. Combine all layers in the Layers panel menu with LAYER/FLATTEN IMAGE. Then save the picture under a new name.

We are now going to show you a slightly different trick with which you can change the skin color. First we need a luminosity mask. Switch to the Channels panel, hold the [⌘]/[Ctrl]-key and click on the RGB-channel. The brightness values are loaded as selection. Use [⌘]/[Ctrl]+[J] to turn them into a layer.

Now click on ADD A LAYER STYLE and choose the layer effect INNER SHADOW.

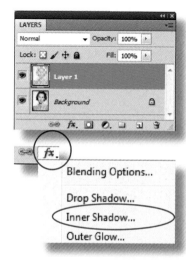

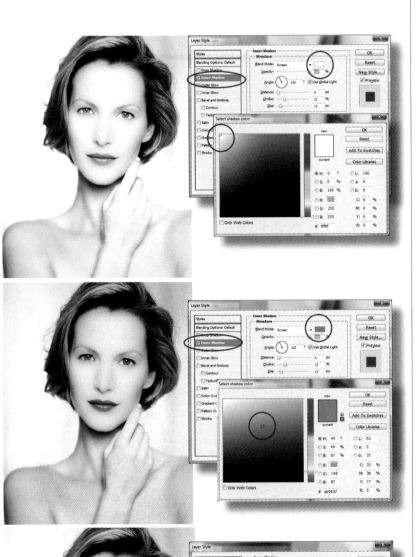

We tried out three different color tones. The following settings remain the same in all three examples:

BLEND MODE:	SCREEN
OPACITY:	100%
ANGLE:	120 degrees
DISTANCE:	4 Pixel
CHOKE:	23%
SIZE:	13 Pixel

The only difference (marked in red) between the three examples is the set color. Click on the color swatch for the shadows to open the Select Shadow Color dialog. If you drag the cursor over the color area, you can see the color changes in the picture straight away.

Try out other colors and settings as well. If you come across interesting results, take a screenshot of the settings and print it with the picture. That way you get a collection of settings and their effects which you can refer to at your leisure. It is worth it.

Correct color cast on skin

Picture analysis

❶ Adapt skin color, remove green and red cast

❷ Neutralize teeth and whites of eyes

The skin tones in this example appear rather unhealthy and not very flattering. In the man's skin color, the red is oversaturated, it looks like a bad case of sunburn. As for the woman's skin, the blue from the swimming pool water reflects onto the face and makes her skin look greenish.

before

after

ch5/couple_at_pool.jpg

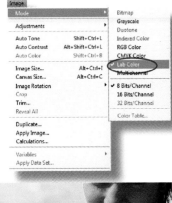

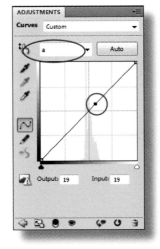

Red-Green correction

We are going to show you a different method for adapting the skin colors than the usual one of Selective Color. Convert the image to LAB mode with IMAGE/MODE/LAB COLOR.

Activate the Color Sampler tool (I) and create a CURVES adjustment layer. Set the drop-down menu at the top of the dialog to the a-channel. That is the red-green channel. We can therefore correct both color casts at once. Hold the ⌘/Ctrl-key and click on a skin color you like. A dot appears on the Curve.

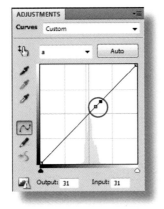

Hold the ⌘/Ctrl-key and click on a color range you want to change. A second dot appears on the Curve.

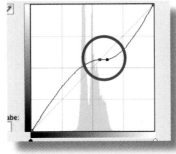

Now drag the second dot to the level of the first. The Reds and Greens adapt nicely to the skin color you first selected.

We only want to recolor the skin, therefore first activate the layer mask and turn it black with ⌘/Ctrl+I. The color correction is hidden. Use white and the Brush tool (B) to paint over all areas you want to correct. To get even results, you need to work with 100% Opacity, otherwise the skin can appear blotchy.

Color correct teeth and eyes

Now we still need to remove the green from teeth and eyes. Create a HUE/SATURATION adjustment layer and set the Saturation to -100%. Fill the layer mask with black and use white and the Brush tool to paint over teeth and whites of eyes.

Brighten teeth and eyes

We want to make teeth and the whites of the eyes a little bit brighter. Create a CURVES adjustment layer and drag the center of the curve slightly upwards.

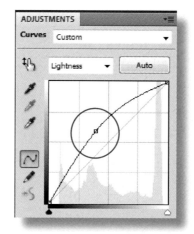

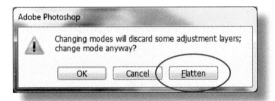

The whole image has changed in brightness. Of course we could paint in a layer mask once again, but we have already done that for the same image areas. Simply hold the [Alt]-key and drag the mask of the "Hue/ Saturation" layer onto the mask of the layer "Curve 2". The mask is copied onto that layer.

Confirm the resulting dialog with OK. This replaces the layer mask and therefore only teeth and eyes are brightened.

If you are not happy with the result, double-click on the Curve layer thumbnail. The dialog reappears and you can change the setting. Then save the file. Now check everything once more. You will notice that the woman's lips are too pale. That is due to the color correction on the layer "Curves 1". Click on the layer mask and remove the correction. The lips are a pretty red again.

Do not forget to convert the image back to RGB-mode, as this offers further editing options.

To avoid color shifts you need to click on the FLATTEN button in the resulting dialog. The file is flattened into the background. Save it under a new name.

Brighten and smooth skin indentations

Picture analysis

❶ Reduce wrinkles and tendons on neck

❷ Smooth abdomen

❸ Perfect body contours

If the model is lying down and there is a lot of skin visible, problem areas are unavoidable, even someone works out regularly. The indentations and dimples in the body are mostly created by the play of light and shadow. Counterbalancing shadows and highlights is the first option we will use.

ch5/sleeping_woman.jpg

before

after

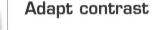

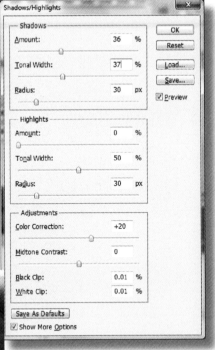

Adapt contrast

Duplicate the background with ⌘/Ctrl+J and convert it to a SMART OBJECT. Choose IMAGE/ADJUSTMENTS/SHADOWS/HIGHLIGHTS. Enter the following values:

SHADOWS
AMOUNT: 36%
TONAL WIDTH: 37%
RADIUS: 30 pixels

Now play around with the settings until the shadows are lighter and match the surrounding brightness of the skin.

To brighten only certain areas, create a layer mask while holding the Alt-key. The layer mask turns black and the brightening vanishes. Now paint with white and the Brush tool over all areas you want to lighten (B, Size 100 pixels, Hardness 0%, Opacity 5%).

You can also work directly in the filter mask.

As mentioned elsewhere in the book, the settings for the tools are not set in stone. You can vary them and adapt them to your individual way of working.

Bear in mind that you can choose the SHADOWS/HIGHLIGHTS dialog again any time and change the settings. Simply double-click on SHADOWS/HIGHLIGHTS in the Layers panel.

Save the image and flatten all layers. Now save the image again under a new name.

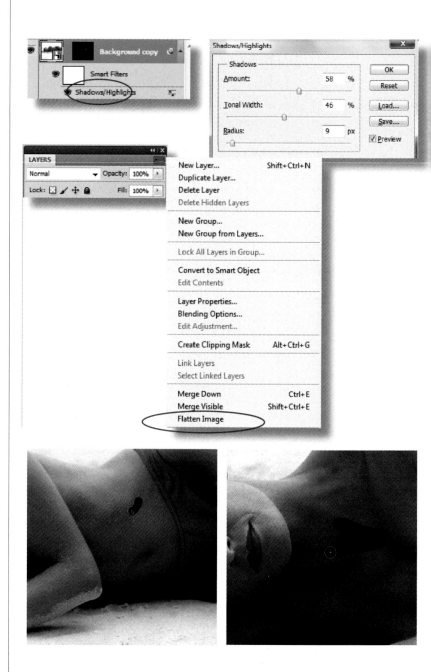

Reduce shadow

Next, we are going to adapt individual dark areas on the abdomen and match their brightness to that of the surrounding skin. Duplicate the background again with ⌘/Ctrl+J, choose the Spot Healing brush (J) and paint over the dark areas (J, Size 30 pixels, Hardness 80%). Only paint in small strokes. That way you can build the picture up gradually. Name the layer "Abdomen".

To remain as flexible as possible, duplicate the retouched layer again and rename it "Neck". Use the same tool to paint over the tendons on the neck.

Copy the layer again. We called it "Neck 2". With the Patch tool ([J]) you can remove the dark areas near the large neck tendon. Edit the other dark areas on the neck as well. If the neck should start looking too unrealistic, reduce the opacity of the layer "Neck 2" until a few contours emerge within the neck. We set the Opacity to 50%.

Perfect contours

To finish, we will improve the curvy shape of the body outline in some places. Save the image, flatten all layers again and save once more under a new name. Copy the background layer ([⌘]/[Ctrl]+[J]) and use the Rectangular Marquee ([W], Feather 2 pixels) to select the upper body.

The body contours on neck, shoulder and waist are not harmoniously curved yet. Use FILTER/LIQUIFY to adapt the shape. Try our settings first.

As you are working on several layers, you can simply delete one of the layers if you happen to make a mistake during retouching, without losing the other editing steps.

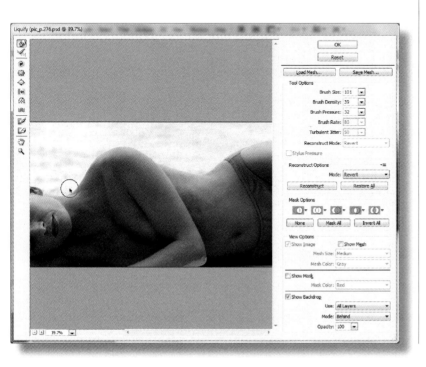

Reduce skin glare

Picture analysis

❶ Reduce glare spots

❷ Desaturate red

Our drummer at the beach has too much glare on his face, but we do not want to remove all of the reflection completely. That would appear very unnatural. A hint of shine often helps to create greater three-dimensionality and make facial features appear more lively.

before

after

ch5/drummer.jpg

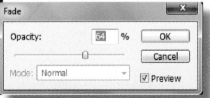

Reduce facial glare

Copy the background layer with ⌘/Ctrl+J. We named the copy "Glare retouching". Zoom into the face with ⌘/Ctrl++. Draw around individual glare spots with the Patch tool (J) and drag the selection to a darker area of skin. Make sure that the skin textures match. The glare has now disappeared completely. To retrieve it again a little bit, press ⇧+⌘/Ctrl+F. In the resulting Fade dialog, reduce the Opacity to about 64%. Try out different settings. Use the Fade option immediately after the Patch tool at every step.

To assess your retouching, the selection border of the Selection tool can get in the way. You can make it invisible with ⌘/Ctrl+H. Nevertheless it stays active. Press ⌘/Ctrl+H before choosing the Fade dialog.

Now you have visibly reduced the shiny areas. Just the fine adaptation left to do.

Brightness mask

It would be a lot of work to use a Curve for darkening and adapting the remaining glare with a layer mask. It is quicker and easier to use a brightness mask.

We will only select the light areas with SELECT/COLOR RANGE.

In the dialog, set Select to SAMPLED COLORS. Click with the Eyedropper on the light area on the forehead and set Fuzziness to 61. Only the light areas in the picture are selected. Only pay attention to the face. In the filter preview window you should see as much black as possible, only a few light areas should remain. Click on OK. Now you can see the selection outlines in the picture.

Switch to the Channels panel. At the bottom edge of the panel, click on the SAVE SELECTION AS CHANNEL icon. The selection is converted to a channel "Alpha 1". This channel appears as new channel in the Channels panel. Now press ⌘/Ctrl+D and the selection is removed.

Click on the "Alpha 1" channel. Only this channel should now be visible and active.

To be able to work better, press ⌘/Ctrl+I and the channel is inverted in its tonal values. Now use white and the Brush tool (B, Size 150 pixels, Hardness 80%, Opacity 100%) to remove all black areas which do not form part of the glare.

We have now removed all black areas, except for just a few in the face. Press ⌘/Ctrl+I once again and the channel is inverted in the tonal values again, as we want to select the light areas. Click on the RGB thumbnail at the top of the Channels panel, so that you are again working on the composite image.

To load the just edited channel "Alpha 1" as selection, drag the channel on the LOAD CHANNEL AS SELECTION icon. The selection is displayed as pulsating selection outline in the picture.

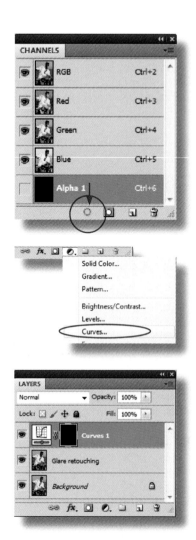

Create a CURVES adjustment layer. Because of the selection you just created, the Layer Mask of the Curve turns almost black, only the selection stays white. Drag the curve slightly downwards in the Curves dialog. In your picture you see that only the selected shine areas are darkened. Let go of the mouse button once you are happy with your results.

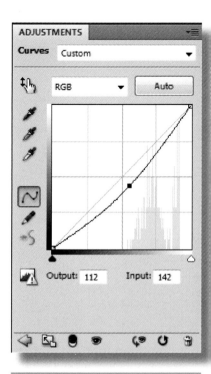

To be able to still correct irregularities, such as near the hair, press and hold the [Alt]- and [⇧]-keys and click on MERGE VISIBLE in the menu of the Layers panel. Make your corrections with the Clone Stamp tool ([S], Size 10 pixels, Hardness 40%, Opacity 30%). Then save the image.

Desaturate red

For the next few steps, flatten the image with LAYER/FLATTEN IMAGE. Save the image under a new name.

We now want to primarily reduce the saturation of the intensive Reds.

First option: If you use HUE/SATURATION to select the Red and then decrease the Saturation, this is applied to all Reds equally, not just the strongly saturated Reds.

Second option: You can load the red channel as luminosity mask by holding the ⌘/Ctrl-key and clicking on the Red thumbnail in the Channels panel. Apply a Hue/Saturation layer to it. The result is much better, but still not perfect.

Saturation mask

Third and best option: We create a
selection based on the color saturation. In this example, the reds on forehead and nose are strongly saturated,
the upper body is hardly affected.

Unfortunately, the HSB/HSL filter
which we need for this is no longer
installed by default in Photoshop. You
need to download it from the Adobe
website.

Did you save your picture? Well
done, now save it again as a copy
– just to be on the safe side, in case
anything should go wrong.

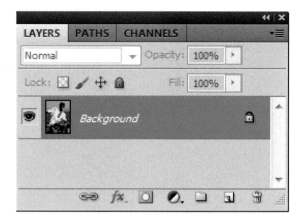

Work on the copy of your image. Choose the filter with FILTER/OTHER/HSB/HSL.

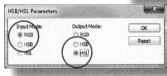

Activate RGB to HSL and click on Ok. The image is converted to HSL color mode. HSL stands for:

H   Hue
S   Saturation
L   Lightness

Your image should now look something like this.

Switch to the Channels panel and activate the Green channel. This contains the saturation information. Select it with ⌘/Ctrl+A and copy it to the clipboard with ⌘/Ctrl+C.

Now open your original image again. Create a new channel in the Channels panel with the CREATE NEW CHANNEL icon and insert the Green channel you just copied with ⌘/Ctrl+V.

To load the selection, activate the RGB composite channel. Drag the new "Alpha 1" channel onto the LOAD CHANNEL AS SELECTION icon.

Switch to the Layers panel and create a HUE/SATURATION adjustment layer. Set EDIT to REDS and drag the Saturation to -50 for now.

Try out other settings as well, for example dragging the Saturation to –100. Even at this extreme setting, the Red is only reduced, it does not disappear completely. For the final result we settled on a Saturation of -80.

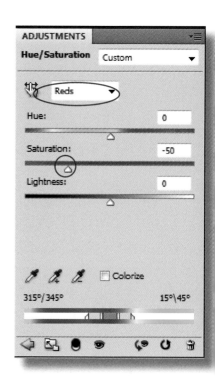

before

after

Even skin tone

Picture analysis

❶ Adapt skin color, remove red

❷ Adapt skin contrast

❸ Create warm skin tone

The colors in this picture are highly saturated. This makes the skin look blotchy. The face, neckline and leg appear rather too red, the abdomen looks pale and yellowish. The skin's brightness varies too much.

ch5/jungle.jpg

Reduce color saturation

First we will change the color saturation. Create a HUE/SATURATION adjustment layer. To reduce the saturation evenly for all colors, set the drop-down menu that determines what to edit to MASTER and the SATURATION to −41.

All colors are desaturated slightly.

Individual colors are still too strong. We will edit those separately. In the drop-down menu you can select the different colors you want to change in your picture. We have chosen the following settings:

REDS
SATURATION: −32

YELLOWS
SATURATION: −20

GREENS
SATURATION: −26

MAGENTAS
SATURATION: −22

Reducing the overall saturation and the Reds is particularly noticeable in the skin. The Yellows and Magentas are present in the skin and not many other areas of the background. Reducing the Greens matches the background harmoniously to the new skin saturation.

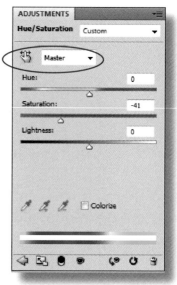

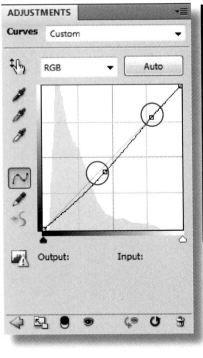

Adapt contrast

The overall contrast is no longer pleasing after the color change. Create a CURVES adjustment layer. We would like to darken the shadows some more.

Click on the curve in the upper highlights. This is an anchor point for the light, to stop it changing as well. Now drag the bottom part of the curve slightly downwards until you are happy with the darkening.

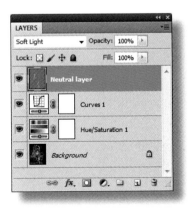

Reduce skin contrast

The contrast on the left arm and the right leg is still too strong. Create a neutral layer by Alt-clicking on the CREATE A NEW LAYER icon. In the dialog, choose SOFT LIGHT and click on FILL WITH SOFT-LIGHT-NEUTRAL COLOR (see Basic Overview "Special Layer Techniques", Chapter 5). Brighten the arm and the leg with white and the Brush tool (B, Size 40 pixels, Hardness 60%, Opacity 10%).

The contrast in the skin is still too strong. Especially the light areas appear too pale. At the top, create a SELECTIVE COLOR adjustment layer. Because we want to change the light or white areas, set COLORS to Whites and increase the Black to +11%. By adding black, the white areas turn slightly darker. We need to exclude the necklace with a layer mask.

Luminosity mask

A luminosity mask will add the finishing touches for adapting the contrast. Hold the ⌘/Ctrl-Taste key and click on the RGB Channel thumbnail in the Layers panel. The brightness values are loaded as selection. Create a CURVES adjustment layer. Due to the selection, it gets a filled layer mask. Drag the center of the curve slightly downwards. Keep watching your image. The light areas are darkened more than the dark ones.

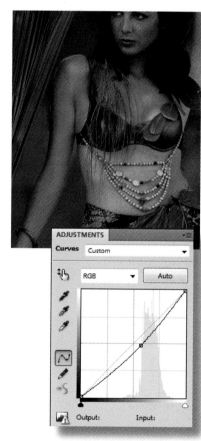

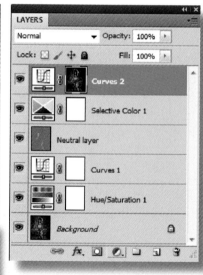

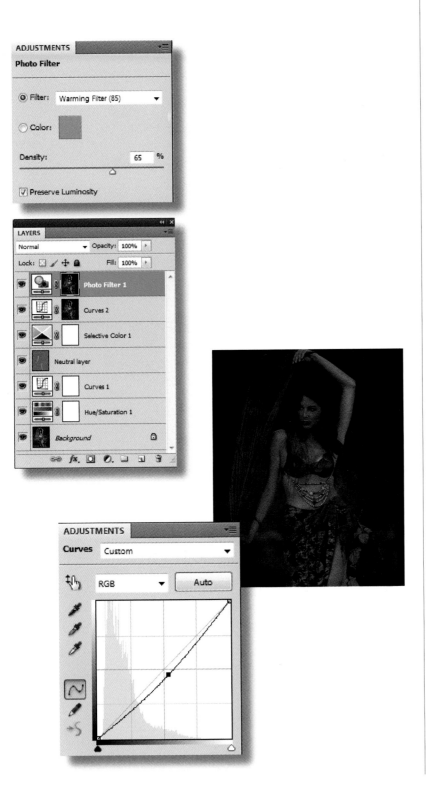

Warmer skin tone

The skin now has even color and brightness values and no longer looks blotchy. To give the skin more color, create a PHOTO FILTER adjustment layer. Set FILTER to Warming Filter (85). Set Density to 65% and check the PRESERVE LUMINOSITY button. Now only the color of the filter is adopted, not the brightness values.

To apply the photo filter more strongly to the light areas, hold the [Alt]-key and drag the mask of the layer "Curves 2" onto the layer "Photo Filter 1". Confirm the dialog asking you if you want to replace the mask.

The abdomen is still too light. Darken it with a CURVES adjustment layer. Fill the layer mask with black and reveal the abdomen again with white. Set the Brush tool to low opacity. You may need to correct the individual beads on the necklace later.

Adapt tone and decolorize skin

Picture analysis

❶ Adapt skin tones

❷ Emphasize details

A simple and often very quick method of adapting skin tones is conversion to black-and-white or partial decolorization. Once this has made the image composition calmer and more harmonious, you can consciously emphasize certain details, such as the eyes, frost-covered faces and fur textures in our example.

ch5/frosty_faces.jpg

before

after

Decolorize skin

First duplicate the background and set the "Background copy" layer's mode to SOFT LIGHT.

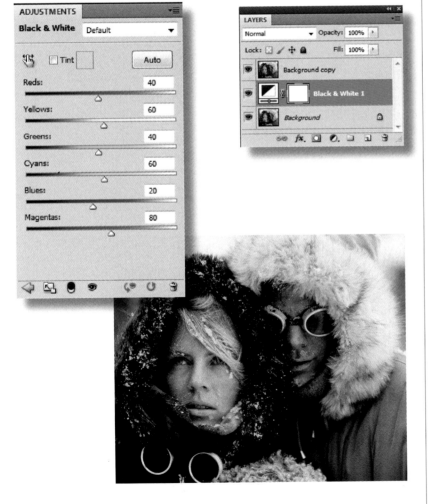

Activate the background layer once more and choose a BLACK & WHITE adjustment layer. This layer is now sandwiched in between the two photo layers. First set the sliders as shown on our picture. If you drag the individual sliders further left, the corresponding color is darkened, if you drag them to right, the colors get lighter. You therefore have infinite possibilities of adjusting the image individually. Pay special attention to the skin tones. Look at the result and then decide which details and areas you want to leave colored, and paint with a layer mask to reveal them again. In our example we want to emphasize the woman's eyes and keep their bright blue. This "sandwich method" also increases the image contrast and lets the ice crystals on the skin really stand out.

Adapt contrast

The image has now become darker especially in the shadows, the black areas. From CS2 onwards, there is a superb way of changing this: the SHADOWS/HIGHLIGHTS adjustment, which from CS3 onwards can be applied as Smart Filter as well. First copy your background layer. The "Background copy 2" has to be directly above the background.

In the pop-up menu of the Layers panel, click on CONVERT TO SMART OBJECT.

Choose IMAGE/ADJUSTMENTS/ SHADOWS/HIGHLIGHTS. Here you can only lighten the shadows and only darken the highlights.

Try the settings shown on the right. Change them until you are happy with the picture. Watch mainly the details in the fur.

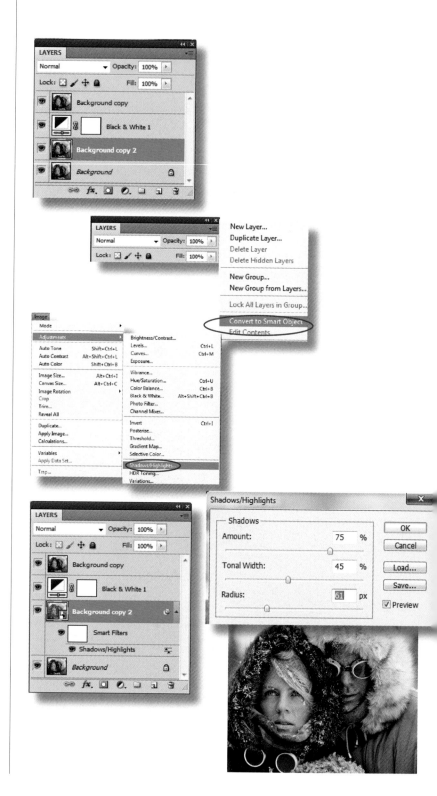

Darken faces

Lightening the shadows has caused the faces and the snow goggles to become lighter as well, but we do not want these areas to be affected.

In the Layers panel, click on the SMART FILTERS mask. Use the Brush tool ([B], Size 100 pixel, Hardness 0%, Opacity 20%) and black to paint over all areas you do not want to be darkened, such as the faces. Hold the [Alt]-key and click on the mask icon to display the mask. [Alt]-click again to reveal the picture.

Tint skin

Picture analysis

❶ Change background color

❷ Tint skin

This picture was taken with very diffuse light. The skin therefore appears very dull and flat, the surrounding area looks bleak and rainy. The customer who works in the tourism business would like the motif in "bright weather".

before

after

ch5/seashell.jpg

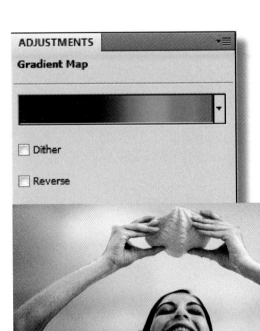

Change background color

To color the background, create a GRADIENT MAP adjustment layer. This allows us to assign different colors to different brightness values of the picture. Don't make any changes in the GRADIENT MAP dialog. Now set the adjustment layer's blend mode at the top left of the Layers panel to COLOR and open the Gradient Map once more by clicking on the layer thumbnail. This is important to ensure you can judge the colors correctly. Click in the gradient to display the GRADIENT EDITOR dialog. Under PRESETS, select a gradient corresponding to your desired colors. You can then edit the gradient in more detail at the bottom of the dialog. The left side applies to the shadows, the right side to the highlights. Click on a color marker and set a color tone in the Color Picker. Simply click underneath the gradient and another color marker appears. You can create as many color markers as you like. You can delete them by dragging the color marker downwards. You can assign a color to each maker. The more similar colors you choose, the more even the color transitions. Click on OK.

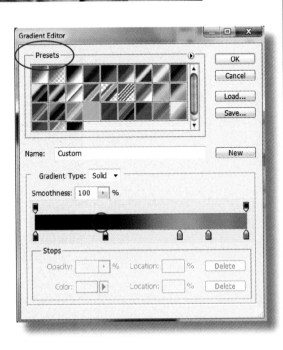

To apply the gradient to the background only, select the background with the Quick Selection tool ([W]) and invert the selection with [⌘]/[Ctrl]+[⇧]+[I]. Click on the mask thumbnail of the layer "Gradient Map 1". With EDIT/FILL/USE/BLACK you limit the color change to the background. Remove the selection with [⌘]/[Ctrl]+[D].

Tint skin

Now we want to match the skin tone to the sky's pretty shade of blue. Create another Gradient Map. This time, we selected different dark skin tones and set the layer's blend mode to COLOR DODGE. This increases the contrast and creates the impression of evening sun of the skin. To restrict the Gradient Map to the skin, hold the [Alt]-key and drag the layer mask of the layer "Gradient Map 1" onto the layer "Gradient Map 2" to copy the mask. Now invert the mask with IMAGE/ADJUSTMENTS/INVERT ([⌘]/[Ctrl]+[I]) to apply it to the model only.

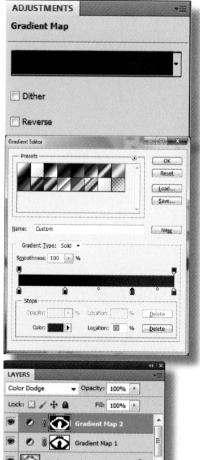

before

after

Various blur effects using channels and filters

Picture analysis

① Silkier skin, keep freckles

We are going to show you several blur effects with which you can create very nice effects. We definitely want to keep the freckles on our model, but they pose a little challenge.

ch5/freckles.jpg

Skin retouching with the Red channel

For this kind of retouching we require the channel with the lowest contrast in our picture. Switch to the Channels panel and look at each channel individually. In most cases, where the skin is concerned, it will be the Red channel, as in our example. Activate it. Select it with ⌘/Ctrl+A and copy it with ⌘/Ctrl+C. Switch back to the Layers panel and insert the copied channel as layer with ⌘/Ctrl+V. Name it "Red channel blur" and convert it to a Smart Object. Set the blend mode to Luminosity.

For the following blur you can use any blur filter. We used the GAUSSIAN BLUR via FILTER/BLUR and set the Radius to 10 pixels. To reduce the effect a little bit, we then set the layer Opacity to 56%.

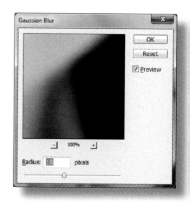

The whole picture is now slightly blurred with gauzy seeming highlights and has a romantic touch. If you only want to blur the skin, proceed with the steps described in the next section.

Reveal shadows and freckles

To bring the shadows and freckles back again, double click on the layer "Red channel blur" to open the LAYER STYLE dialog. We want to reduce the blur only in the dark areas, therefore drag the sliders for THIS LAYER apart while holding the Alt -key. We chose the following settings:

THIS LAYER: 13/116   255

Play around with the sliders until you are happy with the picture. Then click on OK (see also: Basic Overview "Special Layer Techniques", Chapter 5).

Too many other areas are still affected. Create a layer mask on the layer "Red channel blur" while holding the Alt -key. It turns black and the layer effect is removed. Use the Brush tool (B , Size 80 pixels, Hardness 20%, Opacity 20%) and white to paint over all skin areas. The blur reappears. You do not need to work precisely in the dark areas and on the freckles, as these are already protected by the settings in the layer style. If you think the blur is still too strong, reduce the layer Opacity further.

Adapt brightness

The editing has made the face too light. We will fix this with a CURVES adjustment layer. Hold the Alt-key while you creating it. In the resulting dialog, activate the check-box USE PREVIOUS LAYER TO CREATE CLIPPING MASK. The curve now applies only to the layer "Red channel blur". Drag the center of the curve slightly downwards until the brightness values match the overall effect of the picture again.

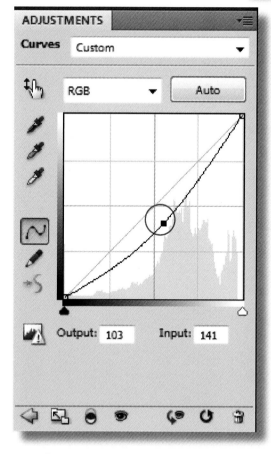

Softer skin with Dynamic Skin Softener

We now want to show you the effects of a few filter plug-ins. You can find demo versions of these for Mac and PC on the DVD included with this book. Install the filter plug-ins following the manufacturer's instructions. After you restart Photoshop, you will find the new filters at the bottom of the Photoshop Filter menu. The Nik filters allow you to achieve completely new effects without requiring a great deal of knowledge.

Open the unedited original image once more and choose the filter with FILTER/NIK SOFTWARE/COLOR EFEX. Click on the PORTRAIT tab on the left. The left filter bar displays the portrait filters. Choose the Dynamic Skin Softener. Set all sliders on the right-hand side to 0% on the left. Choose the eyedropper at the top right corner and use it to click on a color you want to blur, such as a mid-skintone on the left cheek. The color swatch next to the eyedropper displays the selected color. To choose a different color, you need to activate the eyedropper again.

The COLOR REACH indicates how many percent divergence from the selected color you allow. If the slider is set to 0%, only those areas are considered that correspond exactly to the selected color. The higher the value, the bigger the color tolerance. With the next three sliders "DETAILS", the amount you set determines the amount of blur applied to the corresponding areas. "SMALL DETAILS" affects mainly the skin texture, "MEDIUM DETAILS" the freckles and "LARGE DETAILS" cause little change in this picture. You can see our settings on the picture on the right.

Try out various settings because their effect depends on the image resolution as well. You can save and name your settings in the QUICK SAVE SLOTS. This ensures you can access them again later. Click on Ok.

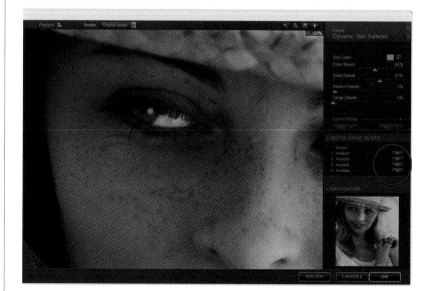

Retrieve detail

We did not copy the background at the beginning. After confirming the filter, it automatically creates a layer with the filter name. Double click on the layer to open the BLENDING OPTIONS.

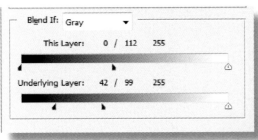

We want to retrieve above all the dark details, such as the freckles. Set the sliders for shadows as follows:

THIS LAYER:
0/112   255

UNDERLYING LAYER:
42/99   255

Create a black layer mask and reveal all skin areas again.

Add glow with Glamour Glow

In a further step we want to add a noble touch to our portrait by adding glow. We therefore need to have all layers on a composite layer. Activate all layers and press ⌘/Ctrl+⇧+Alt+E. A new layer, containing all other layers, appears at the top of the Layers panel. Name it "Composite Layer".

Choose the Nik filter again, select PORTRAIT and click on the filter GLAMOUR GLOW. You can see our settings in the picture at the top.

GLOW: 100%,
SATURATION: 49%,
GLOW TEMPERATURE: 11%,
Drag SHADOWS all the way to the right, HIGHLIGHTS about ⅓

These filters invite you to experiment, so go ahead. Once you have saved your settings, click on Ok. The filter has created another layer with the filter name for you. You can now delete the composite layer, it just takes up space unnecessarily. We used a mask to bring out the eyes, mouth and upper right edge of the hat slightly. If you want to try further filters, you always need to create a composite layer first which contains all other layers.

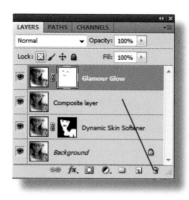

before

after

Reduce overexposure

Picture analysis

❶ Color overexposed skin areas

A problem that occurs frequently with people photography is overexposure, resulting in white areas of skin and clothing, caused by harsh sun light in photographs taken outside. With a little trick, you can recreate texture and bring back color.

ch5/woman_at_beach.jpg

Soften skin

Before we color the overexposed and colorless areas in the skin, we will quickly retouch the skin. You can use any of the many procedures described in this book. Here is just a quick guideline.

1. Duplicate the background.

2. Remove the rougher skin impurities with the retouching tools.

3. Convert the new layer to a SMART OBJECT.

4. Apply the Blur filter of your choice. We chose the BOX BLUR filter with a Radius of 10 pixels.

5. Open the Blending Options by double clicking on the layer and adjust the Shadows slider.

6. Hold the [Alt]-key while creating a layer mask and paint over all skin areas you want to soften.

Choose correct color space

To color skin, you can simply create an empty layer and paint over your portrait with the desired color. That works really well in all brightness areas, except for White and Black.

To demonstrate the effect, we decolorized the picture. It is now black-and-white, but still an RGB image. In the top right picture we created a new layer and filled it with color. We set the layer's blend mode to Color. As was to be expected, all Grays take on the color, but Black and White do not.

In the bottom right example, we did exactly the same, except for one thing. We first converted the image from RGB to LAB. Now, Black and White take on the color, too. Unfortunately, there is a little disadvantage: the color appears slightly changed and no longer seems as pleasing. But this side-effect can easily be fixed later.

Color highlights

Save your picture with the skin
retouching. Then click on FLATTEN
IMAGE in the Layers panel menu.
Save the picture under a different
name.

Change to LAB mode with IMAGE/
MODE/LAB. You can now see the
changed channels in the Channels
panel.

Switch to the Layers panel and create
a new empty layer. Best if you set the
layer's blend mode to Color straight
away. Choose the Brush tool ([B],
Size 100 px, Hardness 40%, Opacity
100%). Hold the Alt-key to turn
the Brush tool into the Eyedropper.
Sample a color in the picture. You
do not need to get the exact skin tone
right now, you can quickly correct it
later. Then paint over all light areas
you want to color.

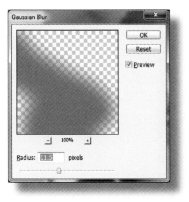

Adapt color

The color we just used still needs to be adapted. The easiest way is using a HUE/SATURATION adjustment layer. But the layer effect should only be applied to the painted color. Hold the Alt -key while choosing the adjustment layer. In the resulting dialog, activate the checkbox USE PREVIOUS LAYER TO CREATE CLIPPING MASK. We only reduced the color saturation to –12. This setting does of course vary depending on the color you are using.

Correct color transitions

If you look closely, you can still see unpleasant color transitions, especially on the forehead and cheeks. To soften the transitions, activate the layer "Skin color" and choose FILTER/BLUR/ GAUSSIAN BLUR. The Radius depends on the brush size, softness and opacity with which you painted on the color. Save the image in LAB with all layers. For further editing, you may need to switch back to RGB mode with IMAGE/MODE/RGB. Some layers will get lost.

To finish, use a SELECTIVE COLOR to adjust the skin tone, if you are not happy with it yet.

Blur skin and increase contrast

Picture analysis

❶ Remove unevenness and soften skin

❷ Improve skin color

The method we used here is especially suitable for almost flawless skin. In just a few quick steps you can achieve a soft, smooth, subtly glowing complexion and healthy skin color.

ch5/woman_with_fan.jpg

before

after

Softer skin

We will remove small uneven areas and create silky soft skin in one step. If your model's skin is not as perfect as on this picture, first remove larger flaws with the retouching tools. Then duplicate the background layer with ⌘/Ctrl+J and convert it to a SMART OBJECT. Choose FILTER/BLUR/BOX BLUR. We set the Radius to 26 pixels.

Reveal structures

The whole picture is now blurred. To change only the skin, double click next to the layer name. The Blending Options dialog appears (see Basic Overview, "Special Layer Techniques", Chapter 5). We want to bring back the original structures in the shadows and highlights and chose the following settings:

THIS LAYER:
9/86   197/255

UNDERLYING LAYER:
22/68   196/255

The eyes, eyebrows, lips, hair and white fan in the foreground are now hardly affected by the blur. To remove the blur from further areas, create a layer mask while holding the Alt-key. The blur becomes invisible. With white and the Brush tool (B, Size 80 pixels, Hardness 40%, Opacity 100%) you can paint over all skin areas you want to soften.

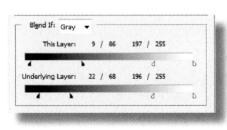

The overall softness is still too
high. Reduce the top layer's
Opacity to about 50%.

More contrast in skin

The blur has caused a loss of
contrast in the skin. To achieve
greater modulation, we are going
to work with a luminosity mask.
Switch to the Layers panel, hold
the ⌘ / Ctrl -key and click on the
RGB CHANNEL. The brightness values are loaded as selection. Switch
to the Layers panel, click on the
Smart Object thumbnail of the layer
"Soft Skin". Copy the selection with
⌘ / Ctrl + J to another layer. Set
the blend mode to SOFT LIGHT and
reduce the Opacity to about 70%.

Reduce red

To make the skin look more tanned,
create a SELECTIVE COLOR adjustment
layer at the top of the Layers panel.
In the Reds, reduce Magenta to –22%
and increase Yellow by +31%. The
slight "sun burn" changes to a pretty
golden tone.

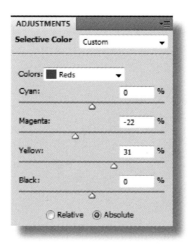

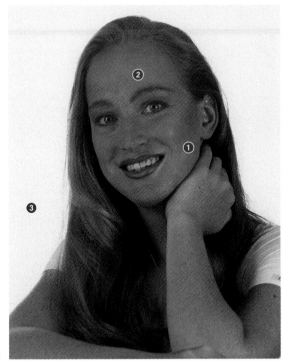

before

after

White skin

Picture analysis

❶ Improve skin texture slightly

❷ Create white skin color

❸ Color background with gradient

This portrait is all wrong. The skin color is oversaturated in the Reds and not very attractive. The light is flat and boring and gives no modulation to the face. The white background appears sterile and the contrast to the rather dark skin tones is too great..

ch5/white_skin.jpg

Retouch skin

First, retouch any unattractive flaws and wrinkles in the skin. To do so, duplicate the background with ⌘/Ctrl+J. The Patch tool works best in this case (J). Do not over-retouch, because the White Skin effect already swallows up much of the texture. You can still refine your retouching later.

White skin

Create a CHANNEL MIXER adjustment layer. Here you can edit the individual color channels. The Red channel lightens the skin color. Green and Blue modulate the face. Enter the following settings:

Output Channel: GRAY

RED	+155
GREEN	+11
BLUE	−66
CONSTANT	0
MONOCHROME	ACTIVATED

The total value should always be 100% to achieve good printing quality.

Set the layer's Blend mode to SCREEN and Opacity to 84%.

Isolate the woman

To get a gradient into the background, we first need to select the background. That looks very easy at first glance, as the background is just a uniform white.

With SELECT/COLOR RANGE you can select color ranges. Set the dialog to: SELECT: SAMPLED COLORS. Click on the background with the Eyedropper and drag the Fuzziness upwards until the background is all white and the woman is as black as possible around the edges. We found a setting of 41 worked best. Click on OK. You now have a selection.

Switch to the Channels panel and click on the SAVE SELECTION AS CHANNEL icon. The selection turns into an Alpha channel. Remove the selection with ⌘/Ctrl+D. Activate the Alpha channel by clicking on it. The background is now nice and white, the woman's outline is black and you paint the inside black with the Brush tool (B) and a large, not too soft tip.

Now the "woman" should look all black in the Alpha channel, only around the edges she may and should be slightly gray, because we are working with an overexposed back light and the contour does not have a clear separation. Activate the RGB composite channel by clicking on it in the Channels panel and then switch to the Layers panel.

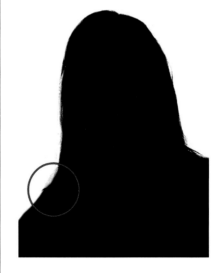

Load color gradient

In the next step, we will add a gradient to the background. Additionally, we put the gradient file of our gradient on the DVD as file. You can find it in the "Settings" folder. To load a finished gradient, activate the Gradient Tool (G). In the Options bar, click on the small triangle on the right of the gradient to open the Presets panel. Then click on the menu triangle and choose Load Gradients. In the resulting dialog, go to the file gradients_V086.drd. Alternatively, you can create a Gradient adjustment layer and work with that.

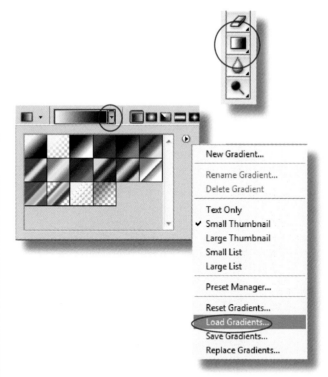

Add gradient to background

Click on the CREATE NEW LAYER icon in the Layers panel. Drag a gradient from top to bottom using the Gradient tool ($\boxed{G}$) Press and hold the $\boxed{\Uparrow}$-key while dragging to make sure the gradient is absolutely straight. Set the blend mode to MULTIPLY.

Channels panel and drag the channel thumbnail to the LOAD CHANNEL AS SELECTION icon.

Switch back to the Layers panel, where the "Gradient" layer is still active. Create a layer mask with the ADD LAYER MASK icon in the Layers panel. This mask protects the background, not the woman. Invert the mask with $\boxed{\mathcal{H}}$/$\boxed{Ctrl}$+$\boxed{I}$.

We want to make the gradient a bit stronger. Instead of experimenting with stronger colors, you can simply copy the "Gradient" layer with $\boxed{\mathcal{H}}$/$\boxed{Ctrl}$+$\boxed{J}$. We now found the gradient too strong and reduced the Layer Opacity to 10%.

Increase contrast

Create a CURVES adjustment layer at the top. Brighten the highlights slightly and darken the shadows a little.

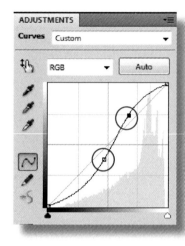

Blur hair outline

The individual hairs that stick out are still too sharp and look too hard. To be able to see the blur better, zoom to 100% by double clicking on the zoom tool. Hide the layer "Gradient copy". Activate the "Gradient" layer mask by clicking on it.

Choose FILTER/BLUR/GAUSSIAN BLUR. We set the Radius to 3 pixels, but here you once again need to experiment until you find your perfect result. Then show all layers again.

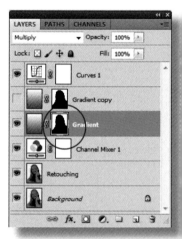

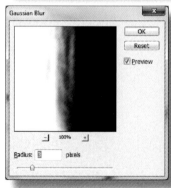

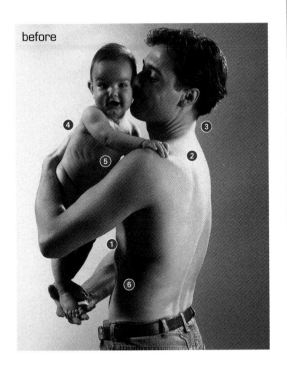

before

Adapt skin contrast

Picture analysis

❶ Neutralize shadows containing color cast

❷ More skin texture for highlights

❸ Reduce skin folds on man's neck

❹ Reduce baby's fat rolls

❺ Soften skin

❻ Lighten shadows

In this portrait, several editing steps are necessary to retouch the various problem zones that were mainly caused by lighting errors. Proceeding in the correct order is often important and can save you time.

after

ch5/man_with_baby.jpg

Remove color cast

The violet color cast in the shadows on the man's abdomen and arm and the child's feet is not easy to remove with corrective layers. We will show you how you can paint over the wrong colors. You will need to have a selection, unless you have a very steady hand. A little trick can help here.

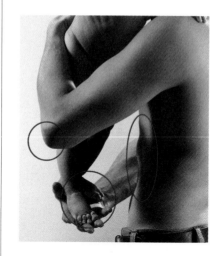

Another way to select

Choose the Quick Selection tool (W, Size 4 pixels, Hardness 100 %). In the Options bar, activate AUTO-ENHANCE and then click only once, for example on the man's elbow. Only a small area is selected.

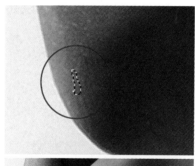

Click on the button SUBTRACT FROM SELECTION or press and hold the Alt-key and drag over all areas you do not want to select. The tool now remembers these areas. At first you will not notice a difference in your selection. Then click on the button ADD TO SELECTION and drag with the same, small tool tip over all areas you require. You can also try out the conventional method without subtracting first, and you will soon see the difference.

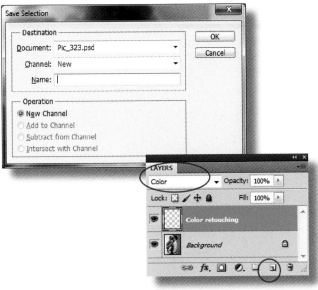

Click on SELECT/SAVE SELECTION. If you do not name the selection, it is automatically designated "Alpha 1".

To paint over the color cast areas, click on the CREATE NEW LAYER icon in the Layers panel. Set the layer's Blend Mode to COLOR.

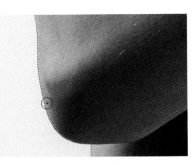

The new color has to consist in different brightness values. Therefore choose the Clone Stamp tool ([S], Size 20 pixels, Hardness 0%, Opacity 100%). Also activate SAMPLE: CURRENT & BELOW in the Options bar, to make the empty layer sample the colors of the layer below but display them on the layer above. As the retouched areas are all on a separate layer, you can easily remove any errors later with the Eraser tool ([E]). Always sample the texture close to the output area and retouch all affected areas.

In some places you will notice that the selection is directly on the color cast edge and therefore not all areas are selected. Enlarge the selection with SELECT/MODIFY/EXPAND. Enter an expansion of 1 pixel. This setting only applies to this picture. It is dependent on the softness of the edge and the image resolution. Usually you need to experiment a bit until you find the right value.

Now edit all violet edges in the image. To finish, flatten the layer "Color retouching" with ⌘/Ctrl+E.

Adjust brightness

Now we want to correct the over-exposed area on the man's back. Unfortunately, we cannot darken the light skin areas here. There is not enough texture and color, the area would turn gray. You therefore need to use the Lasso tool (L, Feather 0 pixel) to select a large piece of skin texture from another area of the upper body. Preferably this selection should not contain any extremely light or dark areas. Copy it to an independent layer with ⌘/Ctrl+J.

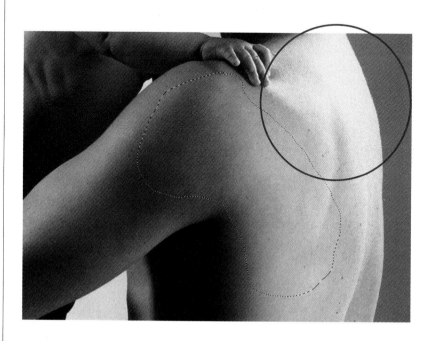

Position the skin texture over the light area. If some parts are not covered, stamp over them with the Clone Stamp tool (⟨S⟩, Size 100 pixels, Hardness 0%, Opacity 100%).

To match the skin more accurately, set the layer's Blend Mode to MULTIPLY.

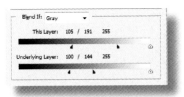

To adapt the brightness, double click on the layer "Skin" to open the Blending Options dialog. Try the following settings:

Blend If: GRAY
THIS LAYER:
105/191   255
UNDERLYING LAYER:
100/144   255

You can split the triangle sliders by holding the ⟨Alt⟩-key and dragging the inside of the sliders (see also Basic Overview "Special Layer Techniques", Chapter 5).

Adapt edges

You can add the finishing touches to the transitions with a layer mask. Hold the [Alt]-key and click on the ADD LAYER MASK icon at the bottom of the Layers panel. The mask turns black and the layer "Skin" no longer has any effect. Now paint over the overexposed areas with the Brush tool ([B], Size 60 pixels, Hardness 0%, Opacity 100%) with a medium gray from the Color panel.

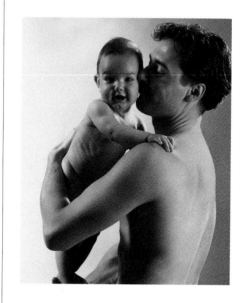

Why we work with gray:

If you paint a white area with black and low opacity, the applied color accumulates the more you paint over one spot. The image or mask will then turn blotchy. If you set the Opacity to 100% and paint with gray, the color does not accumulate. The same level of brightness is maintained. If you want to vary the mask's transparency, you don't lower the opacity but instead choose a different gray.

From CS4 onwards, you can change the mask density in the Masks panel.

Black
100% opacity

Black
50% opacity

Black
25% opacity

Gray
100% opacity

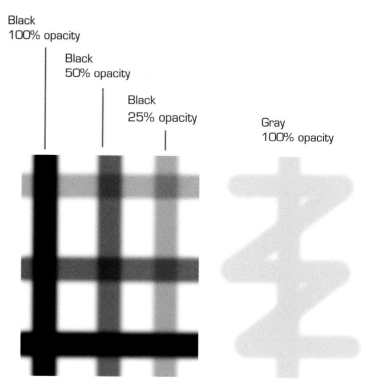

The brightness is better adjusted now, but the transitions on the body are not perfect yet. With the Brush tool ([B]) you will not achieve the desired softness. Activate the layer mask by clicking on it.

Now apply the FILTER/BLUR/ GAUSSIAN BLUR to the mask, with a Radius of 33 pixels. The body transitions now merge into one another nicely. Click on OK. You can also use the REFINE MASK EDGE dialog.

To adapt the back outline, choose the Brush tool ([B], Size 20 pixels, Hardness 40%, Opacity 100%) and black. Remove any skin sections that overlap the edge of the body. With a graphics tablet you can follow the back outline quickly and easily. Or you can select the background, as described in the first section, and work within the selection.

Now check your editing steps. The skin is not absolutely perfect yet. Change the Blend Mode to DARKER COLOR and reduce the layer Opacity to about 66%. Save the image with the layer.

Reduce neck creases

To reduce the creases on the man's neck, merge the image down to one layer with ⌘/Ctrl+E. Save it under a new name.

Duplicate the background with ⌘/Ctrl+J. Use the Patch tool (J) to remove all creases.

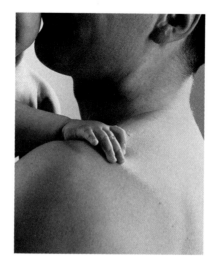

A rotated head completely without any creases would look very unnatural. Create a layer mask and use black and the Brush tool (B) to bring back a few creases. Experiment with the tool tip settings.

Reduce baby creases

We are going to retouch the baby creases on another layer. Use the Rectangular Marquee tool (W, Feather 5 pixels) to select the baby creases around the ribs. Place them on a new layer with ⌘/Ctrl+J. Use the Patch tool (J) again to remove all unwanted creases from the body. To stop the body seeming too smooth, retrieve individual creases slightly with a layer mask. Save the image, flatten it and save it again under a new name. Double click on the magnifying glass and check the picture carefully at 100% zoom.

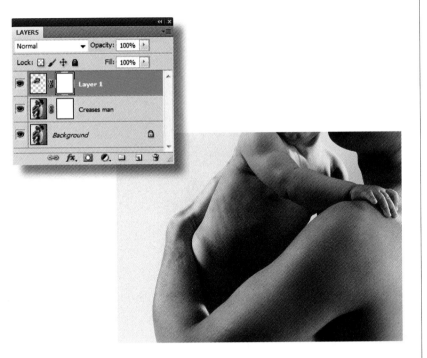

Lighten shadows

The shadows on the man's upper body and the baby's abdomen and legs still need to be lightened a little. Save the image under a new name. Duplicate the background with ⌘/Ctrl+J and convert the layer to a SMART OBJECT.

Lighten the shadows in the Shadows/ Highlights dialog.

Experiment until you have found a setting you are happy with. You can see our values in the SHADOWS/HIGHLIGHTS dialog. To stop the picture seeming too red, set the Color Correction to +8. Use a layer mask to restrict the lightening to the shadow areas.

In a few places the man still looks too red. Use a SELECTIVE COLOR adjustment layer to reduce the Magenta in the Reds a bit.

Quick skin retouching

Photoshop can do a lot, especially if you know the program well and have a lot of time available for editing your pictures. Plug-in filters of other manufacturers can often help you work faster and make editing easier. We are particularly impressed by the Dynamic Skin Softener by Nik Software. You can download an up-to-date demo version from our DVD. After installation, you will find the filter under FILTERS/NIK SOFTWARE/COLOR EFEX (see also Workshop "Various blur effects using channels and filters", page 299).

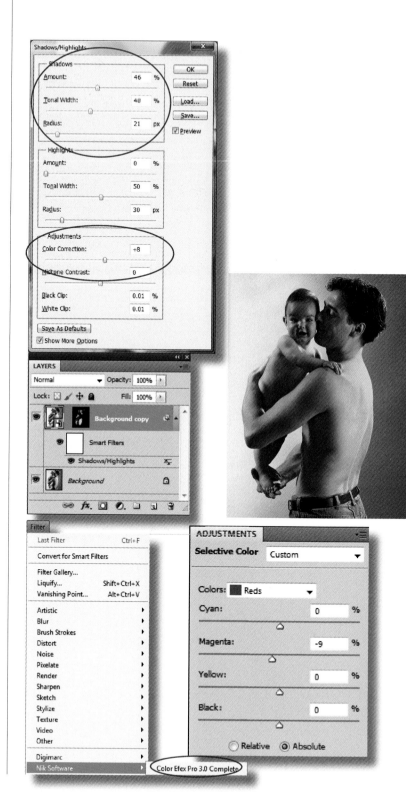

After choosing the command you can activate various filters on the left of the window. Click on the DYNAMIC SKIN SOFTENER filter (1). Always zoom to 100% image view in the filter, using the magnifying glass icon (2) at the top. Set the sliders (3) as in our example. Then you can experiment. You will quickly achieve different types of skin texture. Now click on OK.

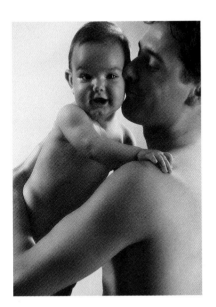

Hold the [Alt]-key and create a layer mask. The layer no longer has any effect. Use white and the Brush tool ([B], Size 30 pixels, Hardness 50%, Opacity 0%) to bring back the soft skin in certain areas. To avoid color changes, set the Blend Mode to LUMINOSITY and the Opacity to 61%.

Rejuvenate man

Picture analysis

❶ Reduce wrinkles

❷ Adapt eyebrows

❸ Smooth over hollows in right cheek

❹ Remove red spots

❺ Adapt skin color

❻ Soften skin texture very slightly

❼ Remove blood vessels (above left eye)

❽ Reduce glare spots

We would like the man in between the two women to look younger, but without losing his distinctive traits and personal charisma. In other words, we do not want to make him look 20 years younger, but would like to tastefully conceal the traces of aging.

ch5/rejuvenate.jpg

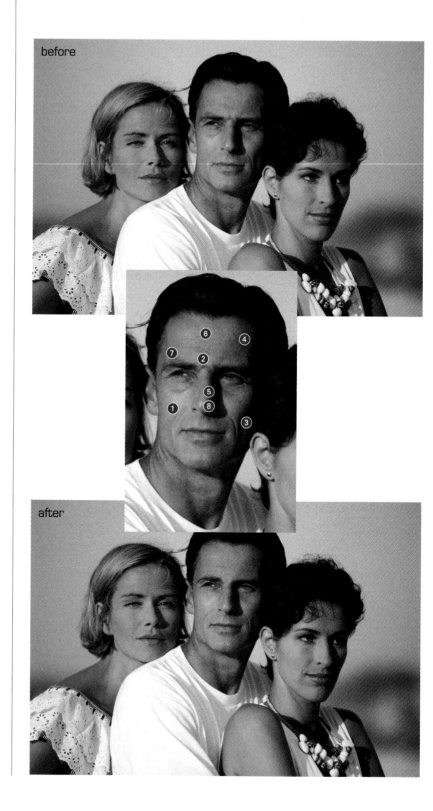

before

after

Retouch wrinkles

With the little wrinkles around the mouth you need to distinguish carefully between fine lines expressing personality, mimic wrinkles showing joy in life, and signs of fatigue that you can quite happily conceal a little. To avoid changing the original, duplicate the background layer (⌘/Ctrl+J). Trace around the individual wrinkles with the Patch tool (J) and drag the selection onto a smooth area of skin. Do not work too quickly, otherwise the next step will not be possible. You should not remove distinctive wrinkles completely. Go to EDIT/FADE and set the Opacity to about 11% in order to reduce them slightly.

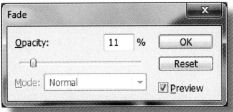

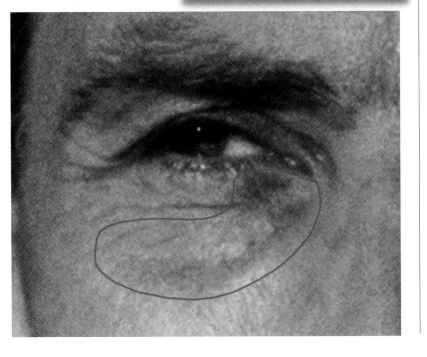

The marked area makes the eye look tired and therefore older. You need to edit this area more strongly than the fine horizontal lines around the eye, which mainly convey experience and wisdom.

Target the Fade function very carefully. Scrutinize each individual wrinkle in order to find the most appropriate reduction in opacity.

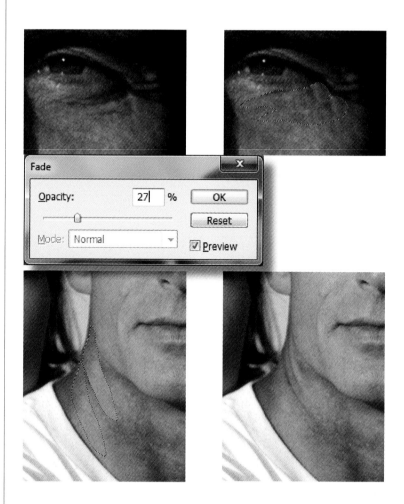

Remove some of the creases on the neck completely. Use EDIT/FADE to bring back the two most pronounced creases.

Set the Opacity in the Fade dialog to 27%.

Remove hairs from root of the nose

Edit the hairs between the eyebrows and the eyebrow shape with the Clone Stamp tool (⑤).

To have greatest possible flexibility, carry out your retouching on a new empty layer.

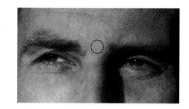

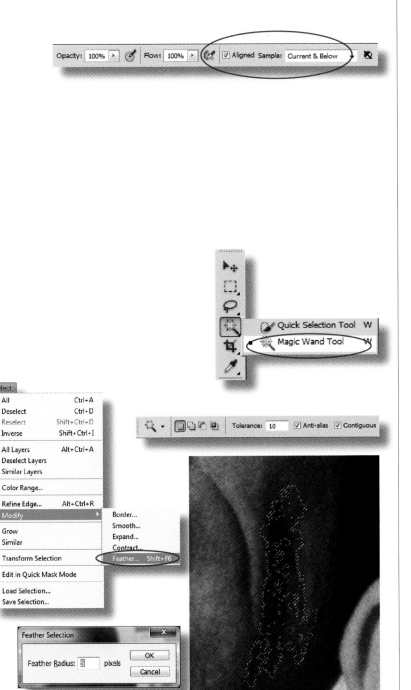

Click on the CREATE A NEW LAYER icon in the Layers panel. Use the Clone Stamp tool to remove the hairs between the eyebrows. Give the eyebrows a better shape by hiding some of the hairs there as well (S, Size 40 pixels, Hardness 0%, Opacity 30%). In the Options bar, set SAMPLE: CURRENT & BELOW. Now the retouching is applied to the empty layer. The original image remains unchanged.

Smooth away hollows

Use the Magic Wand tool (W) and a Tolerance of 10 to select the dark areas in the right cheek. It does not matter that some areas remain unselected, we will fix this in the next step.

Assign a feathered edge of 5 pixels to the selection with SELECT/MODIFY/FEATHER, or use the keyboard shortcut ⌘/Ctrl+⇧+J to display the dialog box.

Now switch from the Magic Wand tool (W) to the Patch tool (J) and drag the selected area to a smooth spot. Immediately after the correction, set the Opacity to 67% with EDIT/FADE.

You can use the Patch tool to drag any selection to another area, regardless of how it was created. The selection has the same properties as if you had used the Patch tool to create it.

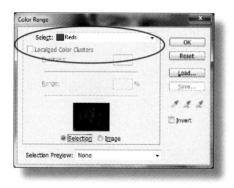

Adapt skin color

In the skin color, we need to correct above all the red. Choose SELECT/COLOR RANGE.

Set the the SELECT box to Reds and click on OK.

You will see a warning: "No pixels are more than 50% selected."

Confirm with OK. You now no longer see any selection edges in the picture. Photoshop cannot display them any more, but they are still there. Create a SELECTIVE COLOR adjustment layer via the Layers panel. Now you are only editing the Reds.

In the Layers panel you can see clearly that the invisible selection has created a layer mask.

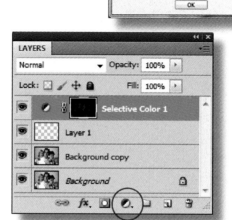

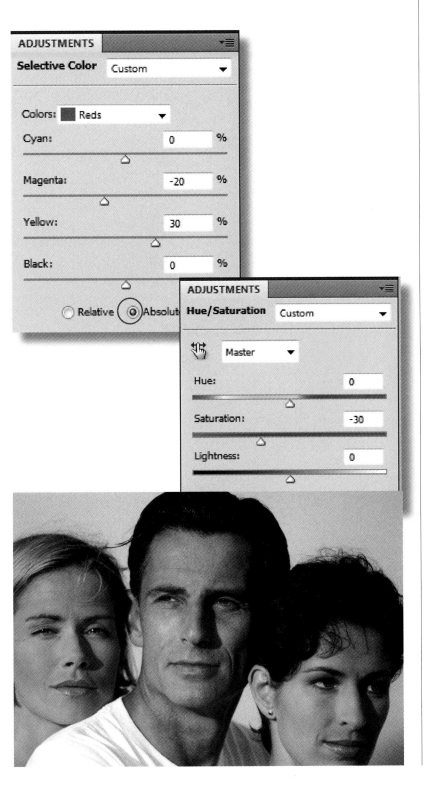

Change the following colors in the Selective Color:

REDS:
MAGENTA   –20
YELLOW   +30

YELLOWS:
YELLOW   +70

You need to set the Method to ABSOLUTE to make sure the increase of saturation in the Yellow works.

Now paint with black ([D]) and the Brush tool over the two women in the layer mask to exclude them from the color correction ([B], Size 150 pixels, Hardness 0%, Opacity 100%).

The man's skin color is still a bit too red after the correction. Create a HUE/ SATURATION adjustment layer and do not change any settings. Now hold the [Alt]-key while you drag the layer mask of the SELECTIVE COLOR layer to the HUE/SATURATION layer. Confirm the REPLACE LAYER MASK dialog with YES.

Then click on the thumbnail of the HUE/SATURATION layer. The dialog reappears.

Reduce Saturation to –30 in the Master channel. The original some-what tired impression has now gone completely.

Basic Overview: Special layer techniques

Smart Object, neutral layer, layer style

Smart Object

If you apply a transformation or a filter to a layer, its pixels are changed. Should you want to alter the setting at a later time, this will result in loss of quality, unless you do it all again. But if you changed the layer to a Smart Object before making your changes, you can change any setting any time you like and as often as you like, without any loss of quality. We are going to demonstrate this with an example. In the image on the right we selected the eyes and copied them to a new layer with ⌘/Ctrl+J. We then copied this layer and converted one of the layers to a Smart Object, but not the other layer.

We now reduce both layers to about 5% with TRANSFORM. Both pairs of eyes on this picture still have the same quality.

But as soon as we enlarge both layers back to their original size, you can see the difference clearly: the Smart Object, at the top of the picture, has not lost any quality, whereas the normal layer at the bottom has lost a lot of sharpness and detail.

Why does this happen?

When we convert a layer to a Smart Object, the layer is integrated into the image as independent file and we only see a preview. If we change the layer, the embedded file is always used to display the preview anew. No pixels are destroyed. Not so in the "unsmart" pixel layer. If we change the size there, Photoshop always interprets the end result as 100% size. For Photoshop, this is the current pixel state of a file and from there the new size is calculated.

Converting

You can convert a layer with FILTER/CONVERT FOR SMART FILTERS or use the menu in the Layers panel, or you can right-click. It is not important which menu item you use to convert a layer to a Smart Object. They just have different names in the different menus. All filters you apply to the Smart Object layers you can call up again by double-clicking on the filter name in the Layers panel. They then open with the last setting. You can now change the setting as many times as you like.

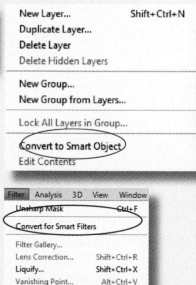

Smart Object and Layer Mask

On the right you can see a picture that has a Smart Object layer and has been slightly transformed. We applied a filter and created a layer mask to adapt the eyes to the surrounding area. In Photoshop versions before CS4, the chain icon between the Smart Object thumbnail and the mask thumbnail would disappear and you needed to re-edit the mask every time you transform the layer again. This problem is fixed from CS4 onwards and the link betweeen mask and layer is maintained.

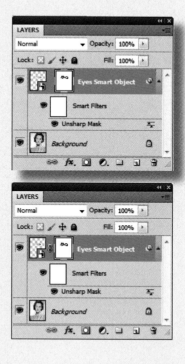

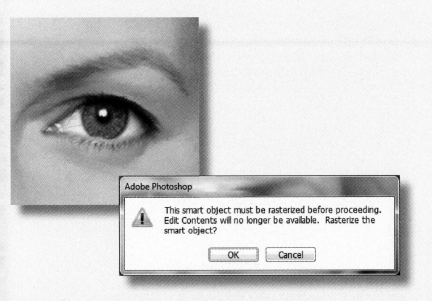

Smart Object retouching

If you still need to make corrections to the Smart Object layer, you will notice that you cannot use any of the retouching tools on it. Instead a message appears, telling you that you first need to rasterize the layer. Click on Cancel. If you were to rasterize the picture, you could neither change the filter setting nor correct a previous transformation without loss of quality.

Of course you can retouch a Smart Object! Just double-click on the Smart Object thumbnail. The resulting dialog now tells you that you have to save the newly opened file in the same place. Click on Ok and a file with the identical layer information opens. You can now edit this file just like any other, without restriction. Once you are finished, simply click on the Close button in the window. The resulting dialog asks if you want to save the image. Confirm with Ok. You immediately see the change in the picture.

Neutral layer

With a neutral layer you can change the brightness values in a picture. The color black darkens, white lightens. Of course grays work too. Only 50% gray won't work, because that is the base color of the layer. You can use it to remove editing errors. You need 50% gray and the right blend mode.

1. Create a new empty layer.

2. Fill the area with EDIT/FILL/ USE/50% GRAY.

3. Set the Layer Mode to SOFT LIGHT. The gray area becomes invisible.

4. Paint into the area with black or white. The contrasts change.

You can also create a separate Neutral Layer for lightening and darkening.

The Dodge/Burn tools are generally not recommended, as they affect the pixels directly. From CS 4 onwards there are improved versions of these functions, but the pixels are still being changed.

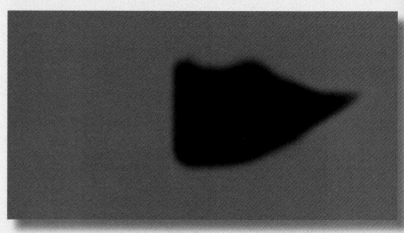

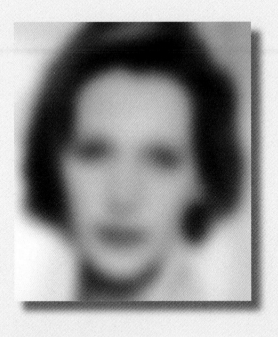

Layer Style/Blend If

With the BLEND IF command in the LAYER STYLE dialog you can display and hide the layer's brightness values and therefore combine layers with high range of contrast. In portrait retouching, this function is frequently used for skin editing. It's easiest to demonstrate with an example.

In this picture, we simply blurred the layer a lot. But we only want to have the blur on the skin . Revealing it via a layer mask would take a lot of time. We use the Layer Style instead.

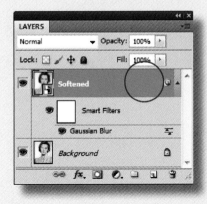

Activate it by double-clicking on the area next to the layer thumbnail. The function is the same for any kind of layer, regardless whether pixel layer, Smart Object layer or adjustment layer. For our workshops the bottom area of the Blending Options dialog, the Blend If box, is of interest. It contains two brightness gradients which symbolize our two layers, the active one and the one below it. Each image contains more or less different brightnesses.

If you drag the top black slider slightly to the right, the dark brightness values of the active layer are hidden and the underlying layer appears.

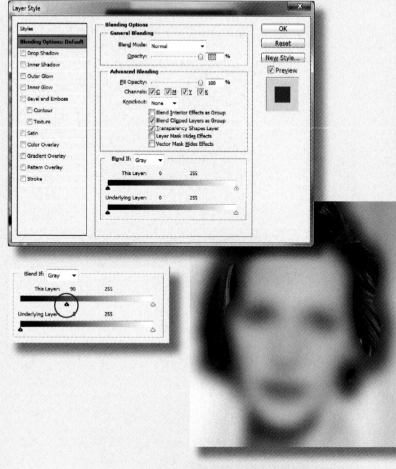

The hidden area is still very hard. You can achieve a softer transition by separating the slider. Hold the [Alt]-key and drag the two halves of the slider apart. You can do this with any of these sliders.

The sliders allow you to hide certain brightness values from the active layer. The sliders of the underlying layer make it possible to show these brightness values in the composite image. Try out different possibilities with your pictures. In our workshops you use various combinations of these settings and become more familiar with them.

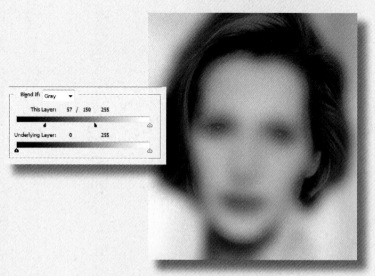

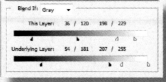

With the setting shown here you can achieve better separation of skin and hairline.

The superfluous blur in the hair, eyes and lips can now be easily removed using a layer mask. The settings in the Layer Style remain the same. The mask no longer has to be as accurate.

Chapter 6
Hair

shapeless shiny strong matte dull healthy scruffy
smooth silky full flat gray colored tinted brittle worn-
out brushed glossy tidy unkempt red flaky greasy
brunette blonde black short long fashionable styled
dandruff curly wavy straight scruffy neat smooth
frizzy split glamorous bouncy layered shapeless
shiny strong matte dull healthy scruffy smooth
silky full flat gray colored tinted brittle worn-out
brushed glossy tidy unkempt red flaky greasy

How to isolate blowing hair from uniform background

How to isolate and recompose hair and transparent areas

How to color dark hair blond-metallic

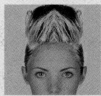

How to bring more texture into a hair-style

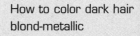

Basic Overview Sharpening

How to trim three-day stubble

How to remove hair-clips

How to add exciting style to hair

Isolate hair from uniform background

Picture analysis

❶ Isolate models

We want to select and cut out these models in order to be able to insert them against a new background. Of course we would like all hair to be maintained. The problem is that the borders always contain some of the background color as well. If we delete the background color, there will be nothing left of individual strands of hair. In this example we will work in three steps:

1. Select the women's contours

2. Select the spaces in between the hair

3. Recolor the blue colored hair

before

after

ch6/isolate_hair.jpg

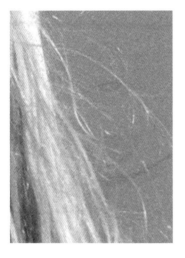

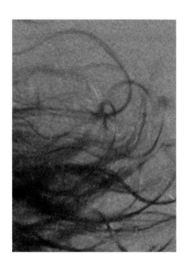

Select contour outline of women

The background only contains one color and the brightness does not vary greatly. With SELECT/COLOR RANGE you can create a selection via the color. In the dialog, choose the setting SELECT: SAMPLED COLORS. Click with the cursor, which has changed to an eyedropper, in the blue sky. The sky is displayed white in the preview window, the models black. Set the Fuzziness to 52. This is the best setting for separating the models from the background. We will edit the spaces in between the hairs later. Some parts of the sky are still gray. To select these as well, click on the middle eyedropper with the plus symbol. Now you can add the gray areas to the selection. Once all the sky areas appear white, click on OK.

Of course there are several ways of achieving what you want. The EXTRACT function works equally well in this case. We decided to use the method with the Color Range because it gives us the best control over the selection.

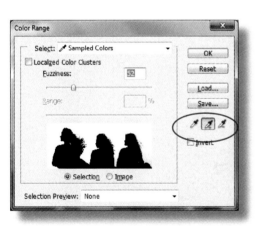

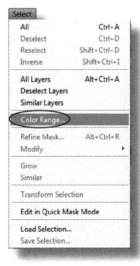

The selection borders indicate that the background is now selected, but you cannot see how exact they are.

Improve edge selection

With SELECT/REFINE EDGE you can make the selection visible and edit various selection parameters.

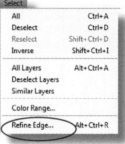

Set the VIEW MODE to On Black (in new versions of Photoshop, via the View drop-down menu; in previous versions via the colored icons at the bottom of the dialog) . The area that is not selected then turns black, in our case the models. We set SMOOTH to 3, adjusted the FEATHER slider (1 pixel) and the SHIFT EDGE slider (−2%). The selection becomes slightly smaller, the FEATHER counteracts this again and allows slight transparency around the edges. This is important to let the new background color shine through later on. Click on Ok.

To be able to check that the selection is absolutely perfect, click on the SAVE SELECTION AS CHANNEL button at the bottom of the Channels panel. This creates an Alpha 1 channel. The selection is still there. Remove it with ⌘/Ctrl+D. Click on the Alpha 1 channel. Only this channel should be active and visible. Now you can see the flaws clearly. Use black and the Brush tool (B) to remove all white and gray areas on the models. But the background white is not perfect either. Use white to remove any black or gray areas in the background.

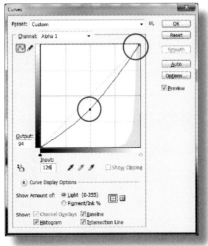

To make sure any remaining gray in the background turns white, create a Curve with IMAGE/ADJUSTMENTS/CURVES or press ⌘/Ctrl+M. Drag the light slightly to the left, all Grays become White, and darken the Midtones a little. Click on OK.

Now the sky is selected perfectly, but really we wanted to select the models. Invert the tonal values with the menu item IMAGE/ADJUSTMENTS/INVERT or press ⌘/Ctrl+I.

Edit spaces between hairs

To check the edge areas and therefore the selection, activate the RGB composite channel. Load the Alpha 1 channel by dragging it to the CHANNEL AS SELECTION icon.

Copy the models to a new layer with ⌘ / Ctrl + J . Click on the background and create a new empty layer which you fill with yellow. Yellow is the complementary color to blue, therefore blue will show best.

The hair edges are now isolated, but the blue of the original background is still present in fine and single strands of hair.

With SELECT/COLOR RANGE you select the sky once more as in the first step. We can now set a higher fuzziness as we only want to concentrate on the blue gaps between the hairs. You can neglect the blue colored hairs and strands of hair for now. Try out various values. Click on OK.

Improve the selection again using the Refine Edge dialog. The values differ from the first version because we are now working with different edge values. Confirm with OK.

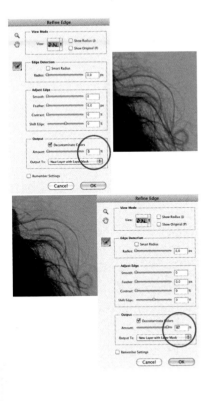

Decontaminate Colors

The new version of Photoshop offers another method for improving selections: the DECONTAMINATE COLORS function. If you activate this checkbox in the Refine Edge dialog, you can refine the selection even more, particularly fine image details such as hair. We set the View Mode to REVEAL LAYER.

Drag the Decontaminate Colors slider to the right and watch what happens to the fine hairs. You can see the result in the picture.
If your version of Photoshop does not have Decontaminate Color, just continue with the next step, below.

Now simply press the Delete key and the blue areas in between the individual strands of hair are deleted. Only single hairs and individual strands of hair are still colored blue. Selection technique will no longer work here, because the hair color itself has been replaced by the blooming effect from the sky in these areas.

Recolor hair

We will now simply paint over these
areas with the appropriate hair color.
First create a new layer above the
layer "Models" while holding the
Alt-key. Click on the USE PREVIOUS
LAYER TO CREATE CLIPPING MASK
icon. The layer appears indented in
the Layers panel and now only applies
to the layer "Models".

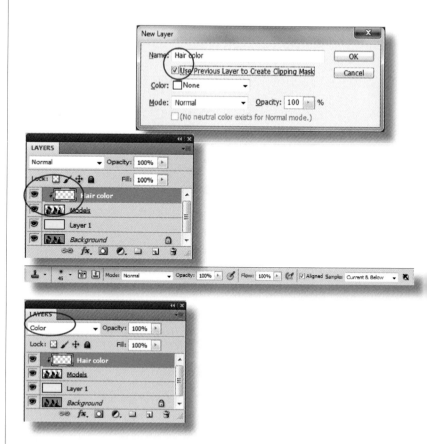

To be able to apply the correct color,
you could of course pick it up with
the eyedropper. But the Clone Stamp
tool works better (S, Size 45 pixels,
Hardness 0%, Opacity 100%). Set
SAMPLE: CURRENT LAYER AND BELOW.
Then set the Blend Mode of the layer
"Hair color" to COLOR. Make sure
you pick up a midtone. Now stamp
over the blue hairs. Because of the
Blend Mode COLOR, only the color
is applied, not the hair texture. Of
course you can also use the Brush tool
to apply color on the same layer. Use
this method to adapt not only the hair,
but all face and body contours.

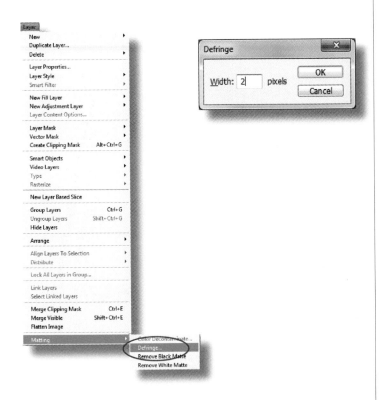

Activate the layer "Models". Give the edges the final touches via the LAYER/MATTING/DEFRINGE menu. First zoom into the picture to 200% with ⌘/Ctrl+[+]. Try out different values for DEFRINGE and make sure you achieve harmonious transitions along the edges. The edge is not literally removed, but the edge pixels are replaced with color from further in which does not contain any blue background color. Save the image. Click on the layer "Hair color" and combine it with the layer below by pressing ⌘/Ctrl+[E]. Now you can insert the models into different backgrounds. You can delete the yellow layer.

Isolate model from structured background for composition

Picture analysis

❶ Isolate model

❷ Insert model into new picture

❸ Adapt model's color and contrast to new background

Other than in the last workshop, we now want to cut out the woman and insert her into another picture. We therefore have to analyze carefully first. There are a lot of problem areas: hair, dress, especially the semitransparent areas. The new background has to shine through these slightly in order to create a realistic effect.

ch6/composition.jpg

ch6/bridge.jpg

before

after

Select the model

First duplicate the background layer by pressing ⌘/Ctrl+J. Select the model with the Quick Selection Tool (W). Use a small brush tip and move it over the model briefly. You only want to select a little. Then, go the Options bar and click on the SUBTRACT FROM SELECTION icon. Brush over all areas you do not want to be part of the selection. You do not always see the change straight away, but Photoshop remembers the areas you want to deselect. Now click on the ADD TO SELECTION icon and move the Quick Selection Tool over any other areas of the model that were missed out before. Selecting the edges on legs and upper body will be easy, but hair and dress will still have messy edges. Not a problem, we will fix this in the next editing steps.

Now click on the ADD LAYER MASK icon in the Layers palette and hide the background layer.

Refine the mask

To refine the mask make sure that the mask is active in the Layers palette. If this is not the case, just click on the mask. Use SELECT/REFINE MASK to bring up the REFINE MASK dialog.

Set VIEW to a mode that shows the edges well and gives you the best overview of your corrections. We selected ON WHITE (W) as VIEW MODE. Now we need to tidy up all the edges and get rid of the remaining colored parts from the original background in the light, overexposed areas.

Bring out hair and hem

Choose the Refine Radius tool (E) in the Refine Mask dialog. Set the Size in the Options bar to 35. Now draw over all edge areas you want to reveal again.

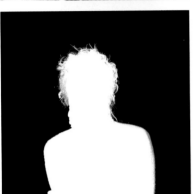

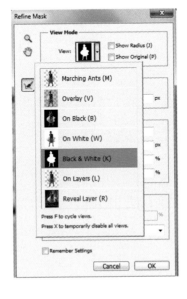

Draw over the edges section by small section, this way you are able to work more precisely on each individual edge. The white background makes the improvement quite hard to see in certain places. To make is easier to assess the corrections you make, occasionally switch the VIEW MODE to BLACK & WHITE (K).

To make the dress translucent, draw over all blue areas on the dress as well. This makes the dress translucent in those places. In some areas, there may be streaks outside of the dress. Use the Erase Refinements tool (E) to remove these.

Check the image once more in Black & White view. This view mode is best to assess the fine hair and translucent areas of the dress.

Hide old background color

The dress still has some blue in it from the old background. Activate the Decontaminate Colors checkbox and set the Amount to 43%. The background color is now hidden. For Output To, set New Layer with Layer Mask and click on OK.

This creates a new layer with a layer mask. Hide the layer below it. You then still have the option to go back to the starting layer in case it becomes necessary to repeat any large corrections. Otherwise you can delete the layer "Background copy".

Go to the mask of the layer "Background copy 2" to make any other corrections that may be required. The shoes, for example, are not yet quite perfect. When you are finished, save the image.

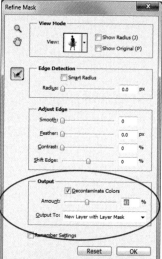

Insert model

Open the bridge image and insert the model: Hold the ⌘ / Ctrl -key and click on the mask icon in the model image. The mask is loaded as selection. Now activate the image thumbnail and copy the model with ⌘ / Ctrl +C. Go to the bridge image and paste the model into it with ⌘ / Ctrl +V.

Adjust sharpness

The bridge shows a diagonal gradient blur. The blur is strongest in the fore-ground and the bottom two thirds of the picture. To adjust the model opti-mally, the level of sharpness has to form a gradient from the bottom front to the top back, therefore touching upper body and head. The other body areas need to be adapted to the blurri-ness of the bridge. We will use a blur filter. First convert the layer "Model" to a SMART OBJECT.

With FILTER/BLUR/GAUSSIAN BLUR and a RADIUS of 8 pixels you can then blur the model.

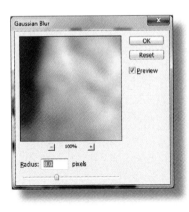

Add a black and white gradient to the mask of the Smart Filter layer, using the Gradient tool ([G]). Make sure that black is at the top and white at the bottom. The blur is now continuously reduced.

Create cast shadow

The model still appears to be somewhat unhappily floating in mid-air. To bring her "down to earth", we need to paint a cast shadow onto the wooden floor. Create a CURVES adjustment layer between the background and the layer "Model". Drag the curve slightly downwards as shown on the right. The new shadow has to show the same degree of blackness as the existing shadow on the bridge. Click on OK. Choose EDIT/FILL/USE/BLACK and paint the shadow with white and the Brush tool ([B], Size 130 pixels, Hardness 40%, Opacity 50%, Flow 100%). Use the edge sharpness of the original shadows on the bridge for guidance.

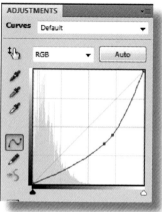

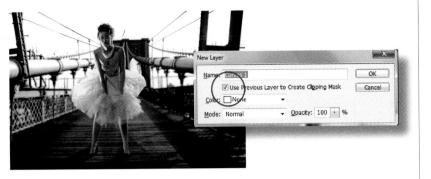

Adapt colors

For a first color adaptation of the model, activate the top layer in the Layers panel and hold the [Alt]-key while you create a Curves adjustment layer. Check USE PREVIOUS LAYER TO CREATE CLIPPING MASK to restrict the correction to the model. To achieve a slight gold tone, adjust the curves as shown on our screenshots on the left. Lightening the Red makes the image more red, darkening the Blue turns it more yellow. Click on OK.

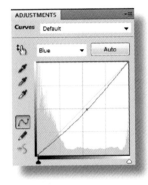

The dress does not look transparent enough yet. The light, overexposed areas still contain the colors of the original background. Create a SELECTIVE COLOR adjustment layer while holding the [Alt]-key. Reduce the Cyan and Black in the Whites a little, this makes the dress look more transparent and white. Increase Magenta and Yellow. This gives the impression that the background shines through the transparent areas.

Using the layer mask, remove this effect on all areas of the dress where the background contains dark bridge areas. Because the dress is still not bright enough in the white areas, we copy the SELECTIVE COLOR and set OPACITY to about 35%.

Color dress seam

Create a new layer while holding the Alt -key and set the Blend Mode to COLOR. Call the layer "Pink". Pick up a color on the dress with the Eyedropper tool (I) and use the Brush tool to paint over all areas that are still too blue-green and need to be recolored.

Improve edges

When you are working with your own files, it may be that the edges still need tidying up even after using the mask or Refine Edges methods. This can soon be fixed.

If, as in this example, you find that the model's contours still appear too sharp, hold the ⌘ / Ctrl -key and click on the layer thumbnail of the layer "Model". The model's contour is loaded as selection. Choose SELECT/MODIFY/CONTRACT to contract the selection by 1 pixel and enter 1 pixel for SELECT/MODIFY/FEATHER. Add a mask using the Layers panel. The model remains visible, only the surrounding area is covered. The model contours become softer and are better integrated into the background. Any details that were lost can be retrieved using the layer mask. Now the composition is perfect.

Bring out hair texture

Picture analysis

❶ Reinforce texture in hair

❷ Lighten face

To give more texture and detail to the dark areas of the hair, we only need to brighten these. The easiest and quickest way to achieve this it with the SHADOWS/HIGHLIGHTS function. It also has a positive effect on other problem areas such as eyes and mouth.

before

after

ch6/hair_texture.jpg

Lighten hairstyle

To give us greater flexibility during editing, we copy the background layer with ⌘/Ctrl+J and choose CONVERT TO SMART OBJECT from the Layers panel menu.

In the IMAGE/ADJUSTMENTS/SHADOWS-HIGHLIGHTS dialog, activate the checkbox SHOW MORE OPTIONS. You can immediately see a change in the picture. The basic setting for SHADOWS/HIGHLIGHTS gives more texture to the dark areas, but also changes the colors. Set the Amount of the Shadows to 55%. Adapt the color change with the Color Correction slider. Drag it to a negative value; we chose –42. We do not want to darken the Highlights. Click on OK.

Of course you can still use a layer mask to hide image areas that you do not want to change. We think that the change applied to the whole picture looks good, and leave it at that.

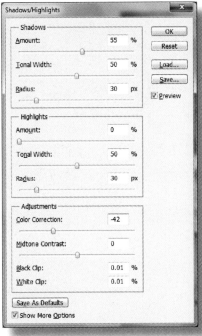

Remove hair clips

Picture analysis

❶ Remove hair clips

before

Want to quickly get rid of these hair clips? No problem. Just select part of the hairstyle, copy it and use the Liquify filter or Warp tool to quickly bend it in the right direction. Or that's what we thought. Unfortunately, it doesn't quite work that way. The image and pixel structure gets warped so much that it becomes completely unsharp. The only way is being patient and stamping lots. But there are a few things to watch out for.

ch6/hairclips.jpg

after

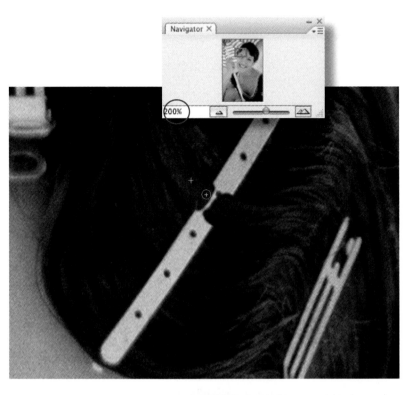

Hair clip removal

The waves in the hair have to continue. The hair texture in front of and behind the clips needs to match, the same applies to brightness and colors.

Start with the simplest area, the long clip on the right. Use the Clone Stamp tool (S, Size 10 pixels, Hardness 50%, Opacity 100%). Stamp from both sides of the hair clip. Change the tool tip occasionally. Work in very small steps and always use a hard brush tip. As soon as the hair and texture become unsharp, your chosen tip is too soft. Work at a magnification of at least 200%, which you can set in the Navigator.

In some places the brightness and color transitions of the hair will look flawed. Don't worry about these areas for now, we will correct them later.

Other areas will show repeating patterns, a clear sign of retouching. Use the Patch tool ([J]) to remove the duplicated patterns by marking them and dragging them to another texture. Quite often it can be sufficient to select parts of the pattern and break it up.

Adapt hair transitions

The hair style shows different areas of sharpness. We therefore have to apply different methods. Use the Patch tool to adapt color and brightness transitions in the unsharp areas. Select the area around the edges to make sure both the light and the dark side are selected. Drag the selection slightly downwards into the light hair area. Use EDIT/FADE to reduce the retouching opacity, in case it is too strong.

The Patch tool can also repair transitions in sharp areas. But here you cannot use the Fade command. The area would become unsharp.

In the picture on the right, the retouching is clearly visible in the hair texture. That is of course unacceptable.

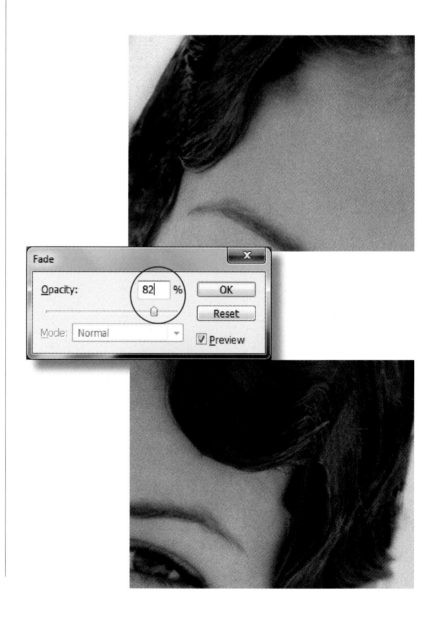

To make the hair look natural again, use the Lasso tool ([L], Feather 5 pixel) to select a few strands and copy them to another layer with [⌘]/[Ctrl]+[J], then convert the layer to a SMART OBJECT. Drag the selected strands onto the hair sections you want to repair. Set the layer's Blend Mode to DARKER COLOR. The texture only becomes visible in the dark areas.

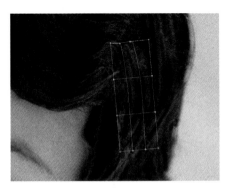

To avoid having the same strands of hair next to each other in the same shape, warp the inserted hair strand a little. The pixel structure becomes unsharp very quickly, therefore be careful not to overdo the warp effect.

Use this method for other image areas as well. Experiment with the layer's Blend Mode. For another area, we set the Blend Mode to LUMINOSITY. Now the brightness values for this area are those of the layer, but the color values are those of the underlying layer.

Fine retouching

After we have removed all the clips and adjusted all the transitions, there is just a minor detail missing for a perfect retouching.

The edited areas need to have a little more contrast and sharpness. We will achieve this with a Noise filter. As our retouchings are on separate layers and we want to maintain these, we first create a neutral layer (see also Basic Overview "Special Layer Techniques", Chapter 5). Hold the [Alt]-key while clicking on the CREATE A NEW LAYER icon. Name the layer "Neutral Layer", set the Blend Mode to SOFT LIGHT and choose the option FILL WITH SOFT-LIGHT-NEUTRAL COLOR. Convert the neutral layer to a SMART OBJECT.

Now activate the filter with FILTER/ NOISE/ADD NOISE and set the Amount to 3%. Check the box MONOCHROMATIC. Confirm with OK.

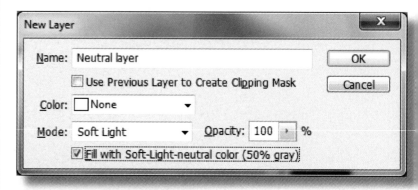

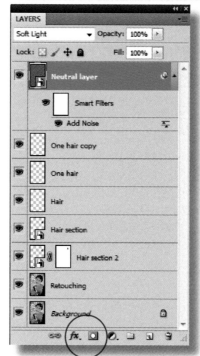

We only want to have noise in certain areas of our picture, therefore we create a layer mask by holding the Alt -key and clicking on the ADD LAYER MASK icon at the bottom of the Layers panel. The mask turns black and the noise disappears. Now reveal the noise again in the overly soft areas by painting over them with white and the Brush tool (B, Size 30 pixels, Hardness 0%, Opacity 40%). The sharpness and contrast, and therefore detail, are improved.

Color hair

Picture analysis

❶ Color hair

❷ Metallic look

We want to give this model a golden metallic look. We will need to experiment a little and use trial and error to find the best effect.

before

ch6/color_hair.jpg

after

Color hair

To give dark hair a lighter color, you need to work in several steps. Create a new Curves adjustment layer. Do not make any changes to the settings. Set the Blend Mode to COLOR DODGE. The picture now has very high contrast. Fill the layer mask with black via ⌘/Ctrl+I. The effect is no longer visible. Use the Brush tool (B, Size 100 pixels, Hardness 0%, Opacity 50%) to bring back the effect in the hair. We limited this first step to the pyramid-like backcombed part of the hairstyle.

Next we want to make the hair shiny and golden. Create a second Curves adjustment layer. Increase the overall contrast in the RGB channel by increasing the highlights slightly and darkening the shadows. Now switch to the individual color channels. For a touch of gold, drag the curve strongly upwards in the Red and Green channel.

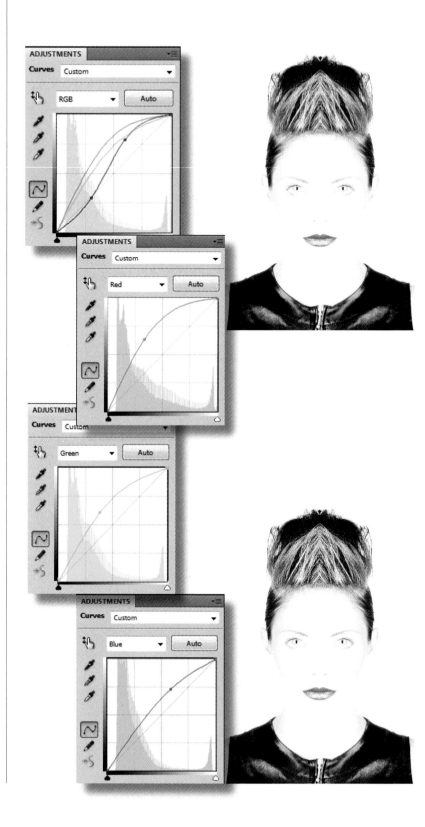

The hair is now too shiny. Drag the curve in the Blue channel up a bit. Blue is the complementary color to Yellow and therefore lessens its intensity.

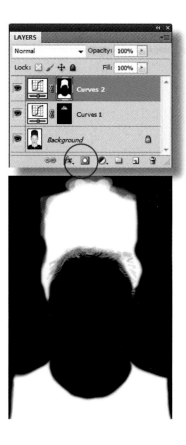

Use a layer mask filled with black to remove all areas that you do not want the curve to affect. We not only left the hair free, but the top as well.

Hold the [Alt]- key and click on the mask thumbnail in the layer. You can now see in the mask that we let the effect peter out slightly around the roots of the hair. Use a fine brush tip and low opacity for painting over the edges, to let the transitions merge softly into the skin. Show the image again by [Alt]-clicking on the mask thumbnail.

The color is not strong enough yet. Duplicate the curve you just created with [⌘]/[Ctrl]+[J]. We then reduced the layer Opacity to 30%.

We are still not happy with the white areas in this picture. In a CURVES adjustment layer we drag the Highlights down by more than a quarter. The white turns into gray and the overall contrast is reduced. The metal effect increases even more.

The disappearance of the highlights is clearly visible in the Histogram.

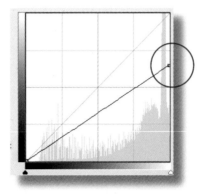

We would like to color the roots of the hairs more. Create a second Curve and drag the composite RGB channel downwards slightly. The picture is darkened.

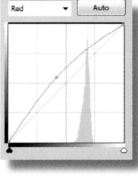

Switch to the Red channel and drag it slightly upwards. The red becomes more intense.

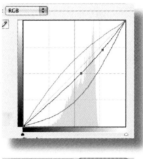

To add yellow, switch to the Blue channel and drag it slightly downwards. The picture becomes more yellow.

Fill the layer mask with black (⌘ / Ctrl + I) and paint with white over the roots of the hair. Use the Brush tool with a soft tip and low opacity. Paint more intensively over individual hairs and increase the effect in order to create a natural shade.

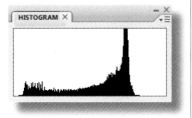

You cannot plan your approach exactly to achieve this effect. Think carefully before each step about what you want to accomplish. Keep watching the Histogram. For printable results it should always be continuous, even if it does not contain any pure White and Black.

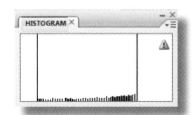

If your Histogram has lots of gaps in it and looks choppy like this, you should not attempt high-quality printing. But if you like the effect, why not.

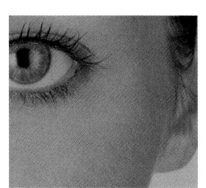

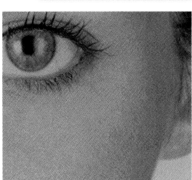

The picture on the left shows the printed result of a continuous histogram, the one on the right that of a noncontinuous histogram.

Remove three-day stubble

Picture analysis

❶ Remove beard stubble

To remove a three-day stubble, you have to dig around more deeply in the Photoshop box of tricks. The biggest problem is that the skin should not be affected. As the stubble has a different brightness than the skin, we can create a selection using the brightness values.

ch6/three_day_stubble.jpg

before

after

Create luminosity mask

In the first step we will select the stubble with a brightness or luminosity mask. Copy the background with ⌘/Ctrl+J , then hold the ⌘/Ctrl-key and click on the RGB channel's thumbnail in the Channel panel. The brightness values are loaded as selection. Bright areas in the picture are selected more strongly, dark ones less strongly. Invert the selection with ⌘/Ctrl+⇧+I. Zoom into the picture to 200% with ⌘/Ctrl++. The selection outlines are always in the way when retouching. Press ⌘/Ctrl+H to hide the outlines, but not remove them. Press ⌘/Ctrl+H again to show the outlines.

Reduce beard stubble

Use the Spot Healing brush (J, Size 9 pixels, Hardness 80%) to remove the stubble. You need to work with great precision. When you are finished, deselect the selection with ⌘/Ctrl+D.

Create skin pattern

There a still a few bits of stubble left. We will remove them with a skin pattern and the Healing Brush tool ([J]). First we need to create the skin pattern.

Create a new file with FILE/NEW with a Size of 100 pixels. Via EDIT/FILL you can enter USE: 50% GRAY.

You can create the skin texture with all filters that create pixelation or graininess. You will find a few under FILTER/ARTISTIC/FILM GRAIN or the Noise filters. Experiment in order to find the right grain for your portraits. The new skin texture is dependent on the file size, display size of the face, ISO sensitivity used and other factors. In our example we used the ADD NOISE filter with an Amount of 1%.

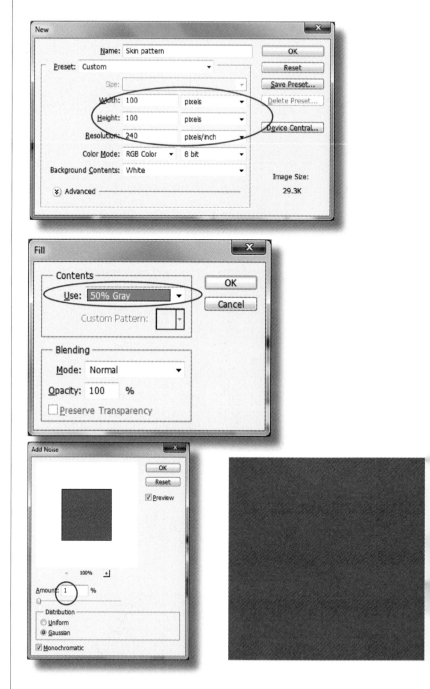

To be able to use the file as pattern, go to EDIT/DEFINE PATTERN. In the resulting dialog, name the pattern "skin 1px". We also enter the filter settings. If a pattern should not be completely right and we need to create another one, we can use these parameters as guidelines. Click on Ok and you will find your new pattern in all pattern related dialogs. You can gradually build a library of skin pattern or other textures. We now no longer need the image file with the pattern. You can find the skin texture we used on the DVD, in the "textures" folder.

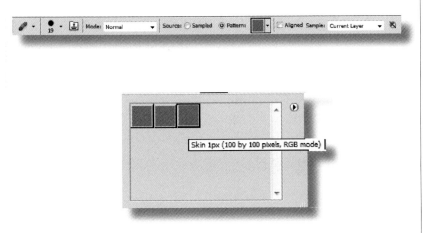

Apply skin pattern

First copy the layer "Retouching"
with ⌘/Ctrl+J and choose the
Healing Brush tool (J, Size 20 pixels, Hardness 0%). Set the Mode to
SCREEN, click on the USE PATTERN
button and select your skin pattern. As
you can see we have created several of
these patterns.

Now paint over the entire beard
area without taking the brush off in
between. Reduce the layer opacity to
about 70% to let the original skin texture emerge slightly. The effect will
only become visible in combination
with the next step.

Copy the layer "Retouching copy"
with ⌘/Ctrl+J. Set the Healing
Brush tool's (J) Mode to MULTIPLY
and improve the beard with the same
pattern. Your picture should now look
similar to this.

Group layers

The entire beard is now reduced
greatly, but the face has lost its modulation in these areas. We will use a
mask to fix this. We need to correct
two layers, but want to use only one
mask. Activate the layers "Retouching
copy" and "Retouching copy 2" while
holding the ⇧-key. In the Layers
panel menu, click on NEW GROUP
FROM LAYERS.

Hold the [Alt]-key and create a layer mask via the mask icon. The mask turns black and your retouching layers become invisible. Now paint with white and the Brush tool (B, Size 20 pixels, Hardness 0%, Opacity 30%) over all stubble areas you want to remove. The facial contours are now clearly visible again.

Recreate shadows

The shadows underneath the nose and below the chin have almost disappeared due to the beard removal. The face is still lacking in contours.

Create a CURVES adjustment layer above the group. Darken the picture slightly.

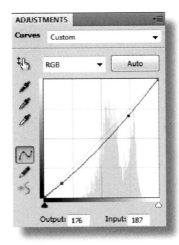

The change affects the entire picture. Therefore fill the layer mask with black ([⌘]/[Ctrl]+[D]) and use the Brush tool ([B], Size 30 pixels, Hardness 0%, Opacity 20%) and white to lightly paint the shadows back in. The curve results in slight color shifts. Set the Blend Mode to LUMINOSITY. Repaint the reduced mimic wrinkles as well, to avoid a mask-like facial expression.

Change hairstyle

Picture analysis

❶ Shiny hair

❷ Remove tiny ponytail

❸ Insert strands of hair

❹ Close up bare patches

To make a hairstyle look fuller, you can either use foreign hairpieces or copy individual strands or whole bunches out of the existing hairstyle and insert them into different places. The advantage of this method: hair texture and color match straight away. The disadvantage: you can easily betray yourself if there are recurring patterns.

ch6/change_hairstyle.jpg

before

after

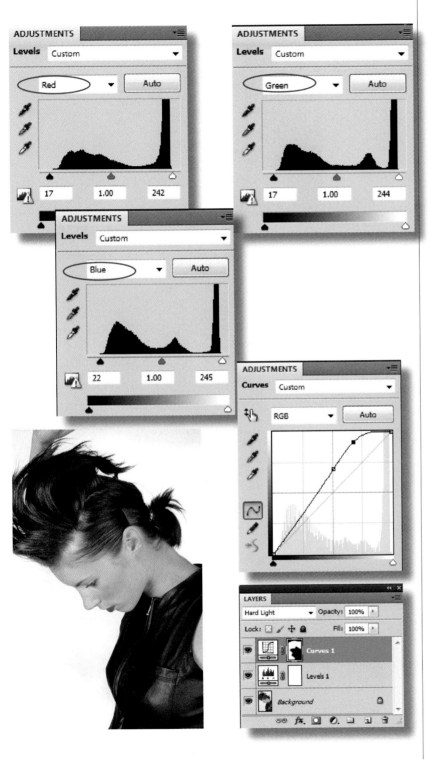

Improve contrast

To give the image more contrast, we will first correct the Levels using an adjustment layer. Correct the picture only in the individual color channels as shown and not in the RGB channel. This gives you better control over colors and contrasts.

Create shine

The hair still looks too dull. Choose a Curves adjustment layer and brighten the highlights strongly. Set the Blend Mode to HARD LIGHT.

With a layer mask in the curve and black you can remove the effect on the face and upper body. Use the Brush tool (B) and vary the size of the brush tip to fit the different shapes such as ear and individual hairs.

To give the hair more shape, create a Curve at the top and increase the contrast with a slight S-curve. Drag the highlights upwards a little and the shadows downwards. Save the image with all layers.

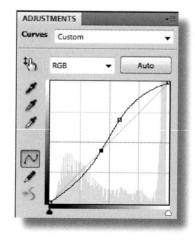

For the next steps, flatten all layers with LAYER/FLATTEN IMAGE. Save the picture under a new name.

Select hairstyle

First use the Clone Stamp tool to remove the ponytail at the back. Then use the Lasso tool ([L], Feather 4 pixels) to select the top hair section. To make it clearer, we have marked the selection in blue on the picture. Copy the section to another layer with [⌘]/[Ctrl]+[J] and convert it to a SMART OBJECT.

Adapt hair

Position the hair and resize it with [⌘]/[Ctrl]+[T]. In the Options bar you can see the changes we made. We squashed the width of the hair section to 87.8% and then rotated it by 50.9 degrees.

Activate the Warp function with EDIT/ TRANSFORM/WARP and change the way the hair falls. Confirm by pressing ⏎.

To give the hair style more volume, we want to add another section of hair near the parting. Copy the layer "Hair section 1" with LAYER/SMART OBJECTS/NEW SMART OBJECT VIA COPY. To let the hair fall downwards, flip it with EDIT/TRANSFORM/FLIP HORIZONTAL. Determine the position again with ⌘/Ctrl+T. You can see the settings in the Options bar.

Use the Warp function again to change the direction the hair falls. It has still the same shape of the previous warp. After making your changes you now have the same section of hair in three different shapes and in different places.

Adjust edges

After we added to the hairstyle, we
now need to work on the hair edges.
Switch to the layer "Hair section 1"
and zoom right into the picture. Now
we can look at the original hair edges
more closely. They are not smooth,
but rather frayed. The edges created
by the Lasso tool ([L]) are soft and
not frayed (see circle).

If you try using a layer mask and a
normal round brush tip for editing
the edges, you won't get very far.
We need to achieve frayed edges.
Photoshop offers the appropriate
brush tip for this purpose. Adapt the
hair edges with a layer mask and the
Brush tool ([B], Size 25 pixels), using
the brush tip shown on the right and
black.

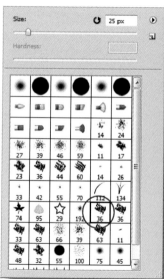

Unfortunately, this brush tip has no setting for a feathered edge and the retouching becomes a bit too hard. With the layer mask activated, soften the mask with FILTER/BLUR/GAUSSIAN BLUR and a Radius of 0.4 pixels. Do this with both sections of hair.

If you show only the two layers with the hair sections in the layer after making your corrections, it should look similar to this. Look at the transparent areas as well, where the background shines through if it is not hidden. Now show the layers again. The Layers panel should look like on our picture.

Fill bald spots

The extreme styling has produced a few bald spots on the scalp. To fill these areas, select the hair with the Lasso tool as shown (⌊L⌋, Feather 1 pixel). Include the roots of the hair, otherwise the transitions will be too hard. Copy the selection to another layer with ⌘/Ctrl+J and push it to the very top of the Layers panel. Adapt the shape with EDIT/ TRANSFORM/WARP. Drag the two left corner points to the left until the bald spots are covered.

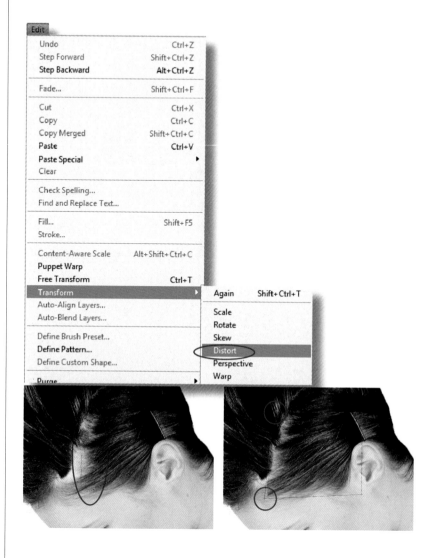

Now adapt the hair edges with a layer mask again.

The transition between the inserted piece of hair and the scalp does not look good yet.

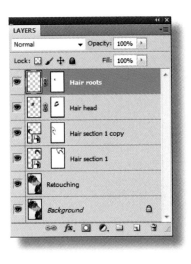

Activate the layer "Retouching" and hide all layers above it. Use the Lasso tool ($\boxed{\text{L}}$, Feather 1 pixel) to select the the roots of the hair at the problem area. Copy this section with $\boxed{\text{⌘}}$/$\boxed{\text{Ctrl}}$+$\boxed{\text{J}}$ and push the layer to the top of the Layers panel. Now you can see the original hair roots in this area again, which were destroyed by the shine-creating curves.

Carry out your adaptation with another layer mask.

To finish, check all transitions and edges carefully and watch out especially for duplicated structures caused by multiple insertion of the same copied section of hair.

Basic Overview: Sharpening

In the age of digital photography, we are dealing with three different kinds of sharpening. If you develop a RAW image in Camera-Raw, you can sharpen it there, the same if you are scanning image material. This so-called Capture Sharpening compensates for shortcomings of the capture system. Then there is Creative Sharpening, if you just want to sharpen lips, eyes or individual strands of hair in a portrait in order to draw more attention to these areas. And finally there is Output Sharpening, which only takes place at the very end of the image editing process, because it has to be adapted to the output process. Arrange the sharpening with your printer and do a test print if possible.

What happens during sharpening?

Sharpening is a change of contrast. After sharpening, light areas are represented lighter and dark areas darker. If you look at the black-and-white gradient, you can see clearly that it becomes sharper and has more contrast after we apply a sharpen filter. But at what price? Details will be lost, soft transitions become hard and quite often the colors are not right any more either. This more or less happens with any kind of sharpening. If you sharpen an image or part of an image, you need to have at least 100% zoom to make sure that one image pixel is represented as one pixel on the monitor. Multiples of 100% are also okay, such as 200% or 400% etc. You need to consider carefully whether sharpening will actually improve your picture.

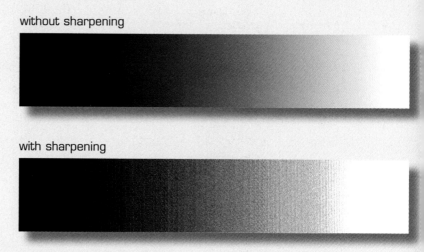

without sharpening

with sharpening

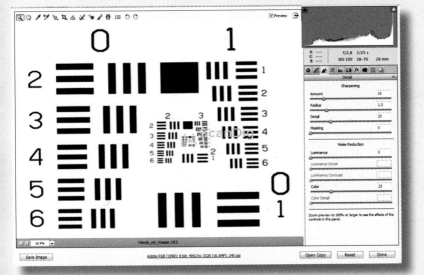

Capture Sharpening

To avoid unnecessary oversharpening, test your camera with all lenses. There are special test cards for this purpose. Correct any errors you come across in Camera RAW.

Here is a quick overview of the slider functions in Camera RAW:

AMOUNT: Sets the strength of the sharpening you want to apply.

RADIUS: Determines the width of the edges to be sharpened. If the radius is too high, fine structures can get lost and a light margin can appear around the edges.

DETAIL: Determines how much you want to sharpen even the finest, high-frequency details. If you [Alt]-click on the slider you can see a preview of the areas that will be sharpened.

MASKING: Here you can influence to what extent homogenous areas are sharpened. The higher the value, the less the areas are sharpened.

LUMINANCE: Reduces the brightness of your camera noise.

COLOR: Reduces the color noise of your camera.

Creative Sharpening

We already used creative sharpening in some of our workshops. We would like to show you a few others interesting approaches. The sharpening effect is different for each picture. Try out the various methods for your pictures. With creative sharpening, there is no right or wrong way.

Sharpen with the Emboss filter

Here we applied the Emboss filter to a copy of the background.

You should try it out yourself in order to get a feel for the effects of the different sliders. You can see our settings in the dialog shown on the right. It is important to set the layer mode to HARD LIGHT. We restricted the sharpening to eyes, mouth and fur texture, using a layer mask or with the filter mask.

Of course you can just as well work within the Smart Filters mask.

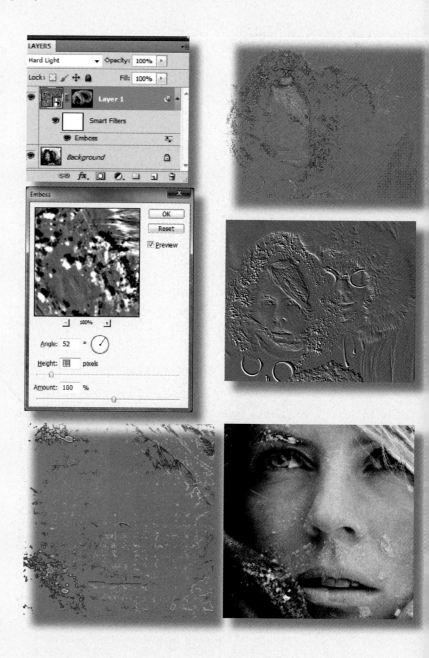

Extreme contour sharpening

To sharpen only the contours, we need a selection that protects the areas but leaves the edges free for editing.

After selecting the image, copy the entire image. Create a new channel in the Layers panel. It is called "Alpha 1" by default. Insert the picture and then remove the selection outline.

Emphasize the edges with FILTER/STYLIZE/FIND EDGES.

Use Levels or Curves to increase the contrast as shown on our picture.

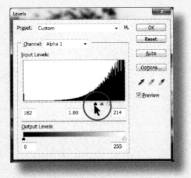

Blur the channel with the Gaussian Blur.

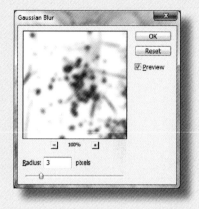

Increase the channel's contrast again.

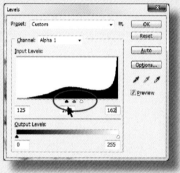

Then activate the RGB composite channel and switch to the Layers panel to the layer "Background copy".

Choose SELECT/LOAD SELECTION and activate the INVERT button. Now only the edges are selected. Choose any Sharpen filter and experiment with the settings.

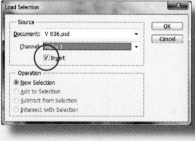

Sharpen with Luminosity Mask

Sometimes you only want to sharpen certain brightness areas in a picture. In this example, the hair, eyebrows and lips could use a bit more sharpness. The tonal values in these areas are darker than the skin. So why not select just the dark tonal values and sharpen those?

Load the brightness values via the Channels panel while holding the ⌘ / Ctrl -key. Invert the selection and apply a Sharpen filter.

Output Sharpening

Sharpening for a specific output, such as a high gloss print or newspaper print, should only be done at the very end. As you may need your image for different output forms, you should never sharpen the original image. Save your picture with all layers and then flatten them. Remove all Alpha channels and paths from your picture, if you do not need these for a layout program. Save the image under a new name. Now you can sharpen this copy for a specific output or print size.

Determine sharpening

The question is always which amount to choose. Until you like the picture? No, the danger of oversharpening is too great. To find the right parameters, we will give you a few tips. First you need to know the resolution of your picture. Under IMAGE/IMAGE SIZE you can see the resolution. Make sure it is set to PIXELS/INCH. Copy the layer and convert it to a SMART OBJECT. Select the UNSHARP MASK filter via the Filter menu. The Radius is calculated with the following formula: image resolution 210 : 150 = 1.4 pixels. The divider 150 is a value based on printing experience. Set the Amount to 100% if the image resolution is 300 ppi. If the resolution is lower, you can increase the Amount, in our case to about 130%. With a higher resolution, you reduce the amount accordingly. Drag the Threshold value up so that the skin is not sharpened, only the edges. Set the layer's Blend Mode to Luminosity to avoid color shifts.

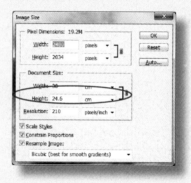

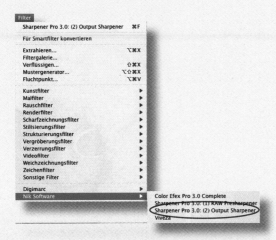

Filter plugin for output sharpening

There are lots of filter plugins with sharpening functions. But only a few are really useful if you want to achieve the right sharpening for output. The Nik Sharpener Halftone is one of these. For the right sharpen setting, you not only need size and resolution of an image, but also information about paper quality, such as newspaper, matte or highgloss paper. How big is the viewing distance to the printed image? Normal reading distance in case of a magazine, or will the picture be displayed on the side of a house ten meters away? What is the printing resolution? You can enter these parameters in the HALFTONE filter. You will then get a sharpening matched to your settings.

In the Filter dialog under HALFTONE you will also find Sharpen filters for output on various ink jet printers and other requirements.

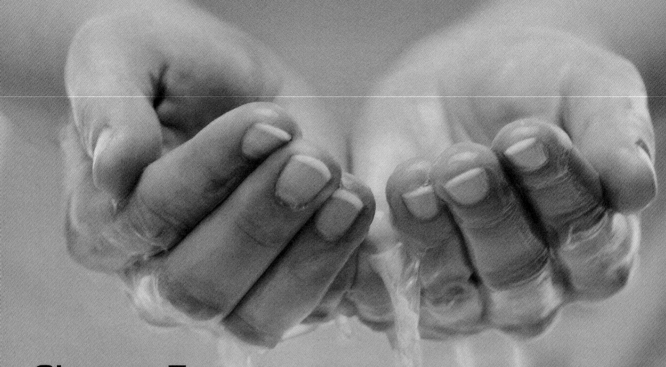

Chapter 7
Hands and feet

aesthetic blotchy tender chapped soft sore gnarled long short youthful large **pampered** negle
manicured wrinkly straight strained ugly dry silky strong **fine** small rough veiny plump br
beautiful **supple** powerful nimble dry aesthetic blotchy tender chapped pampered soft sore gna
long short youthful large neglected manicured wrinkly straight strained ugly dry silky strong
small rough veiny plump broad beautiful supple nimble aesthetic blotchy **tender** chapped pampe
soft sore gnarled long short youthful large neglected manicured wrinkly straight strained
silky strong fine small rough veiny plump broad **beautiful** supple powerful nimble aesthetic
tender chapped pampered soft sore gnarled long short youthful large neglected manicured wr

 How to refine the
shape of individual
toes and foot contours

 How to shape
fingernails and
create perfect
varnish

 How to reinforce
the effects of aging
in hands

 Basic Overview
Paths

 How to improve
skin color and
fingers in a few
quick steps

 How to use exact
paths to make
hands and nails
look pretty

Change foot contours

Picture analysis

❶ Adapt big toe

❷ Narrower left foot

❸ Rounded toe tips

Not many of us probably have naturally "beautiful feet" in the classical sense, with straight and well-proportioned toes. Often we force our feet into shoes that are too tight, which does not improve their shape. In this example, we want to edit the main problem areas. To achieve perfect feet we need to reshape almost every single toe.

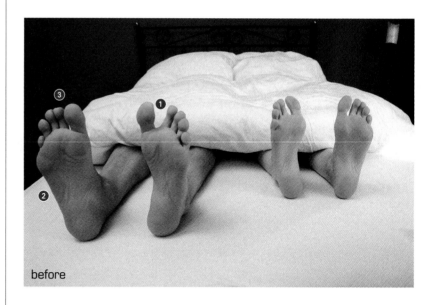

before

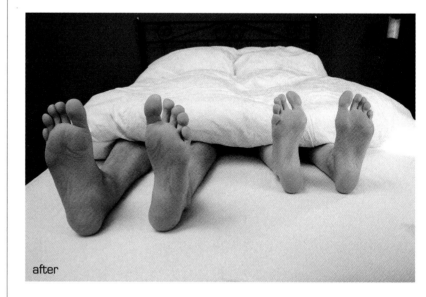

after

ch7/feet.jpg

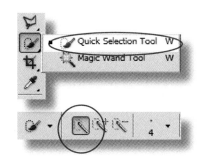

Select foot in three steps

The man's right big toe is too splayed. To reposition the big toe, we first need to select it. The simplest method is to use the Quick Selection tool (W). Set the tool tip to a small Size, for example 4. Keep this size for the next three steps.

1. Click once on the big toe. Only a small selection appears.

2. Hold the Alt-key and drag over all areas of bed and duvet that you do not want to select. You will not see any change in the selection, but the tool remembers what areas you don't want selected.

3. Release the Alt-key (if necessary, click on the Add to Selection icon in the middle) and drag over the toes and foot. Now you have a perfect selection. Copy the foot to a new layer with ⌘/Ctrl+J and name this layer "Foot".

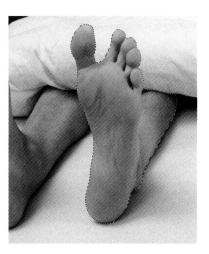

Move over, big toe!

To make sure the original toe and parts of the foot do not get in the way while we reposition the big toe, we will remove these parts first. Hide the layer "Foot". Click on the background layer and copy it to a new layer with ⌘/Ctrl+J. Use the Clone Stamp tool (S, Size 40 pixels, Hardness 40%, Opacity 100%) to separate the toe from the foot as shown, otherwise the Patch tool (J) will not work properly. Then draw around the rest of the toe with the Patch tool (J) and drag the selected area left onto the duvet. The toe is gone.

Change back to the Clone Stamp tool (S) and roughly remove the neighboring areas in the foot as well.

Show the layer "Foot" again. For the moment, we only need the big toe and the left side of this foot. Select this area with the Lasso tool (L) and copy it to a new layer with ⌘/Ctrl+J. Name the layer "Big toe".

Create a SMART OBJECT from the layer with the command in the Layers panel menu.

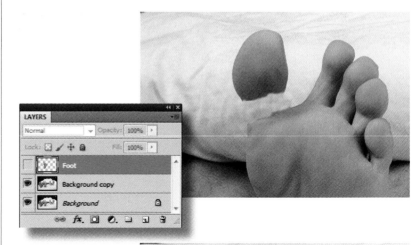

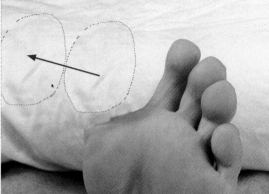

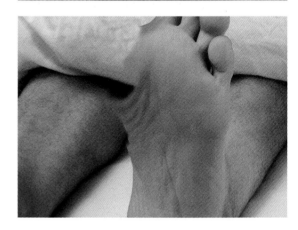

If you hide all other layers, the layer "Big toe" should look something like this. Show the layers "Background" and "Background copy" again. But not the layer "Foot", otherwise you would see the big toe twice, which would be confusing.

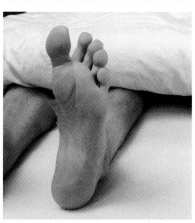

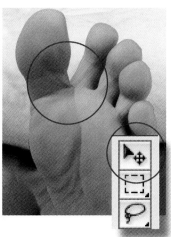

Now drag the layer "Big toe" a bit to the right with the Move tool ([V]). Position the toe in about the same way as shown on this picture.

With [⌘]/[Ctrl]+[T] you rotate the toe slightly clockwise. We rotated it by 2.8 degrees. Watch the value at the top of the Options bar.

The big toe has now moved much closer to the other toes. The lower part of the foot is still not quite right. The foot itself should remain unaltered. Use EDIT/TRANSFORM/WARP to match the left side of the layer "Big toe" to the left side of the original foot. The two edges should meet up in the marked circle. Use the picture on the right for guidance. Depending on how you selected the big toe earlier you can of course end up with slightly different settings.

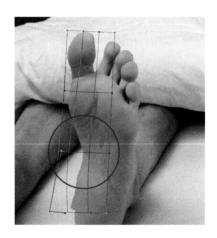

The transitions between the foot edges do not match yet. Create a layer mask with the ADD LAYER MASK icon in the Layers panel and use black ([D]) to remove the areas that stick out on the left. Create soft transitions within the sole of the foot.

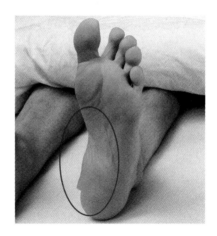

If you hide the underlying layers, you can see what is left of the original selection after editing in the mask.

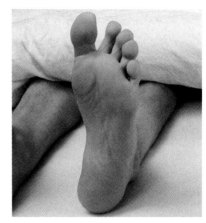

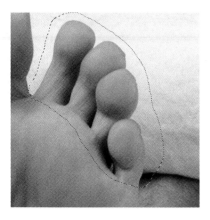

Adjust little toes

To reduce the gap between the big toe and the second toe even more, we now edit the other four toes. Activate the layer "Foot" again and make it visible. Use the Lasso tool (L, Feather 1 pixel) to select the remaining toes, copy them with ⌘/Ctrl+J and convert them to a SMART OBJECT. Name the layer "Toes". Hide the layer "Foot" again.

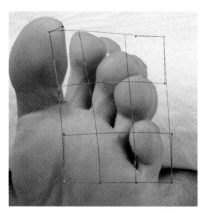

Use the Warp tool to bend the toes to the left. Follow your own aesthetic instincts. You will see the original toes emerge from underneath. We will soon change that. Confirm with the ↵-key when you are happy with the result.

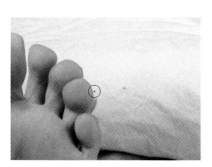

To remove the duplicated toes, click on the layer "Background copy". Use the Clone Stamp tool (S, Size 30 pixels, Hardness 0%, Opacity 100%) to remove the superfluous areas.

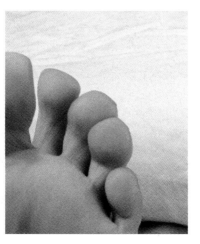

Narrow left foot

On closer inspection we notice that the man's left foot looks rather wide in comparison to the other foot. We need to correct that a bit. Select the foot with the Lasso tool ($\boxed{\text{L}}$, Feather 1 pixel) and copy it to a new layer with $\boxed{\mathcal{H}}/\boxed{\text{Ctrl}}+\boxed{\text{J}}$. Convert the layer to a SMART OBJECT and name it "Left foot".

Click on the layer "Background copy" and remove large areas from the left side of the foot with the Clone Stamp tool ($\boxed{\text{S}}$, Size 50 pixels, Hardness 0%, Opacity 100%). In this case it is better to remove more rather than not enough.

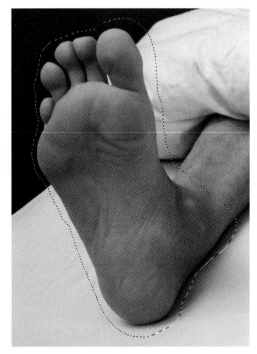

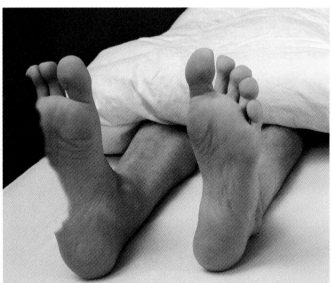

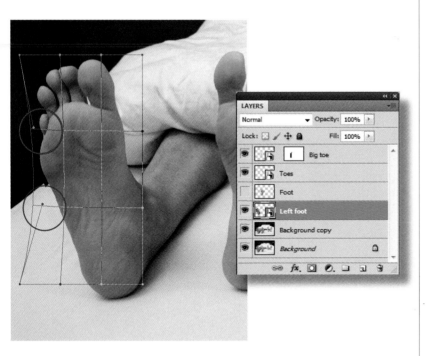

Select the Warp tool and drag the two tangents on the left side slightly to the right. The foot becomes narrower and there are no flawed transitions, except for the left edge of the bed. Confirm with the ↵-key.

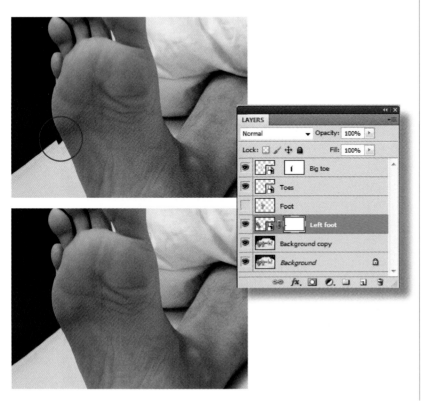

Create a layer mask and use the Brush tool (B) with a very small brush tip and black to remove the little gap between bed edge and foot.

Save the picture with all layers.

Fine-tuning

For fine retouching, merge all layers with the background via the command MERGE VISIBLE. Save the picture under a new name to make sure you keep all layers.

Some areas are still not perfect. The ball of the foot below the little toe needs to be smaller. The toe tips have to look more rounded and the transition between our reattached big toe and the other toes is not quite right.

Copy the background layer with ⌘/Ctrl+J. Select the left foot with the Rectangular Marquee tool (M, Feather 5 pixels).

The shape corrections can be carried out with the Liquify filter. Activate it with FILTER/LIQUIFY. Follow roughly our tool settings, but try others as well. Set the center of the tool outside the foot and push the edge slightly inwards. Create a nicely rounded shape.

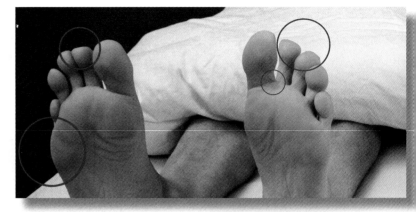

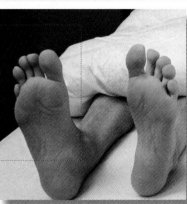

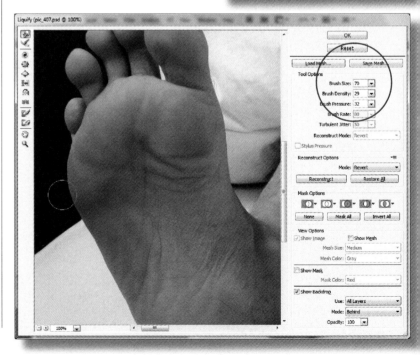

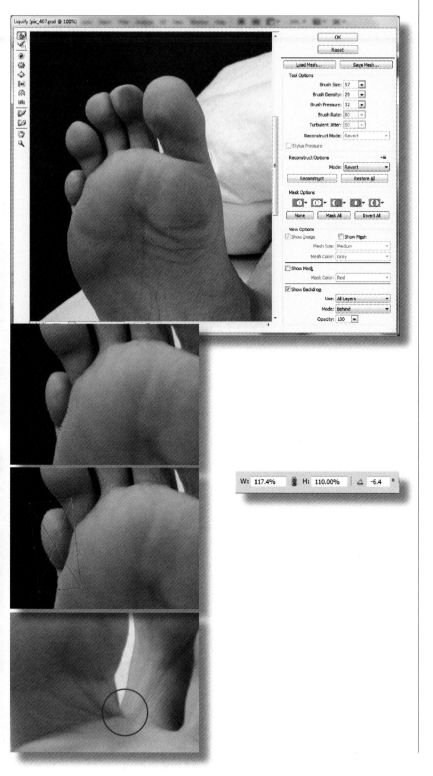

Proceed in the same way with the toe tips that look squarish. This time you push the edge upwards to achieve a nice rounded shape. Keep perfecting the toes and feet in this manner.

The left little toe almost disappears behind the foot. To enlarge it a bit, select it with the Lasso tool (L, Feather 1 pixel) as shown on the picture and copy the little toe to another layer with ⌘/Ctrl+J. After converting it to a SMART OBJECT, resize the width of the toe to about 117% and the height to about 110%. Then rotate the toe slightly by about -6.4 degrees and confirm with the ↵-key. Use a layer mask to adjust the transitions between the new toe and the original foot.

Finally, correct the small edge between the toes. Now the feet are looking much better.

Emphasize age

Picture analysis

❶ Increase effect

Wrinkles and pigment spots are not necessarily little blemishes that need to be inconspicuously concealed. On the contrary, here we want to rein-force the symbolic power of the motif by emphasizing the traces of time.

after

ch7/old_hands.jpg

Increase signs of aging

Usually you would use the SHADOWS/HIGHLIGHTS dialog to add more definition to the shadows and highlights. But it can also help you achieve dramatic effects.

Copy the background with ⌘/Ctrl+J and click on FILTER/ CONVERT FOR SMART FILTERS. This is important to be able to carry out fine changes later on. The SHADOWS/ HIGHLIGHTS function does not exist as adjustment layer. Display the dialog with IMAGE/ADJUSTMENTS/SHADOWS-HIGHLIGHTS.

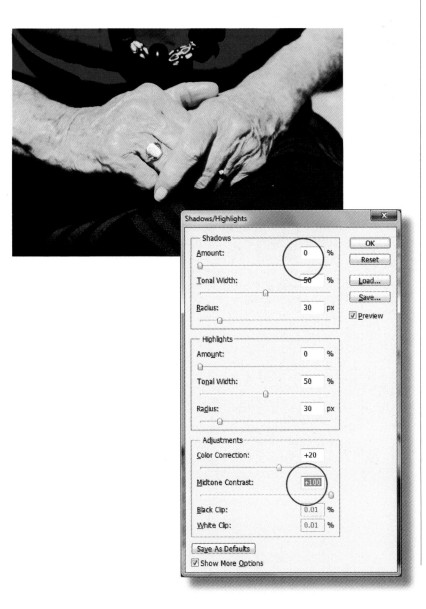

We do not want to lighten the SHADOWS in this picture, we therefore set the AMOUNT for Shadows to 0%.

We want to improve the details on the hands. We achieve this by increasing the contrasts. First drag the MIDTONE CONTRAST to 100%. You are going to see the effect in the next step.

Now drag the AMOUNT for HIGHLIGHTS to about 97%. You can also set it to 100% or 90%. Corrections can still be made later.

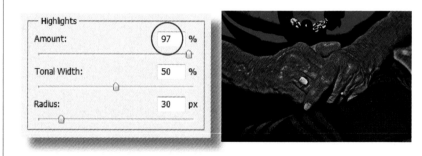

To be able to assess the image more clearly, reduce the color intensity. Drag the COLOR CORRECTION slider to a negative value. We set it to –15.

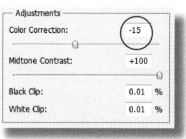

Now drag the RADIUS for HIGHLIGHTS slightly to the right and keep watching your picture. We liked the look of the picture at a RADIUS of 352 pixels. Click on Ok.

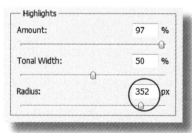

We left the TONAL WIDTH at its default settings. The smaller the tonal width, the fewer tonal values in highlights and shadows are affected by the modification. The bigger, the greater the modification.

The contrast is still not high enough and we are not happy with the color change in the hands caused by the Shadows/Highlights adjustment. Create a new BLACK & WHITE adjustment layer with the NEW FILL OR ADJUSTMENT LAYER icon at the bottom of the Layers panel.

Contrast through color change

After creating the adjustment layer, the whole picture is black and white, but we want to keep a slight coloration. Do not change any settings in the Black&White Adjustments panel. Reduce the Layer Opacity until you achieve a pleasing skin tone; we chose 68%.

We want to bring the skin texture out a bit more via the individual color channels. To change the brightness of the individual colors, we need to go back to the Black&White dialog in the Adjustments panel once more.

Change the color tones as shown on our picture. Keep in mind that the colors are darkened in the minus range and lightened in the plus range. Try out all colors. The Reds and Yellows are the most obvious. Arms and hands change dramatically. The Blues and Cyans affect the clothing very noticeably. But the material also contains Greens, and even Magenta has an effect on the picture. To be able to assess the changes better, you need to zoom to greater magnification. Only then will you notice that the bright edge on the jewellery changes.

Keep watching the Histogram, to avoid the shadows running together.

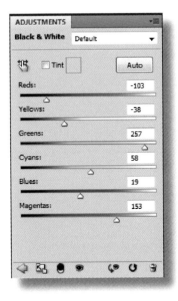

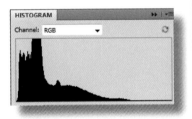

Now we still want to increase the contrast slightly. Create a new CURVES adjustment layer via the CREATE NEW FILL OR ADJUSTMENT LAYER icon in the Layers panel.

First drag the ❶ white input slider to the left until it touches the histogram. This way you assign white to that brightness value. Because we do not want to darken the shadows, place a ❷ lock-down point at the bottom left of the curve. Simply click on it. Now drag the ❸ curve slightly upwards in the top range, the highlights. Keep watching the two end points of the histogram. They should not be touching the very right nor left. That would mean loss of quality.

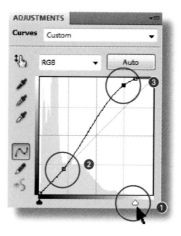

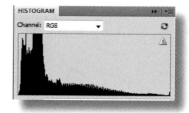

The Curve has affected the colors as well. Set the layer's Mode to LUMINOSITY. Now only the brightness values are modified.

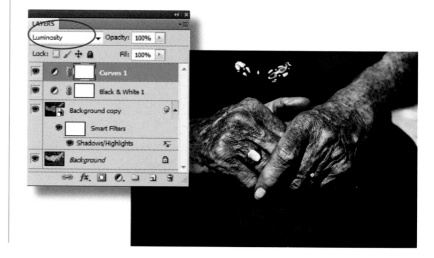

To finish we want to further reduce the colors. Create a new HUE/SATURATION adjustment layer via the CREATE NEW FILL OR ADJUSTMENT LAYER icon.

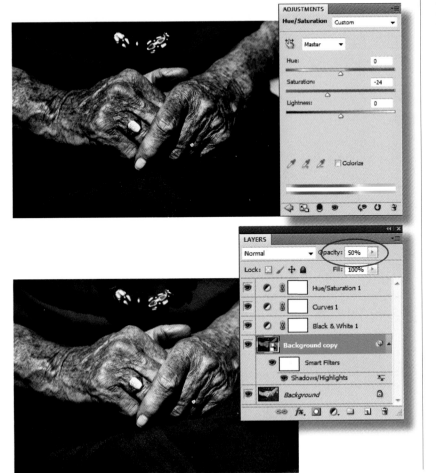

Drag the SATURATION slider back until you are happy with the colors. We set it to –24.

Reduced version

To demonstrate the full effect of this example, we chose a very extreme setting for the first SHADOWS/HIGHLIGHTS correction. If we reduce the Opacity to 50%, the effect is more aesthetically pleasing.

Expressive hands

Picture analysis

❶ Reshape fingernails

❷ Whiten nail edges

❸ Bring out skin color and texture

When photographing hands, you should always check how big an individual fingernail will appear when reproduced in the final picture. With a large reproduction scale, every single tiny detail will be visible. If well-manicured fingernails are important to you, then you are faced with extensive retouching. You should definitely consider before the photo session if a professional manicure would be cheaper than editing 30 fingernails afterward, as in this example.

ch7/circle_hands.jpg

before

after

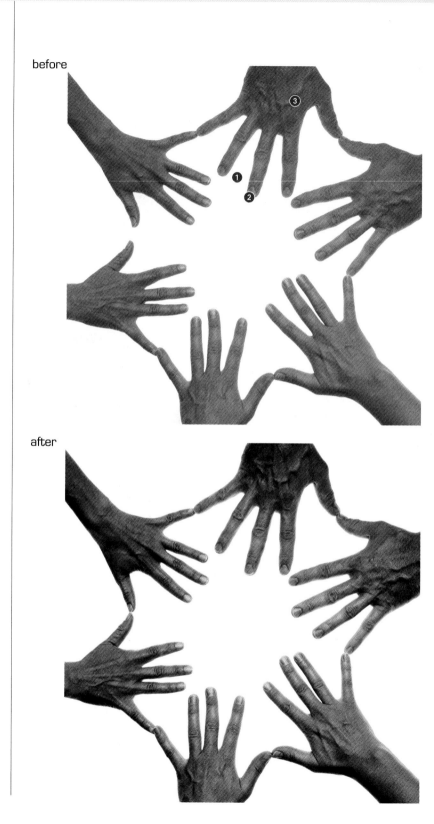

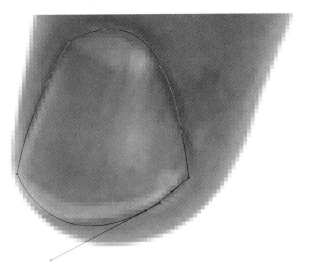

Select fingernail

For retouching we need to have the fingernails separately on individual layers. Magnify one of the finger-nails with the zoom tool by pressing ⌘/Ctrl+[+]. We selected the nail with the Pen tool (P) to have good control over the nail shape. Place the path so that it already outlines the new shape of the nail.

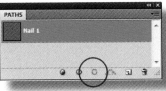

Save the path in the Paths panel. You can now load the path by dragging it to the LOAD PATH AS A SELECTION icon at the bottom. With SELECT/MODIFY/FEATHER you give the selection a feathered edge of 1 pixel.

Copy the nail to a new layer with ⌘/Ctrl+[J].

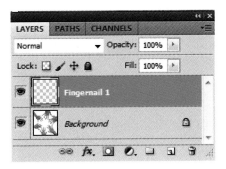

Shape fingernail

Hide the background to see the nail shape more clearly. Click on the buttons FIX TRANSPARENT PIXELS and LOCK POSITION in the Layers panel. This ensures that we do not accidentally retouch over the transparent areas or move the fingernail.

To give the edge of the nail a nice rounded shape, we need to create exact paths again.

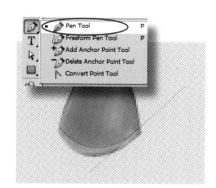

Also create a path around the white area near the base of the nail, the halfmoon. Deactivate all paths by clicking on a blank area in the Paths panel. You may need to drag to make the panel a bit bigger.

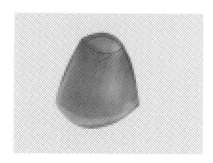

Now use the retouching tools to remove the left edge and the white of the nail and reduce the reflection slightly. After retouching, convert the layer to a SMART OBJECT.

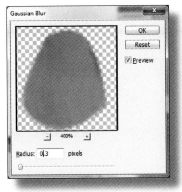

To make the nail surface nice and soft and therefore let the fingernail appear more manicured and shinier, apply a Gaussian Blur with a Radius of 0.3 pixels (FILTER/BLUR/GAUSSIAN BLUR).

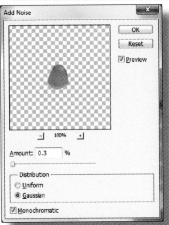

This causes it to lose pixellation. Add it again with a noise filter. We used FILTER/NOISE/ADD NOISE with an Amount of 0.3%.

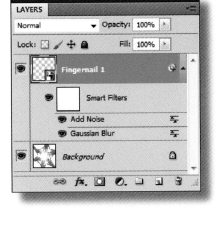

Color edge of nail

To create a light or white edge for the nail, create a new empty layer at the very top. Load the path "Nail edge" as a selection. Click on the Brush tool (B, Size 10 pixels, Hardness 0%, Opacity 100%). Now pick up a light fingernail color while holding the Alt-key. By pressing the Alt-key, the Brush turns to an Eyedropper; when you let go of the Alt-key, it turns back into the Brush. If there is no suitable color in the picture, go to the COLOR PICKER and select your color there.

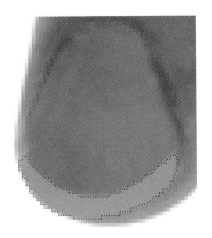

To integrate the white edge better into the nail, blur it with a Gaussian Blur via FILTER/BLUR/GAUSSIAN BLUR and a Radius of 0.3 pixels. Then apply the Noise filter again with an Amount of 0.3%.

Create another new layer for the light root of the nail and proceed as in the previous section. For a better overview hold the Shift-key and click on the layers "Nail white", "Nail white edge" and "Fingernail 1". Combine them into a group by clicking on NEW GROUP FROM LAYERS in the Layers panel menu. Do the same with all badly manicured nails. Make sure that the nail-edge is some degrees lighter than the half-moon. Set the brightness and color settings for all fingers of each person to the same values.

When you have finished retouching the fingernails, save the picture with all layers. Then merge all layers. Click on the "Background" layer and copy it with ⌘/Ctrl+J. Finally, retouch all fingernail edges and skin impurities and save the picture under a new name. This ensures you keep all the layers and the file size does not get too large.

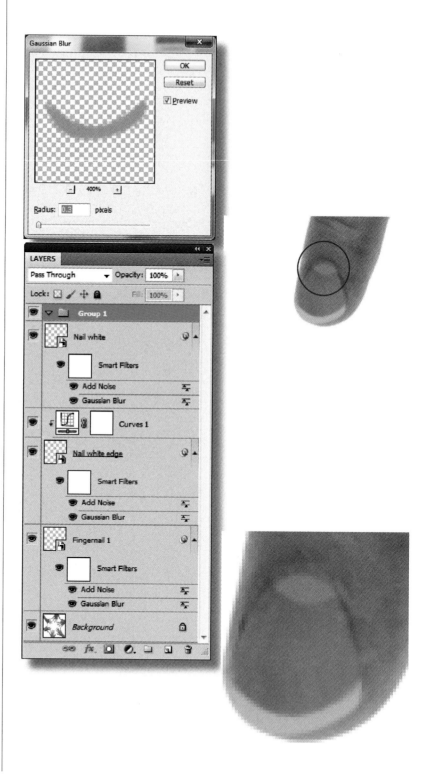

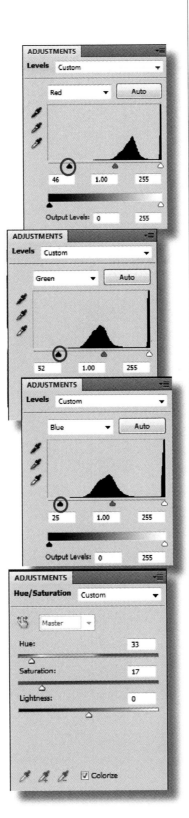

Enhance texture

With pictures that were taken without using hand models, the question arises: should we get rid of tendons, veins, pigment spots and the like, or emphasize them? The motif we have here has strong symbolic character, this is not a beauty shot, therefore we decide to make the hands as expressive as possible with emphasized skin texture.

First we are going to increase the contrast using a LEVELS adjustment layer. Adjust the Shadows slider in the individual color channels until the skin texture emerges nicely.

Adapt skin colors

To give the hands an even and pleasing coloration, create a HUE/SATURATION adjustment layer and activate the COLORIZE button. The HUE slider determines the color and the SATURATION slider the vividness of this color. We decided to use a light brown shade. We leave the LIGHTNESS unchanged.

Metallic look

To emphasize the distinctive properties of the individual hands even more
we would like to achieve a metallic
look. Before taking the photo we
could easily have achieved this by
applying metallic make-up. Create a
BLACK&WHITE adjustment layer by
clicking on the icon in the Layers
panel. We dragged the Reds and
Yellows into the negative area. This
gives the hands even more emphasis.

For the metallic effect, set the
"Black&White 1" layer's Blend
Mode to LINEAR LIGHT and reduce the
Opacity until you are happy with the
effect.

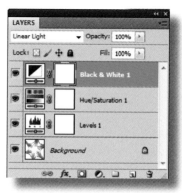

The fingers are now a bit too shiny
and have lost their shape. With a
SELECTIVE COLOR adjustment layer,
you add some black to the color
WHITE. The light areas in the hands
gain emphasis. Save the picture with
all layers.

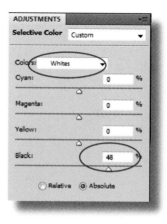

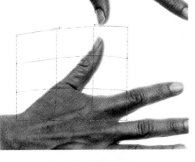

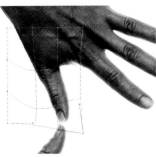

Close the circle

To make the picture perfect, we now need to close the gaps between the two thumbs on the left side. Flatten all layers and save the picture under a new name. Now use the Lasso tool (⌊L⌋, Feather 5 pixels) to select the thumb of the bottom hand and the surrounding area and copy it with ⌘/⌈Ctrl⌉+⌊J⌋. Convert the layer to a SMART OBJECT with the panel command. Choose EDIT/TRANSFORM/ WARP and drag the thumb upwards by about half the missing distance. Then press the ⌊↵⌋-key. Edit the top thumb in the same way, but this time transform it downwards.

Get fingernails into shape

Picture analysis

❶ Lengthen fingernails and create even shape

❷ Place light reflections

All seems perfect in this picture. But if you look closely, you will notice the fingernails which need some attention.

To edit each nail individually would mean a lot of work. It is much easier to edit one nail to perfection and then simply copy and insert it onto each fingertip, adapting the shape as required.

ch7/nail_varnish.jpg

before

after

Shape fingernail

To reshape a nail perfectly, use the Crop tool ($\boxed{C}$) to select a fingernail and the surrounding area. Double-click in the selection and save the section under a new name. We named it "Fingernail 1".

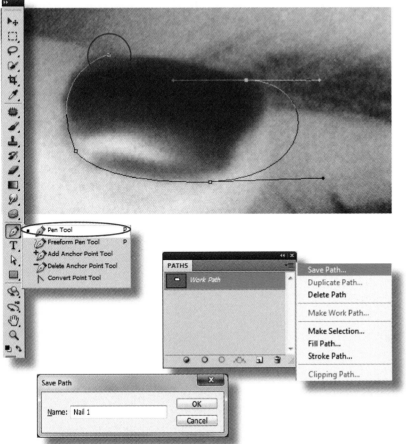

For the new nail we require a selection that corresponds to the new shape.

Magnify the picture "Fingernail 1" with a strong zoom by pressing $\boxed{\mathbb{H}}$/$\boxed{\text{Ctrl}}$+$\boxed{+}$ repeatedly.

Use the Pen tool ($\boxed{P}$) to create a path around the fingernail. The path traces the correct shape and size of the newly created nail (see Basic Overview "Paths", Chapter 7).

After finishing, save the path in the Paths panel. We named it "Nail 1".

The path should still be active. If not, click once on the path in the Paths panel. Now it should appear as activated. Click on MAKE SELECTION in the Paths panel menu.

Enter 1 pixel for RENDERING/RADIUS. Change to the Layers panel, activate the background and copy the selection to a new layer with ⌘/Ctrl+J. Name it "Nail". Now hide the background.

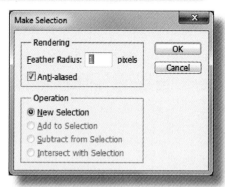

Complete fingernail

Use the Clone Stamp tool (S, Size 35, Hardness 40%, Opacity 100%) to stamp perfect varnished areas over the flawed parts. Deselect the selection by pressing ⌘/Ctrl+D.

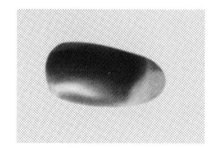

Place highlight

Click on the CREATE A NEW LAYER icon at the bottom of the Layers panel. Name the new layer "Highlight". Make sure that the LOCK-PROTECT TRANSPARENT AREAS button is active again.

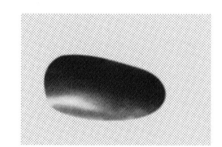

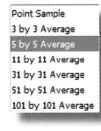

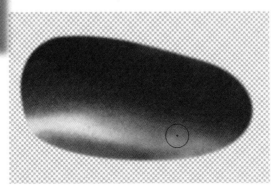

Paint the light reflection with the Brush tool ([B]).

Use the Eyedropper tool ([I]) to pick up a color in the mid-brightness of the reflection. Set the Eyedropper tool to SAMPLE SIZE of 5x5 AVERAGE in the Options bar.

Paint with the chosen color and the Brush tool ([B], Size 50 pixels, Hardness 0%, Opacity 6%) from about the center of the reflection towards the tip. Keep repeating this until a gentle, even reflection appears. Once you are happy with the nail, merge the layers "Nail" and "Reflection" into one new layer. To that purpose, activate both layers, hold the [⇧]+[Alt] keys and choose MERGE VISIBLE in the Layers panel menu. The two layers are merged into a new layer, the original layers remain intact.

Rename this new layer to "Composite".

Now copy this layer with ⌘/Ctrl+J and name the duplicate "Blur". The transparency of the layer has to stay locked. Choose FILTER/BLUR/GAUSSIAN BLUR and set the Radius to 2.8 pixels.

Hold the Alt-key and click on the mask icon in the Layers panel. The added layer mask is black and the Blur effect is no longer visible. Now paint over the fingernail with the Brush tool (B, Size 80 pixels, Hardness 0%, Opacity 10%) and the color white until you are happy with the degree of blur. Then merge the two layers "Blur" and "Composite" by activating the top layer and pressing ⌘/Ctrl+E.

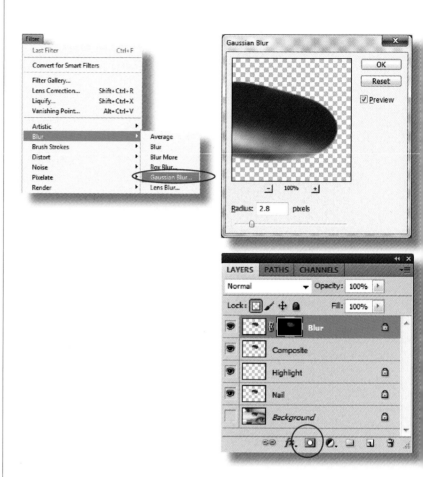

Replace fingernails

The blur may have caused the shape to be less exact. To make the nail edges more accurate again, switch to the Paths panel and load the selection of the path "Nail 1" again. Enter 1 pixel for RENDERING/ RADIUS. Invert the selection with ⌘/Ctrl+⇧+I and press the Delete key. Then deselect the selection. Open the original image again and copy the newly created fingernail into it. Name this layer "Nail LIF" (for "left index finger") and convert it to a SMART OBJECT.

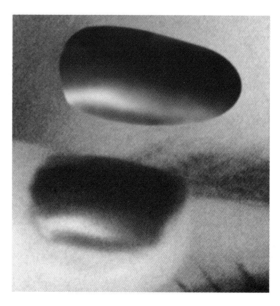

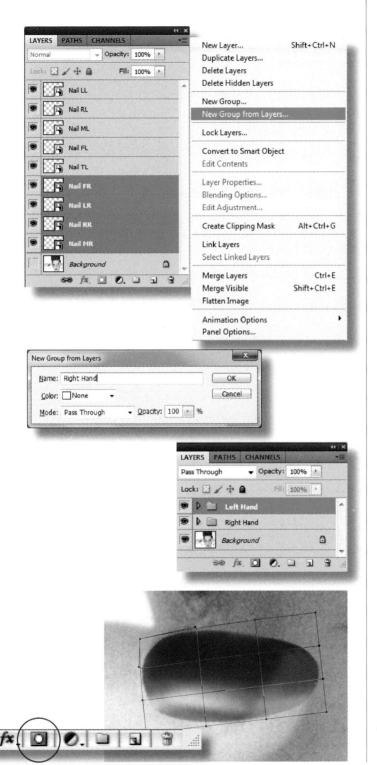

Organize layers

Copy this layer "Nail LIF" eight times with the command LAYER/SMART OBJECTS/NEW SMART OBJECT VIA COPY and give each layer a new name to create individual, independent layers. If you duplicate the layer with another method you risk that an adaptation or modification affects all other layers. It is very important to remember this when working with a Smart Object. Name each individual nail, such as "Little finger right hand" would be "LR".

The Layers panel has now become rather long. To have a better overview, hold the ⇧ - key and select all layers of the right hand. Via the Layers panel menu, choose NEW GROUP FROM LAYERS... and enter for example the name "Right Hand" into the window that opens. Confirm the dialog. Proceed in the same way for the layers of the left hand. The Layers panel is now much more manageable.

Adapt fingernails

Open the group "Left Hand" and activate the layer "Nail ML".

To be able to align the old and new nail more easily, reduce the layer Opacity of "Nail ML" to 50%. Now you can see the original nail shine through. Position the new nail on top of the old nail. After the modification, set the Opacity back to 100%.

Because of the Smart Object conversion you can try out different sizes and nail shapes without losing quality. After the final position has been determined, create a layer mask by clicking on the mask icon at the bottom of the Layers panel. Use black (D) to adapt the edges of the new fingernail to the surrounding area.

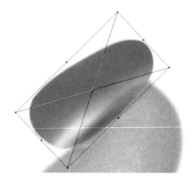

In the dialog shown here, activate the option "DON'T SHOW AGAIN".

The thumb nail is only visible from the side. Rotate the layer "Nail TL" with ⌘/Ctrl+T until it has the correct angle.

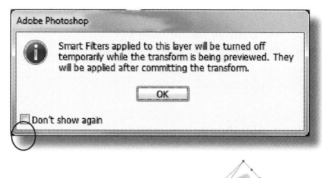

Squash the width of the thumb severely by simply dragging the marked point downwards. Then correct the shape again with a layer mask. Now adjust the other seven fingernails with the same method.

Add noise

The fingernails do not quite fit the surrounding area yet. Finish by adding a slight noise to each nail with FILTER/NOISE/ADD NOISE. First merge all nails into one composite layer. Activate the nails and press ⌘/Ctrl+E. First double-click on the Zoom tool to see the filter effect at 100% zoom.

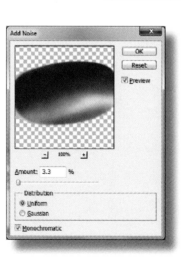

Recolor fingernails

Hold the [Alt]-key and create a
HUE/SATURATION adjustment layer.
Holding the [Alt]-key displays the
Options. Click on USE PREVIOUS
LAYER TO CREATE CLIPPING
MASK, then click on OK. You can
recognize the clipping mask as it
appears indented.

In the HUE/SATURATION dialog,
click on COLORIZE. Now you can
adjust each desired color with the
HUE slider. You can also modify
the SATURATION and LIGHTNESS of
the color. Drag the sliders until you
have found the right color.

Black nails

To color the fingernails black, it is
not sufficient to set the Lightness
of HUE/SATURATION to –100. The
fingernails do turn black, but the
light reflections are lost. To maintain these, double click in the blank
area on the right of the layer thumbnail and set UNDERLYING LAYER to
157/255. You can split the triangles
by [Alt]-dragging the inner part of the
slider. The light areas of the underlying layer become visible on the layer
above and the shine is back (see
also Basic Overview "Special Layer
Techniques", Chapter 5).

Beautiful hands in a few quick steps

Picture analysis

❶ Correct skin color

❷ Improve fingernails

Many hands appear older than they are and rather unattractive simply due to their red cast and too dark color. During the RAW conversion you can reduce this impression greatly. At small image scale or, as in our example, low sharpness of detail due to an even layer of water on the hands, the remaining flaws are easy to remove.

ch7/hands_with_water.CR2

before

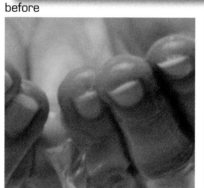

after

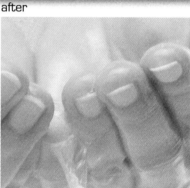

RAW Conversion

When you open this picture, the RAW Converter opens automatically. The basic setting (click on Default) shows the picture too dark, with strong colors and a red cast (see previous page). But for beauty shots, light and pastel skin shades with a low Red content create the best effect. We adjust the lightness with the EXPOSURE. We entered a value of +1.25. The whole picture becomes lighter.

The Histogram shows that there are large unstructured white areas. Click on the top right button in the Histogram (HIGHLIGHT CLIPPING WARNING). On this picture you can see the areas in question colored red. This is called clipping. Such a button also exists for the SHADOWS at the top left of the Histogram. In a picture that is too dark, it would represent the black areas without details in blue. Because we want the background in our example as pure white, we do not need to pay any attention to the clipping.

To get more detail into the over-exposed body areas, drag the RECOVERY slider slightly to the right until the highlighting color disappears in those areas. The RECOVERY slider can darken very light areas without affecting lightness elsewhere, but of course only to a certain extent. To increase the brightness in the midtones and therefore make the skin appear more pastel shaded, drag the BRIGHTNESS slider to +50. The color is too strong, so set the VIBRANCE value to –10. VIBRANCE reduces the colors but maintains the difference between colors. SATURATION would desaturate everything evenly.

The skin still contains too much red. Via the HSL/GRAYSCALE tab you access the color settings. Click on the Reds tab and drag the reds slowly to the right until you like the skin tone. Go to SATURATION and lower the saturation a bit more.

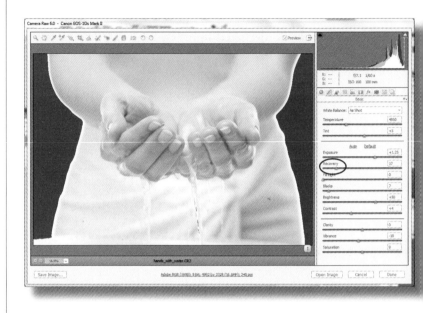

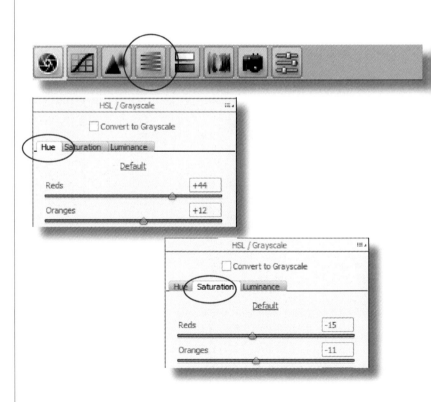

The red in the body disappears. Click again on the HIGHLIGHT CLIPPING WARNING at the top of the Histogram, and the marking color disappears.

We cannot do any more in the RAW Converter. Click on OPEN IMAGE and save the picture as PSD file for further editing.

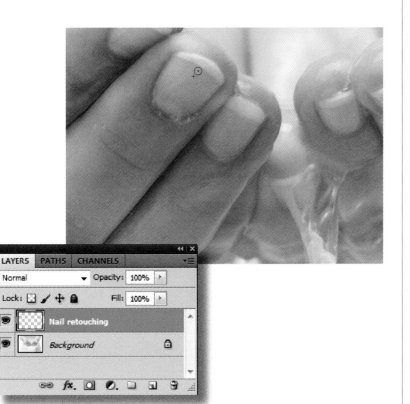

Correct fingernails

This time, we can correct the fingernails without elaborate paths. The fine layer of water on the surface of the skin makes the fingers appear slightly unsharp and we can reshape the nails free-hand with the Stamp tool and the Brush tool (B). Create a new empty layer and name it something like "Nail retouching".

Activate the Stamp tool ($\boxed{\text{S}}$, Size 50 pixels, Hardness 25%, Opacity 100%) and set the Options bar to SAMPLE: CURRENT & BELOW. Now the retouching is applied to the empty layer and the original image remains unchanged. Give all nails approximately the same length and rounding. The white nail edge should be even in all fingers as well. Adapt the tool tip to the various areas in softness, opacity and size.

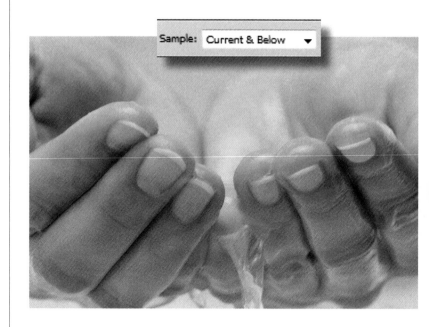

Brighten nail edges

To brighten the white nail edges and adjust their lightness, create a "Neutral Layer" (see Basic Overview "Special Layer Techniques", Chapter 5). Paint with white over the nail edges that are too dark, using a Brush tool ($\boxed{\text{B}}$) adjusted in size depending on the retouching area in question and a very soft feathered edge. The tool opacity should not exceed 10% to allow you to check the brightening and adjust it if needed. The half-moons at the nail base and the gaps between the fingers can be brightened in the same step.

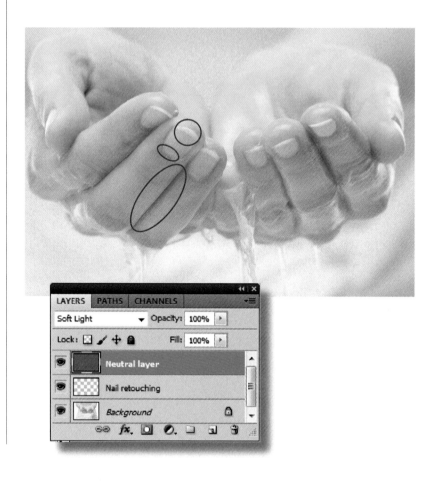

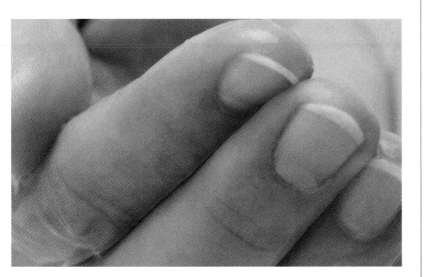

Fine retouching

Finally, switch back to the background layer and retouch any unattractive skin textures, undesirable water bubbles or other flawed areas with the Patch tool (J).

Basic Overview: Paths

Paths are vector based resolution-independent curves. They do not belong to any particular layer but can be saved and converted to selections. Paths are very good for selecting clearly defined edges, such as body shapes and machines. Hair, fur and other textures rich in detail on the other hand are unsuitable. Paths are the graphic designer's daily bread; everyone else looks at them with suspicion because they take some getting used to. But once you are a bit more familiar with paths, you won't want to manage without them.

More info on using paths

The paths you use in our workshops are created with the Pen tool ([P]).

Use Path Selection tools to modify a finished path's position, size and shape.

Simple triple-click on the image area to create two paths with an anchor point/corner point. You can place as many anchor points as you wish.

Double-click and then drag over the image at the same time as the third click. This creates a curve, the corner point is now a curve point.
In the workshops you always need to close a path by clicking on the starting point. You will see a circle next to the cursor.

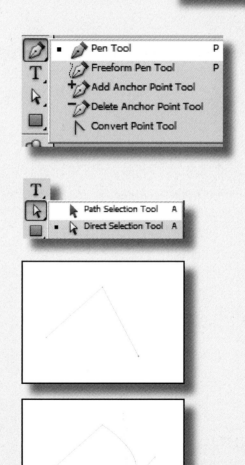

The Paths panel

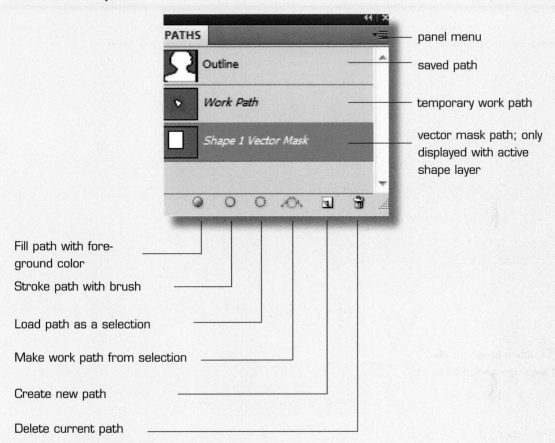

panel menu

saved path

temporary work path

vector mask path; only displayed with active shape layer

Fill path with fore-ground color

Stroke path with brush

Load path as a selection

Make work path from selection

Create new path

Delete current path

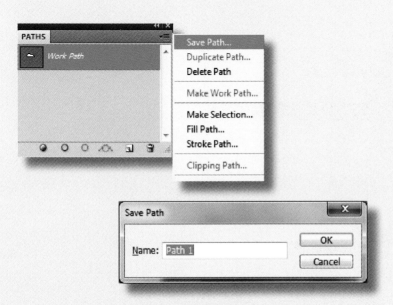

Saving paths

When you use a Pen ($\boxed{P}$) or Shape tool to create a path, it appears as temporary work path. To make sure it is not lost, you need to save it via the Paths panel menu. Give the path a descriptive name. One quick alternative: Double-click on the path name. This also saves the path.

Online Workshops

The Online Workshops for this book can be found on the book's Web Site. Visit www.wiley.com/go/bodyshop.

1 Stay Young

2 Snapshot

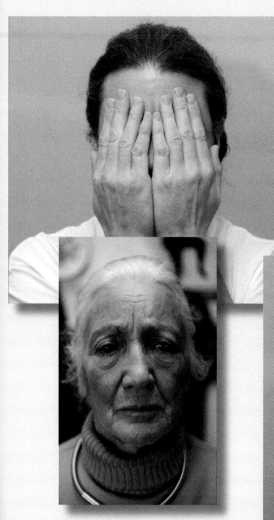

3 Mother and Son

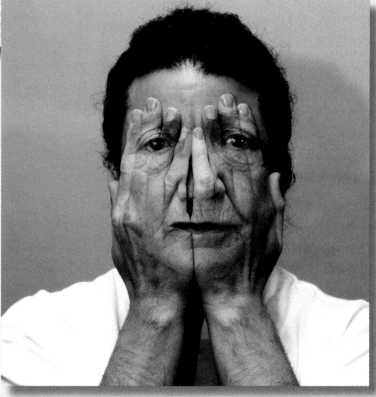

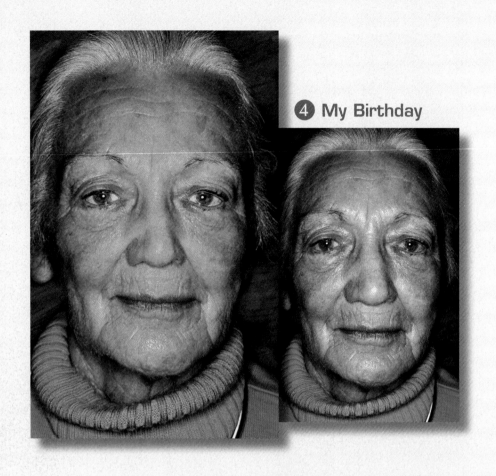

④ My Birthday

⑤ Cool

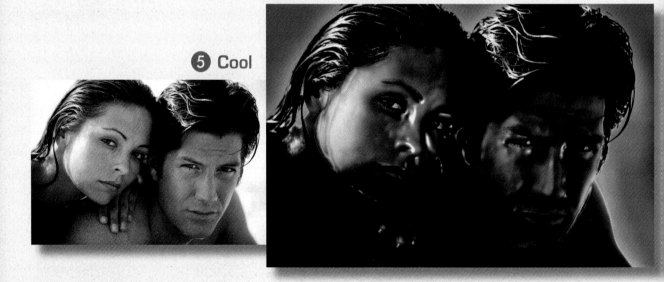

6 Bodypainting

⑦ **Mallorca**

8 Queen of the Beach

9 The View

10 Bathing Beauty

⑪ **Successful**

⑫ **Monroe Pose**

⑬ After Skiing

⑭ Hangover

15 Dreaming

16 Single Again

⑰ Who Am I?

18 1, 2, 3, Cheeeese

19 Gorbi, Erich and us

Index